LIFE IN
EARLY PHILADELPHIA

Also by
Billy G. Smith:

The "Lower Sort":
Philadelphia's Laboring People, 1750–1800

Also edited by
Billy G. Smith:

with Richard Wojtowicz

Blacks Who Stole Themselves:
Advertisements for Runaways in
the Pennsylvania Gazette, 1728–1790

with Susan E. Klepp

The Infortunate:
The Voyage and Adventures of
William Moraley, an Indentured Servant

LIFE IN
EARLY
PHILADELPHIA

*Documents from the Revolutionary
and Early National Periods*

Edited by
BILLY G. SMITH

The Pennsylvania State University Press
University Park, Pennsylvania

Library of Congress Cataloging-in-Publication Data

Life in early Philadelphia : documents from the Revolutionary and
    early national periods / edited by Billy G. Smith.
        p.   cm.
    Includes bibliographical references and index.
    ISBN 0-271-01454-7 (cloth)
    ISBN 0-271-01455-5 (paper)
    1. Philadelphia (Pa.)—History.   2. Philadelphia (Pa.)—History—
    Revolution, 1775–1783.   I. Smith, Billy Gordon.
    F158.44.L54   1995
    974.8′1103—dc20   94-49343
                                                                  CIP

Published by The Pennsylvania State University Press,
University Park, PA 16802-1003

Second printing, 2003

It is the policy of The Pennsylvania State University Press to use acid-free paper
for the first printing of all clothbound books. Publications on uncoated stock
satisfy the minimum requirements of American National Standard for Information Sciences—Permanence of Paper for Printed Library Materials, ANSI
Z39.48–1992.

For Michelle Maskiell and Sage Adrienne Smith

CONTENTS

PREFACE

Those who use the past to criticize the present should be put to death, together with their relatives.
—Li Si, Chinese prime minister, 3rd century B.C.

The meaning of history, as Li Si recognized, is extremely important and always contested. Recent world events have once again demonstrated how our assessment of the past shapes our understanding of the present. One reason for the self-destruction of the Soviet Union, for example, was that its citizens learned about and were repulsed by Stalin's atrocities. As the Chinese become aware of the previous excesses of the ruling Communist Party, many have begun to question the legitimacy of their government. The "culture wars" currently being waged in the United States are being fought in part over how Americans living in a multicultural society interpret and teach their history. A central issue in the battle concerns the nature of the story itself. Is it a tale characterized primarily by material success and individual freedom? Should it be depicted mainly as the exploitation of women, poor white males, and minorities? Is it described best as the process of conflict and cooperation among numerous groups of Americans?

This collection of records produced in Philadelphia during the Revolutionary and Early National periods is designed to permit people to enter the debate about the American past by using primary historical sources to interpret history for themselves. The Continental Congress, which produced the Declaration of Independence in 1776, the Constitutional Convention, which drafted the United States Constitution in 1787, and the federal government, which established the new nation's political institutions in the 1790s, dominate the history of late eighteenth-century Philadelphia, the city that hosted all these assemblies of rich and powerful men. Until recent decades, scholars of Early American history devoted a great deal of their attention to analyzing these critical events and the famous participants in them. As a result, we often view the history of Philadelphia through a lens that magnifies famous figures like Benjamin Franklin but obscures the great majority of its residents. A particular flaw in this vision is that the city's ordinary inhabitants are seen to be important only insofar as they participated in major political events. But the ways in which they led their lives, the forces that shaped their experiences, and the manner by which they helped fashion contemporary and future American society are largely ignored. The documents selected for this volume are intended to convey the diversity of life and the range of conditions in America's premier urban center during this period and to indicate the variety of evidence historians can use to reconstruct the past.

Life in Philadelphia during the closing decades of the eighteenth century is not representative of the entire country, since only one of every twenty Americans lived in an urban center at that time. But studying Philadelphia is a good way to begin to understand the history of America, because the City of Brotherly Love was on the leading edge of change and represented the nation's future in many ways. In Philadelphia, the struggle to gain political independence from Great Britain and to establish a republican form of government took shape early; the meaning of "human rights" and "equality" was debated fiercely; the conflict over the transition from mercantilism to capitalism emerged plainly; the problems of growing economic inequality and poverty appeared clearly; the two-century decline in the country's birth and death rates began haltingly; many African Americans resisted slavery and exploitation forcefully; and a multicultural and multiracial population attempted to coexist peacefully. In all these matters, the sails of America's future society were visible in the harbor of its premier city.

Each chapter in this book contains lengthy excerpts from one or two sources written in Philadelphia during the Revolutionary or Early National years. The introduction to each chapter provides necessary background and essential information about the documents, but leaves the interpretation of the records largely to the reader. The ten chapters are organized into five sections. Part One (Chapter 1) includes descriptions of the city offered by two contemporaries and an introduction that sketches various aspects of urban life neglected by those reports.

While most historical documents are biased toward wealthier, literate people, the sources included in Part Two chronicle the lives of marginalized Philadelphians—the poor, the imprisoned, and the fugitives, who generally were "down and out." Specifically, the Daily Occurrence Docket of the city's almshouse (Chapter 2) consists of the clerk's comments about people applying for admission to that institution, the predicaments that caused them to seek refuge, and life inside that asylum. The Prisoners for Trial Docket and the Vagrancy Docket (Chapter 3) depict conditions of individuals either incarcerated for alleged crimes or confined to the workhouse by their masters during the 1790s. Of particular note in the Vagrancy Docket are numerous slaves jailed for refusing to obey their owners. Chapter 4 reprints newspaper advertisements offering rewards for runaway slaves, indentured servants, and apprentices. These notices sketch the personal and physical characteristics of the escapees and their modes of flight, as envisioned by their masters.

Part Three spotlights the daily lives of two women. Chapter 5 contains excerpts from the journal of Elizabeth Drinker, a conservative Quaker who belonged to the "better sort" of Philadelphians. Drinker comments on topics ranging from medical practices to domestic activities, and from the experiences of wealthy women during the Revolutionary War to the nascent movement for women's rights at the end of the century. Chapter 6 includes portions of the memoirs of Ann Baker Carson, a woman who came from a middle-class background and worked intensely to maintain her position. Unlike Elizabeth Drinker, Ann Baker Carson embraced many of the ideals associated with the American Revolution and attempted to apply them to her own life. She comments on a host of issues pertinent to understanding the place of women and men in the new nation.

Part Four considers demographic issues concerning marriage, mortality, and migration. The registers of Gloria Dei (Chapter 7), a church that served the middle and lower classes predominantly, provide information about their marriages and deaths. The rector's extensive notations about each person are also suggestive about the nature of their housing, health, material conditions, premarital sexual behavior, and familial relationships. Zachariah Poulson's Bills of Mortality (Chapter 8) provide a statistical portrait of the demographic characteristics of the entire city from 1788 through 1801, allowing us to assess the community's health and to measure its birth, death, growth, and migration rates. Poulson's unusually detailed records differentiate among the experiences of women and men, blacks and whites, and various religious groups.

Part Five addresses the struggle by the city's middle and lower classes to institute their ideals during the Revolutionary War. The collection of broadsides in Chapter 9 reveals much about the concerns of many wage-earners and poorer artisans, especially the ways in which they understood such key concepts as "equality" and "justice," and how they wanted their radical ideas implemented in practical terms. The final chapter, Chapter 10, deals primarily with the debate in Philadelphia over the workings of the economy, although the implications of the debate extend far beyond that topic. When artisans and ordinary working people attempted to impose price controls during the inflationary years of the war, they entered into a momentous moral confrontation with merchants and other Philadelphians about the character of the new American society itself. Since this book encourages readers to reach their own understanding of history, it is instructive to note that the two historians who edited the documents in Part Five differ in their assessments. Steve Rosswurm depicts poorer Philadelphians as having been primarily deferential and politically inert before becoming active in 1775, while Ronald Schultz describes the city's artisans as constantly opposing the ruling elite since the city's founding.

The Appendix contains the prices of a few common items, the cost of firewood, clothing, and rent, and the wages earned by members of five occupational groups. These data should help readers to evaluate monetary amounts that appear in the various documents. The Glossary provides definitions for words and terms that appear in the records but that are no longer commonly used. For ease of reference, definitions often appear in the footnotes as well as in the Glossary. The Selected Bibliography and Further Reading will help readers locate books and articles written by historians about various topics relevant to the sources reprinted in this book.

Finally, in all the documents except those in Chapter 9, punctuation occasionally has been altered silently, and abbreviations and ampersands have been expanded to make the text easier to read.

This collection of primary sources originated nearly a decade ago when I served for two years as Documents Editor for the journal *Pennsylvania History*. Various scholars submitted to the journal edited records, portions of which appear in this book. I especially thank the historians who have contributed to this volume for caring enough about the sources to spend the necessary time to make them available to a wider audience. One personal reason for editing this volume is that I have a deep affection for historical records, both because they constitute the "stuff" of history but also because I simply enjoy the smell, sight, and feel of the documents for entirely irrational reasons.

Because of my own work patterns and the intrusions of everyday life, this book has come together quite slowly, and I am grateful to everyone involved for their patience. I am pleased to acknowledge the helpful suggestions offered by Peter Potter, the editor at Penn State Press, and the conscientious copy-editing performed by Peggy Hoover. Konstantin Dierks meticulously created the indexes. John K. Alexander and Ned Landsman offered good criticism of the entire book. I appreciate the financial support provided by the Research/Creativity program at Montana State University, by a research grant from the American Philosophical Society, and by an American Antiquarian Society–National Endowment for the Humanities Fellowship. The Philadelphia Center for Early American Studies—including its director Richard Dunn, Simon Newman, Susan Klepp, Leslie Patrick-Stamp, George Boudreau, Gabrielle Lanier, Susan Stabile, Cynthia Van Zandt, Rick Beeman, Michael Zuckerman, Stevie Wolf, and the other people associated with the Center—provided a wonderful place to complete the book's final details. As always, Betty Smith, Jack Smith, Carol Smith, Barbara Gibson, and James Gibson have been loving and supportive. Michelle Maskiell is a wonderful partner, and Sage Adrienne Smith is one of my life's new joys.

PART ONE

The City

CHAPTER 1

Philadelphia

The Athens of America

BILLY G. SMITH

When I resided in the Athens of America. . . .
—Gilbert Stuart

Philadelphia was the premier city in North America during the Revolutionary and Early National era. Much like Athens in ancient Greece, the City of Brotherly Love was the political, economic, and cultural center of the colonies and the new nation. It served as the de facto capital of the country during the final decades of the eighteenth century, the site of not only the Continental Congress, which declared national independence in 1776, but also the Convention that wrote the United States Constitution in 1787, and the three branches of the federal government during the 1790s. Philadelphia was also the wealthiest urban area in America; its financial institutions, such as the Bank of the United States (see Figure 1), anchored the new nation's economy. As the home of Benjamin Franklin, the Quaker City reaped the fruits of Franklin's

Fig. 1. "Bank of the United States, with a View of Third Street, Philadelphia," 1798. The Bank was at the center of both the nation's and the city's financial affairs. From W. Birch and Son, *The City of Philadelphia . . . As It Appeared in 1800*. Courtesy of the Historical Society of Pennsylvania.

tremendous energy and intellect. Many of its inhabitants embraced both his scientific approach to knowledge and his deep commitment to improving the community. Philadelphians thus established the American Philosophical Society, the College of Physicians, and the University of Pennsylvania to advance philosophical and practical wisdom, and they supported a host of private and public measures designed to aid the needy, cure the sick, educate the children, clean and light the streets, combat fires, and regulate markets.

The excerpts below from two contemporary accounts, the first written by Clement Biddle for the City Directory he compiled in 1791 and the second penned by James Mease in 1811, provide detailed descriptions of the city.[1] Biddle locates Philadelphia geographically, discusses the nature of its government and the number of its inhabitants, sketches its religious, charitable, and educational institutions, and comments on the health of its residents. Like promotional literature produced by modern Chambers of Commerce, Biddle's glowing account exaggerates the wonders of the city, and it should be interpreted accordingly. James Mease highlights the operation of urban markets and the ways in which the streets were patrolled, cleaned, and lighted. The remainder of this introduction considers aspects of the city's economic, occupational, social, and physical structure that Biddle and Mease did not cover.

Philadelphia's economy rested squarely on the foundation of commerce, and water dominated material life in the port city. Contemporary observers agreed that "everybody in Philadelphia deals more or less in trade" and that "their chief employ, indeed, is traffick and mercantile business."[2] These comments simplify but still capture the essence of the city's primary business enterprise. The majority of Philadelphians depended, either directly or indirectly, on commerce with people scattered throughout the Atlantic world, from small farmers and storekeepers in the neighboring countryside, to large manufacturers and merchants operating from the West Indies to Lisbon and London.[3]

The hundreds of ships that annually docked at wharves lining the city's eastern edge formed the backbone of the economy. They disgorged molasses from the West Indies and manufactured goods from Europe, which were dispersed throughout the city and the surrounding countryside. The abundant grain and livestock products of the city's rich hinterlands, encompassing parts of Pennsylvania, New Jersey, Delaware, and Maryland, were loaded onto vessels sailing to Europe and the Caribbean. Pro-

1. Clement Biddle, *The Philadelphia Directory* [1791] (Philadelphia: Johnson, 1791); and James Mease, *The Picture of Philadelphia* (1811; reprint, New York: Arno Press, 1970). On Philadelphia in general, see Russell F. Weigley, ed., *Philadelphia: A 300-Year History* (New York: Norton, 1982).

2. The first comment is from "Journal of Lord Adam Gordon," in *Narratives of Colonial America, 1704–1765*, ed. Howard H. Peckham (Chicago: R. R. Donnelley, 1971), 262; and the second is from Carl Bridenbaugh, ed., *Gentleman's Progress: The Itinerarium of Dr. Alexander Hamilton, 1744* (Westport, Conn.: Greenwood Press, 1973), 23.

3. The city's economy is discussed by Gary B. Nash, *The Urban Crucible: Social Change, Political Consciousness, and the Origins of the American Revolution* (Cambridge: Harvard University Press, 1979); Thomas M. Doerflinger, *A Vigorous Spirit of Enterprise: Merchants and Economic Development in Revolutionary Philadelphia* (Chapel Hill: University of North Carolina Press, 1986); and Billy G. Smith, *The "Lower Sort": Philadelphia's Laboring People, 1750–1800* (Ithaca, N.Y.: Cornell University Press, 1990).

Fig. 2. "The Arch Street Ferry," as it appeared in 1800, suggests the commercial activity of the city's waterfront. The foreground depicts coopers finishing barrels and laborers and draymen unloading ship cargo. From W. Birch and Son, *The City of Philadelphia . . . As It Appeared in 1800*. Courtesy of the Historical Society of Pennsylvania.

ducing, transporting, and selling these commodities created a complex economy involving thousands of individuals. Mariners staffed ships, stevedores moved cargo, and carters and laborers transferred merchandise between vessels and warehouses. Waggoners, farmers, and flatboat operators carried flour, bread, and other foodstuffs into the city and returned to the countryside ladened with shoes, textiles, and other processed goods. Coopers fashioned barrels to hold items bound for the sea (see Figure 2), while shopkeepers and grocers peddled both foreign and local merchandise in retail stores. Subsidiary sectors of the economy provided jobs for workers in the construction of houses and ships, encouraged artisans to fashion wares for local consumption, and stimulated the service roles played by keepers of boardinghouses, inns, and taverns as well as by smiths, farriers, wheelwrights, riggers, sailmakers, and chandlers who cared for horses, carts, and boats. All the while, merchants, clerks, and other tradespeople directed and organized the entire system.[4]

People in these occupations were divided roughly into three "classes" or, in eighteenth-century terminology, "sorts." Among the "lower sort" were unskilled laborers who worked with their hands cleaning chimneys, excavating cellars, draining swamps, hauling building materials, and stowing and unloading ship cargoes. Hundreds of sailors also belonged in this category because they shared with laborers a minimal living standard, low status, and limited occupational and economic mobility.[5]

The "middling sort" was comprised mostly of artisans or craftspeople, who fashioned items by hand. While most artisans belonged to this category, they were a somewhat amorphous group spread along the spectrum of wealth, ranging from impoverished apprentice shoemakers to affluent master carpenters. The bottom end of the scale—tailors, shoemakers, and coopers—had much in common with sailors and laborers, including low income, uncertain prospects for advancement, and, in most cases, exclusion from the ranks of property holders (and therefore from the ranks of voters before the Revolution). At the upper end were tanners, bakers, sugarboilers, brewers, goldsmiths, and some construction contractors. Artisans, however, rarely reached the pinnacle of the social hierarchy.[6]

In addition to these differences among artisans, every craft was divided into three tiers: masters, journeymen, and apprentices. The generally older masters were experienced at their craft, almost always worked for themselves, and usually owned their place of business or operated out of their homes. Journeymen hired out to masters for wages for specified periods of time, and they probably possessed their own tools. Apprentices, generally in their teens, learned "the art and mysteries" of the craft under contractual arrangements with a master, who often also served as surrogate father. This craft system was the most popular way for youngsters, mostly males, to get vocational training in an urban environment. In theory, a youth moved from one tier to another, spending approximately seven years as an apprentice and perhaps an equal

4. Smith, *The "Lower Sort,"* chap. 3.

5. Steven Rosswurm, *Arms, Country, and Class: The Philadelphia Militia and the American Revolution* (New Brunswick, N.J.: Rutgers University Press, 1987); and Gary B. Nash, Billy G. Smith, and Dirk Hoerder, "Laboring Americans and the American Revolution," *Labor History* 24 (1983): 415–19.

6. Ronald Schultz, *The Republic of Labor: Philadelphia Artisans and the Politics of Class, 1720–1830* (New York: Oxford University Press, 1993).

Fig. 3. "View in Third Street, from Spruce Street Philadelphia," 1800. William Bingham, one of the city's wealthiest merchants, constructed the mansion in the foreground between 1786 and 1788. From W. Birch and Son, *The City of Philadelphia . . . As It Appeared in 1800.* Courtesy of the Historical Society of Pennsylvania.

number as a journeyman. The transition from journeyman to master may not have been so easy to achieve, however.

Many merchants and a few substantial shopkeepers belonged to the "better sort." Of course, not all merchants were wealthy; some were grocers who lived no better than prosperous master craftspeople. But the pillars of the mercantile community sometimes amassed fabulous fortunes, dressed in fashionable finery, and constructed marvelous mansions (see Figure 3). Doctors, lawyers, clergymen, government officials, and other professionals also enjoyed high social status even if their wealth rarely matched that of merchants.[7]

Outside these occupational and social horizontal layers stood nonfree

7. Doerflinger, *Vigorous Spirit of Enterprise.*

people of two kinds. Indentured servants (mostly European migrants) were bound to individual masters for as many as three or four years, and their liberties were greatly restricted while under indenture. African and African American slaves were owned perpetually by another person, their human rights were abridged, and their position was hereditary. These nonfree people worked in all aspects of the city's economy, from sailors to servants and from caulkers to clerks.[8]

The city's occupational structure changed slightly during the final quarter of the eighteenth century, but for every twenty men the following breakdown roughly applied: three or four servants or slaves, six sailors or unskilled laborers, seven artisans (divided equally among apprentices, journeymen, and masters), one person engaged in a miscellaneous trade or service (including clerks, carters, porters, and barbers), one shopkeeper, one merchant, and one official or professional person.[9]

While Philadelphia's economy was generally prosperous, it was characterized by frequent financial oscillations that buffeted the inhabitants. In general, conditions deteriorated in the decade before the Revolution, the economy suffered a crisis during and immediately after the war, and the years after 1793 were particularly good ones. The way in which the economy grew, however, benefited some residents greatly and others hardly at all. Those at the top possessed enough resources to cushion fiscal shocks and to take advantage of available opportunities during both good and bad times, and at the end of the century they were better off financially than at the time of the Revolution. The middling sort enjoyed mixed success, with advantages for some craftspeople counterbalanced by a decline in the material welfare of others.[10]

The lower sort, however, did not enjoy an overall improvement during the century's final decades. Not only did economic inequality increase, but the living standards of poorer Philadelphians failed to improve. Laboring Philadelphians generally led intensely insecure economic lives throughout most of this period. Disease, epidemics, injuries, business cycles, political turmoil, wars, and seasonal unemployment created times of personal financial crisis and pushed many unskilled and lesser skilled

8. Sharon V. Salinger, *"To Serve Well and Faithfully": Labor and Indentured Servants in Pennsylvania, 1682–1800* (New York: Cambridge University Press, 1987); and Gary B. Nash, *Forging Freedom: The Formation of Philadelphia's Black Community 1720–1840* (Cambridge: Harvard University Press, 1988).

9. Nash, Smith, and Hoerder, "Laboring Americans," 435.

10. Smith, *The "Lower Sort,"* chap. 3.

workers below the subsistence level. As many fell into poverty, they turned to public assistance and private relief agencies to supply the basic necessities of life.[11]

Women accounted for nearly half of the city's population, although their social and economic status usually was determined by their husbands and fathers. The vast majority of adult women married, and only a few of those whose husbands could support the family worked outside the home. A great many women, however, who were married to men who did not earn enough to support them, sought employment in the public sphere. But social custom limited their opportunities primarily to jobs as teachers, nurses, seamstresses, milliners, hucksters, maids, servants, and laundrywomen. Some kept shops, inns, taverns, and boardinghouses, while others had little choice but to engage in prostitution to support themselves and their children.[12]

Philadelphia was one of the most multicultural cities in the Western world. As the primary American port of immigration, it experienced an influx of thousands of migrants during the late eighteenth century. While most Europeans quickly passed through the city to the countryside, enough settled in Philadelphia to help make it the continent's largest metropolitan center. Its population mushroomed from approximately 24,000 in 1765 to nearly 70,000 in 1800. The tide of European migrants, mostly Germans and Scots-Irish, crested during the quarter-century before the Revolution, then subsided during the war itself. After a brief hiatus, a smaller wave of migrants flowed through the city during the 1790s as the Irish, refugees from revolutions in France and Saint Domingue (now Haiti), and itinerants from other parts of America arrived in the Quaker City. Among the latter group were thousands of newly freed and escaped slaves who took refuge in Philadelphia and successfully created a vibrant black community there. The result was a city marked by remarkable ethnic and racial variety, containing natives from northern Europe, Africa, the West Indies, and various parts of North America.[13]

11. John K. Alexander, *Render Them Submissive: Responses to Poverty in Philadelphia, 1760–1800* (Amherst: University of Massachusetts Press, 1980); Gary B. Nash, "Poverty and Poor Relief in Pre-Revolutionary Philadelphia," *William and Mary Quarterly*, 3rd ser., 23 (1976): 3–30; and Billy G. Smith, "Poverty and Economic Marginality in Eighteenth-Century America," *Proceedings of the American Philosophical Society* 132 (1988): 85–118.

12. Smith, *The "Lower Sort."*

13. Susan E. Klepp, ed., *The Demographic History of the Philadelphia Region, 1600–1860* (Philadelphia: American Philosophical Society, 1989); Smith, *The "Lower Sort"*; and Nash, *Forging Freedom*.

Philadelphia was an extremely hazardous place to live, considerably more unhealthy than American rural areas of the day and many European cities. Sickness and death were part of the day-to-day lives of the residents of the Pennsylvania capital, and mortality was particularly heavy among new arrivals, who entered an unfamiliar disease environment. Smallpox, the greatest menace in the pre-Revolutionary years, was gradually brought under control, at least for those both willing and financially able to undergo immunization. But residents still worried about contagious diseases, particularly because yellow fever epidemics devastated the city during the 1790s. Remarkably high birth rates offset the elevated death rates to create a small natural increase of the population throughout much of the period. This growth, combined with the large influx of migrants, skewed the city's age structure: children and young adults greatly outnumbered those in the older age-groups.[14]

Because all but the wealthiest Philadelphians relied on walking as their principal form of transportation, the main markets and prime residential and business districts were located in the center of town. During the closing decades of the eighteenth century, Philadelphia increasingly assumed the classic preindustrial urban residential pattern, consisting of concentric rings radiating from a nucleus of wealthy residents in the center of the city through bands of successively poorer inhabitants toward the fringes. During these years, residents behaved as if Philadelphia rotated on an axis running through the eastern end of High (or Market) Street in the middle of town (see Map 1). The laws of motion affected the various classes in different ways: centrifugal force dispersed poor folk to the perimeter, while centripetal force propelled the wealthier people to the core. By 1800, laborers and mariners congregated in the northern, southern, and western areas of the city and its suburbs of Southwark and the Northern Liberties, while most of the wealthy lived around several of the eastern blocks of High Street near the Delaware River. Yet the classic pattern did not completely materalize. While the lower sort dominated the city's periphery and suburbs, many of them continued to inhabit the central city, crowding into cheap shelter in alleys, courts, and lanes and leaving the major thoroughfares to the middling and better sort of citizens.[15]

14. Susan E. Klepp, *Philadelphia in Transition: A Demographic History of the City and Its Occupational Groups, 1720–1830* (New York: Garland, 1989); and Smith, *The "Lower Sort,"* chap. 2.

15. Smith, *The "Lower Sort,"* chap. 6.

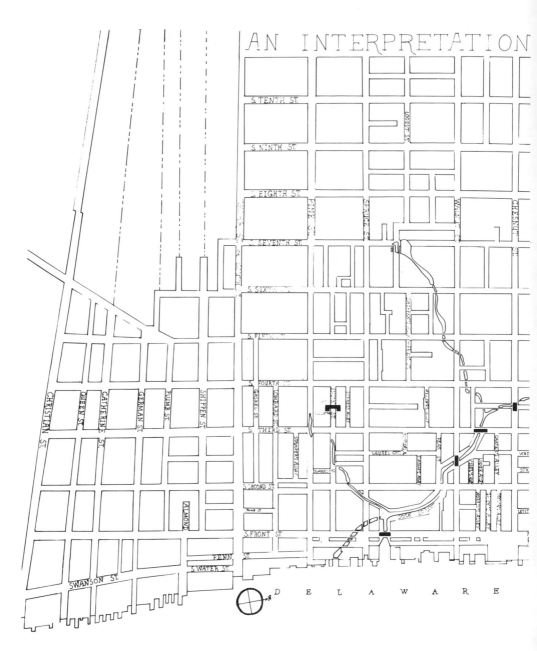

Map 1. Philadelphia, 1796. Drawing by Peter E. Daniels in 1982.

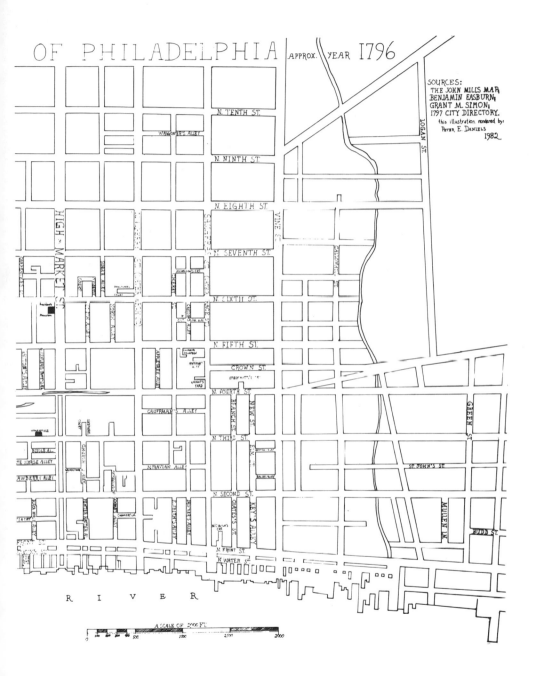

OF PHILADELPHIA APPROX. YEAR 1796

SOURCES:
THE JOHN MILLS MAP
BENJAMIN EASBURN,
GRANT M. SIMON,
1797 CITY DIRECTORY.
this illustration rendered by:
PETER E. DANIELS
1982

LOGAN ST.

N. TENTH ST.

WAGGONER'S ALLEY

N. NINTH ST.

N. EIGHTH ST.

VINE ST.

N. SEVENTH ST.

HIGH & MARKET ST.

N. SIXTH ST.

N. FIFTH ST.

CROWN ST.

N. FOURTH ST.

CAUFFMAN'S ALLEY

NEW ST.

N. THIRD ST.

MORAVIAN ALLEY

ST. JOHN'S ST.

GREEN

N. SECOND ST.

BUDD ST.

MULLEN LN.

N. FRONT ST.

N. WATER ST.

R I V E R

A SCALE OF 2000 FT.
0   100 200 300 400   500   1000   2000   3000

Philadelphia experienced both changes and continuities from the Revolutionary through the Early National years. The population expanded enormously, augmented primarily by successive waves of migrants that had broken over and occasionally nearly drowned the city. Still, the racial and ethnic diversity of Philadelphia remained relatively constant. The overall mortality level lessened as smallpox, the most devastating disease before the Revolution, was gradually brought under control. Yet periodic yellow fever epidemics wrought incredible destruction of human life during the 1790s. Philadelphia's prosperity increased significantly, but its basic economic structure did not change. The primary business activities still entailed exporting the region's grain products, importing British manufactures, constructing housing and ships, and distributing the handmade goods of urban craftspeople throughout the area. Commercial success was shared unequally, as the richest citizens accrued control of more of the wealth while poverty increased. This growing inequality was reflected in a more clearly defined pattern of residential segregation by class. Meanwhile, political events deepened the commitment of many radical and liberal Philadelphians to notions of freedom, independence, and equality, although the same ideas often scandalized their more conservative neighbors.

The following documents provide further important details about everyday life in the City of Brotherly Love.

I

From Clement Biddle, *The Philadelphia Directory* (Philadelphia: Johnson, 1791):

Information Concerning the City of Philadelphia

The city of Philadelphia, capital of the state of Pennsylvania, and seat of government of the United States of North America, lies . . . upon the

Western bank of the river Delaware, which is here about a mile in breadth, about one hundred and twenty miles from the Atlantic Ocean . . . and about fifty-five miles from the sea, in a South-Eastward direction [see Map 2]. The Delaware is navigable from the sea to the falls of Trenton, about thirty miles above the city, by vessels of considerable burthen; and by boats of twenty and thirty tons, and by large rafts in the time of freshes,[16] near two hundred miles into the state of New-York.

It was laid out by William Penn, the first proprietary and founder of the province, in the year 1683 and settled by a colony from England, which arrived in that and the preceding years, and was increased by a constant and regular influx of foreigners, to so great a degree, that in less than a century, and within the life time of the first person born within it of European parents, it was computed to contain 6,020 houses and 40,020 inhabitants in the city and suburbs [in 1783].[17]

The ground plot of the city is an oblong square, about one mile North and South, and two miles East and West, lying in the narrowest part of the isthmus between the Delaware and Schuylkill rivers, about five miles in a right line above their confluence [see Map 3]. The plane is so nearly level except upon the bank of the Delaware, that art and labour were necessary to dig common sewers and water courses in many places to drain the streets. In the beginning of this settlement it was expected, that the fronts on both rivers would be first improved for the convenience of trade and navigation, and that the buildings would extend gradually in the rear of each until they would meet and form one town extending from East to West, but experience soon convinced the settlers that the Delaware front was alone sufficient for quays and landing places, and that the Schuylkill lay at too great a distance to form part of the town on its banks; whence it followed that the town increased Northward and Southward of the original plot, upon the Delaware front, and now occupies a space near three miles in length, North and South, while the buildings in the middle where they are most extended, do not reach a mile from the Delaware.

The city has been twice incorporated, and the limits thereof restrained to the oblong, originally laid out by William Penn, without including the Northern or Southern suburbs. This plot is intersected by a number of streets at right angles with each other, nine of which run East and West

16. This occurred when the Delaware River was at its height during the Spring runoff.
17. Historians have estimated that the population of Philadelphia and its two "suburbs" in 1783 was 39,277; see Smith, *The "Lower Sort,"* 206.

Map 2. Pennsylvania, New Jersey, Delaware, and Maryland. Drawing by Adrienne Mayor in 1989.

from Delaware to Schuylkill, and twenty-three North and South, crossing the first at right angles, forming one hundred and eighty-four squares of lots for buildings. The streets running East and West are named (except High Street near the middle of the city) from the trees found in the country upon the arrival of the colony: Vine, Sassafras, Mulberry, High, Chestnut, Walnut, Spruce, Pine and Cedar Streets, and those running North and South from their numeral order, Front, Second, Third, Fourth, etc. to Broad Street, which is midway between the two rivers. . . .

Of these, High Street is 100 feet, Broad Street 113, Mulberry 60, and all the others 50 feet wide. Within the improved parts of the city they are

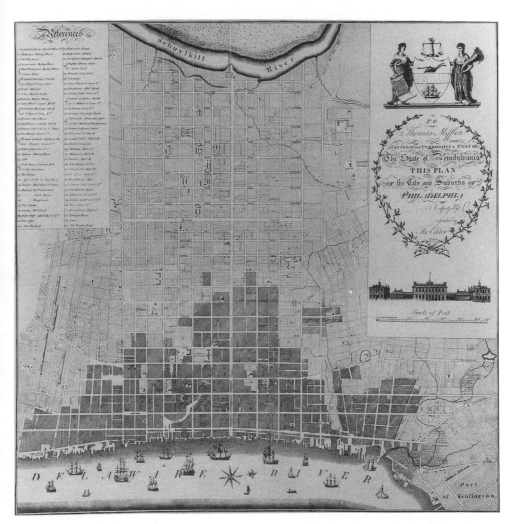

Map 3. "Plan of the City and Suburbs of Philadelphia," 1794. The shaded area indicates densely settled neighborhoods. Southwark is adjacent to the Delaware River at the city's southern end, while the Northern Liberties parallel the river to the north. Courtesy of the Historical Society of Pennsylvania.

paved, in the middle with pebble stones, for carts and carriages, which usually contains three fifths of the whole breadth, and on each side with bricks for foot passengers; between the brick and stone pavements, are gutters, paved with brick, to carry off the water, and the foot-ways are defended from the approach of carriages, by rows of posts placed without the gutters at the distance of 10 or 12 feet from each other. Besides the forementioned main streets, there are many others not originally laid down in the plot, the most public of which are Water Street and Dock Street. . . .

The general assembly in the winter sessions of 1789, favouring the wishes of the citizens, passed an act intitled an act to incorporate the city of Philadelphia, which with a supplement passed in 1790, constitutes the present city charter. . . . The common council consists of two branches: fifteen aldermen are chosen by the freeholders to continue in office for seven years; they chuse a recorder from the citizens at large for seven years, and a mayor from their own number for one year. Thirty common council men are chosen by the citizens at large, entitled to vote for representatives in assembly, to continue in office for three years; these were intended to form a balanced government upon the principle, that the choice by freeholders, and for a longer term would produce a more select body of aldermen, and that the citizens at large would chuse characters fitter to represent and form the popular branch of city government. . . .

There is not perhaps in the world a more liberal plan of city government, every class of citizens have an opportunity of representing and being represented. The body . . . possesses the powers of legislation and taxation in all cases necessary for the well governing and improving the city . . . and from the many improvements already introduced, there is reason to hope that its police will be equal to that of any modern city.

A city court is held by the mayor, recorder and aldermen four times a year, and hold cognisance of all crimes and misdemeanors committed within the city. A court of aldermen having cognisance of debts above forty shillings, and not exceeding ten pounds, is held every week beginning on Monday morning, and setting by adjournments until the business of the week is finished. Each alderman has separate cognisance of debts under forty shillings.

The number of inhabitants within the city and suburbs (including the district of Southwark and the compactly built part of the Northern Liberties, which to every purpose but as to their government, are considered as parts of the city) is found by the late census to be 42,400, and the number of houses 6,651, and stores or work shops 415.[18]

18. According to the first census, 42,520 people lived in Philadelphia, Southwark, and the urban portion of the Northern Liberties in 1790. U.S. Bureau of the Census, *Heads of Families at the First Census of the United States Taken in the Year 1790: Pennsylvania* (Washington, D.C.:

Fig. 4. "High Street, with the First Presbyterian Church," 1799. This westward view depicts the church on the north side and the city's central market house, with a meat hook at its top, on the south. From W. Birch and Son, *The City of Philadelphia . . . As It Appeared in 1800.* Courtesy of the Historical Society of Pennsylvania.

The houses for public worship are numerous, the principal of which are as follows: Of the church of Rome three, of the Protestant Episcopal church three, of the people called Quakers five, of the Presbyterians of different sects six [see Figure 4], of the Baptists one, of the German Lutherans two, of the German Calvinists one, of the Moravians one, of the Methodists two, of the Universalists one, and of the Hebrews one.

The city is provided with a number of public and private charitable institutions; the principal of which are, the house of employment, a large

Government Printing Office, 1908), 10. See the corrections made to this figure by John K. Alexander, "The Philadelphia Numbers Game: An Analysis of Philadelphia's Eighteenth-Century Population," *Pennsylvania Magazine of History and Biography* 98 (1974): 314–24.

commodious building, where the poor of the city and some adjoining townships are supported, and employed in coarse manufactures to aid in defraying their expences, under the care of the overseers and guardians of the poor, who are a corporate body created for this purpose by act of assembly, with power to lay taxes for its further support.

The Pennsylvania hospital, an institution erected at first partly by the bounty of the legislature, and partly by private subscription; its funds, arising mostly from the latter source, are considerable, and are under the care of twelve managers, chosen annually by contributors to the amount of ten pounds or more, who are incorporated by act of assembly. In this house, insane persons and the friendless sick and wounded, are taken care of and provided with every necessary and comfort their situation requires, and are attended by six of the ablest physicians and surgeons, who are annually chosen by the managers, and who chearfully give their time and advice to the patients, for whose use a well furnished shop is kept in the house, by a skilled apothecary, who makes up the medicines prescribed.

The Quakers alms house is supported by that society for the use of their own poor; it is divided into a number of separate houses and rooms, for families of single persons who have fallen into decay; most of them contribute by their industry towards their own support, but are supplied with whatever their industry falls short of procuring, by a committee of the society, and live more comfortably than many who, in full health and unhurt by accident, provide for their own subsistance. . . .

The dispensary, a very useful institution, supported by voluntary annual subscriptions; it is under the care of twelve managers, chosen annually by the subscribers, who choose physicians and surgeons to attend the sick and wounded at their own houses, and keep a large apothecaries shop to supply medicines; each subscriber paying a guinea annually, has a right to recommend two poor patients at a time, and, to the honor of the faculty, it is mentioned, that the poor thus recommended, are attended gratis, with equal care and tenderness with those who are able to pay them, and many thousands have received the benefit of this institution, who otherwise would have languished, or perhaps perished for want of medical assistance and by the quackery of pretenders to the healing art.

Almost every religious society has a fund under proper direction, some of which are incorporated for the relief of the widows and children of their clergy or other distressed members of their communion. There are also societies formed for the relief of particular descriptions of persons, with funds raised by subscriptions or otherwise, for the purpose, such as the sea captains society, the Delaware pilots society, separate societies for the relief and assistance of emigrants and other distressed persons, from England, Scotland, Ireland, Germany, etc. some of which are incorporated, so that there can scarce happen an instance of individual distress, for which a mode of advice, assistance or relief is not provided without resort to public begging.

Seminaries of learning are established upon the most enlarged and liberal principles, of which the principal are: The university of Pennsylvania, founded and endowed by the legislature of the state. Professorships are established in all the liberal arts and sciences, and a complete course of education may be pursued here, from the first rudiments of literature, to the highest branches of science. . . .

Almost every religious society have one or more schools under their immediate direction, for the education of their own youth of both sexes, as well of the rich, who are able to pay, as of the poor, who are taught and provided with books and stationary gratis; besides which, there are a number of private schools under the direction of masters and mistresses, independent of any public body; and there are several private academies for the instruction of young ladies in all the branches of polite literature, suitable to the sex . . . let it suffice, that there is no individual, whose parents or guardians, masters or mistresses will take the trouble to apply, but will be admitted into some one of these schools, and if they are unable to pay, will be taught gratis; it ought not to be omitted, that there is a school for the Africans of every shade or colour, kept under the care and at the expence of the Quakers, into which are admitted gratis, slaves as well as free persons of whatever age of both sexes, and taught reading, writing, arithmetic, knitting, sewing and other useful female accomplishments; this school was originally instituted by private subscriptions of the society, with a view to prepare that degraded race for a better situation in civil life; but the will of the late Anthony Benezet,[19] of benevolent memory, a considerable donation from the society in England, and some other charitable devices,

19. Anthony Benezet, a Philadelphia Quaker, was a leader in the early antislavery movement and an advocate for the education of African Americans—both slaves and free people. Benezet, who died in 1784, founded the Quaker African School, located in Willing's Alley in the center of the city.

have provided funds adequate to its future support, and it will no longer be burthensome to individuals.

Sunday schools for the instruction of children who would otherwise spend that day in idleness or mischief, have lately been instituted, and it is to be hoped will tend to amend the morals and conduct of the rising generation.

The public library of Philadelphia is a most useful institution; it contains near ten thousand volumes, well selected, for the information and improvement of all ranks of the citizens; they are deposited in an elegant building lately erected, in a modern stile, and are accessable every day in the week, except Sunday. . . .

The corporation have lately ordered the streets, lanes and alleys to be marked at every intersection with each other, and the houses to be numbered. . . . The numbers in the streets, etc., lying East and West, begin with No. 1 on the North and No. 2 on the South sides at the river Delaware or other Eastern beginning of the street, and proceed regularly in the excess of two Westward, hence all the houses marked with odd numbers are on the North sides of the way, and all those marked with even numbers on the south. The numbers in the streets lying North and South, begin at the several corners of High Street, with No. 1 on the East and No. 2 on the West sides. . . .

The city within a few years past has experienced a very remarkable revolution in respect to the healthiness of its inhabitants; the bill of mortality proves that the number of deaths has considerably decreased since the year 1783, notwithstanding the great increase of its population; this change in favour of health and life is ascribed by physicians to the cooperation of the following causes. 1st, The arching the dock [Dock Creek], whereby a very noxious and offensive nuisance was removed.[20] 2d, The cultivation of the lots adjoining and partly surrounding the city, whereby another extensive source of putrid exhalations is dried up. 3dly, An increased care in cleansing the streets. 4thly, An increase of horticulture, and consequently greater consumption of vegetable elements. 5thly, The institution of the dispensary, which has extended medical aid to many hundreds in a year, who either perished for the want of it or were sacrificed by quacks. 6thly, The more improved state of physic, whence several

20. Dock Creek flowed sluggishly through the center of the city and emptied into the Delaware River. By the end of the Revolution, Dock Creek had become a virtual sewer filled with human and animal waste that emitted strong noxious odors. The city covered the creek with a low brick arch in the late 1780s.

diseases formerly fatal in most instances are better understood and treated, and therefore more generally cured. And 7thly, From a general diffusion of knowledge among all classes of people from our libraries, our numerous societies, monthly, weekly and daily publications, whence the people at large are better acquainted than formerly with the means of preserving their health, as may be exemplified in one instance: there was but one death last summer from drinking cold water, whereas some years ago twenty has not been an uncommon number from this single cause. . . .

II

From James Mease, *The Picture of Philadelphia* (1811; reprint, New York: Arno Press, 1970):

Markets—Provisions

The first Market house built in High street [see Figure 5], was a range of wooden stalls from Front to Second street. In the year 1720, the first part of the market in High street west of the old court house was built. . . . In proportion as the population of town and country increased, the market house was extended until at present it reaches from Front to Sixth street. . . .

By the law authorizing the continuation of the market, it is provided that the western half of the stalls is to be let to the people of the country, and to no others: and the other half to butchers. . . .

The market house in south Second street, was built for the accommodation of the citizens in the southern part of the city, and has been enlarged from time to time until it now extends from Pine to Cedar street, a distance of about 440 feet. At each end a room is erected, for the meetings of the commissioners, fire companies, and of the citizens. . . .

As mentioned earlier, the hill on Market street is allotted for the sale of fish. This traffic, except in the case of those who bring fish preserved in ice, in waggons from the sea, is carried on chiefly by women, many of whose husbands are employed in catching the fish. . . .

Fig. 5. "High Street Market, Philadelphia," 1799. This engraving of the interior of one of the three market houses during a nonmarket day conforms with a traveler's description of the market as "a covered building, 420 of my steps, in length, exclusive of the intersections of streets, and I calculated my step to be a yard; but only five feet in breadth, including the butchers' benches and blocks" (Charles William Janson, *The Stranger in America, 1793–1806*, ed. Carl S. Driver [New York, 1971], 185). From W. Birch and Son, *The City of Philadelphia . . . As It Appeared in 1800.* Courtesy of the Historical Society of Pennsylvania.

The days appointed by law for holding markets in High street, are Wednesday and Saturday; and Tuesday and Friday, for the Market in south Second street. . . .

The quantity of provisions, animal and vegetable, brought to market during the year, is immense, and much beyond the wants of the inhabitants. . . . It may be safely asserted, that in no city in the world, is more animal food consumed, in proportion to its size, than in Philadelphia. It constitutes the substantial part of the dinner of every adult in the city, and most labourers and mechanics eat a portion of it at breakfast and supper. . . . [21]

The task of attending to the execution of the regulations of the markets, is attached to the duties of the clerks of the market. . . . Seizures are often made of butter, lard, and sausages, for being deficient in weight. Half of the quantity seized, is sent to the alms-house, and the other half is the perquisite of the clerks. . . .

Preservation of the Peace

There are fourteen constables, one for each ward; and until the present year, one high constable, who is required to walk through the streets daily with his mace in his hand, and examine all vagrant and disorderly persons, and upon refusal to give him an account of their residence and employment, or not giving a satisfactory account, to carry such persons before the mayor or an alderman to be dealt with according to law. . . .

Watching and Lighting

There are thirty-two watchmen who cry the hour, and six who visit the boxes of the others, to insure a punctual performance of their duty; the whole are under the direction of the captain of the watch, who attends at the old court house in Second street, every night, to receive the vagrants, rioters or thieves, who may be taken up by the watchmen; and to take care of the oil, wick, etc. of which he must render an account to the city commissioners. . . .

Cleansing the Streets

To accomplish this, the city is divided into districts, and one commissioner attends to the cleanliness of a district. The street dirt is scraped by scavengers into small heaps, and men follow with carts, to take it away to

21. Although meat was inexpensive by European standards, the assertion that most laboring Philadelphians ate meat regularly is probably false, because they did not earn enough to afford to purchase beef daily (Smith, *The "Lower Sort,"* chap. 4).

the commons, where it is deposited in heaps, and disposed of occasionally by auction, for manure. . . .

Fuel—Wood Corders—Public Landings

The principal article of house fuel in Philadelphia, is hickory, oak or maple wood. Pine wood is used chiefly by brick burners and bakers. . . .

During the continuance of the navigation in the Delaware, fire wood is brought in shallops from both sides of the river, above and below the city; but in winter, when from the obstruction by ice, the supply in that way is cut off, wood is brought by land. In all cases, it is measured by sworn corders, at certain fixed rates. . . .

No person is permitted to buy wood in the city to sell again, from September to March inclusive, under a penalty of two dollars for every cord sold. . . .

PART TWO

Down and Out

CHAPTER 2

The Institutional Poor

The Almshouse Daily Occurrence Docket

BILLY G. SMITH

As the distribution of wealth has become more unequal and the "underclass" even more permanent in the United States during the late twentieth century, considerable study has been devoted to the contemporary and the historical dimensions of poverty. American welfare policies have been fashioned out of centuries of experience, scholars reason, and a clearer understanding of the evolution of attitudes and practices during the past will enable us better to evaluate current programs and proposed solutions.[1]

1. See Michael B. Katz, *In the Shadow of the Poorhouse: A Social History of Welfare in America* (New York: Basic Books, 1986); and Walter I. Trattner, *From Poor Law to Welfare State: A History of Social Welfare in America* (New York: The Free Press, 1989).

Historians have been interested in the level, causes, and nature of poverty in early America for other reasons as well. The character of indigents and the way in which they are treated reveals a great deal about their society. The ideological commitment to equality during the American Revolution, for example, would not rest in easy accord with the existence of widespread impoverishment amid plenty. Given the rich natural resources and the general scarcity of labor in early America, many scholars have concluded that the poor were relatively few in number and that they consisted primarily of the sick, aged, widowed, and orphaned. Most unfortunates, especially healthy young men, were able to improve their economic situation. Other analysts disagree. They detect growing indigence during the eighteenth century, especially in the urban centers, and argue that the specter of poverty began to cast its shadow over able-bodied adults as well as those who chronically suffered the darkness of deprivation. This phenomenon could have played an important role in the American Revolution if the economic difficulties encountered by many lower-class people weakened their allegiance to the British Empire and to their own domestic political systems.[2]

The level of indigence in Philadelphia during the first half of the eighteenth century appears to have been low; rarely did more than 1 percent of its residents depend on public relief. But the financial problems of the less fortunate grew substantially during the Seven Years' War (1756–63), and, by the late 1760s and 1770s, approximately 5 percent of the city's inhabitants received public aid. Philadelphians responded to poverty in ways similar to their counterparts in other American metropolitan areas. When taxes to aid the poor escalated, officials devised more-stringent residency requirements for potential aid recipients and forced some destitute nonresidents to leave the city. In the 1760s the overseers of the poor began to abandon the traditional system of providing cash, firewood, and food to families in their own homes in favor of an institutional solution. City leaders thus financed the construction of a "bettering house" with tax money and placed it in the hands of a private corporation. This almshouse-workhouse combination (see Figure 6) was designed to serve the dual purpose of minimizing the cost of care for indigents and forcing capable paupers to labor for their livelihood. During the century's final

2. Two studies of Revolutionary Philadelphia that differ in their assessment of poverty are Doerflinger, *Vigorous Spirit of Enterprise;* Nash, *Urban Crucible.* For a brief overview of poverty in Colonial America, see Billy G. Smith, "Poverty in Early America," in *Encyclopedia of the North American Colonies,* ed. Jacob Ernest Cooke et al., 3 vols. (New York: Charles Scribner's Sons, 1993), 1:483–94.

Fig. 6. "Alms House in Spruce Street," 1799. The brick walls surrounding the almshouse confined inmates to the grounds. Robert Honyman offered the following description of the structure in 1775: "It is built of Brick, & consists of a Main Body & two wings, & in the two corners are two square buildings, higher than the other parts, which are two stories high, besides a ground & Garret story. It has Piazzas round on the Inside" (Philip Padelford, ed., *Colonial Panorama 1775: Dr. Robert Honyman's Journal for March and April* [San Marino, Calif., 1939], 17). From W. Birch and Son, *The City of Philadelphia . . . As It Appeared in 1800.* Courtesy of the Historical Society of Pennsylvania.

decades, private citizens established a host of organizations, associated primarily along ethnic, occupational, or religious lines, to supplement government relief.[3]

Public welfare dependents continued to comprise roughly 5 percent of

---

3. Alexander, *Render Them Submissive;* Nash, "Poverty and Poor Relief," 6, 9, 25, 28; Smith, "Poverty and Economic Marginality," 96–97. On welfare policies in other American cities, see Robert E. Cray Jr., *Paupers and Poor Relief in New York City and Its Rural Environs, 1700–1830* (Philadelphia: Temple University Press, 1988); and Raymond A. Mohl, *Poverty in New York, 1783–1825* (New York: Oxford University Press, 1971).

Philadelphia's inhabitants during the final quarter of the eighteenth century. However, this figure does not include those who received aid from public or private agencies for which records no longer exist, men and women who did not qualify or apply for public assistance, slaves and servants who were prevented from receiving help, or working people who daily lived at or just above subsistence. Although precise statistics are impossible to calculate, all of these people constituted as many as one-third or, during hard times, one-half of the residents of the Quaker City during the late eighteenth century. Almshouse inmates thus represented only a small proportion, albeit the most desperate, of Philadelphians who constantly struggled with poverty.[4]

The lack of primary documents has contributed to the disagreements among historians about the nature of poverty in early America. As has been the case throughout history, the middle and especially the lower classes left many fewer records than the elite did, and that is true of Philadelphia as well. Only when the destitute came into contact with government officials was information about their lives routinely recorded for posterity. Such was the case when indigent Philadelphians applied for relief from the city's almshouse. The almshouse "Daily Occurrence Docket," a portion of which is reproduced below, contains the clerk's observations about thousands of needy people admitted to or discharged from that institution. Although brief, these comments are the most complete available descriptions of poverty-stricken individuals who left behind virtually no other written records. These accounts provide a great many details about the lives, difficulties, and subsistence strategies of the institutional poor.[5]

A host of problems caused people to apply for admission to the almshouse. As was the case throughout the eighteenth century, officials in 1800 and 1801 often dispensed aid to the "traditional" poor—the sick, the aged, the widowed, and the very young. Some 5.7 percent of all inmates were "old," 43.1 percent were "sick," 10.2 percent endured venereal disease, 3.1 percent were alcoholics, and 4.8 percent were judged to be mentally deranged (see Table 1). Approximately 18.2 percent of almshouse admittees in 1800–1801 were children, many of whom were too young to be apprenticed. The Docket excerpts reprinted below contain

4. Smith, The "Lower Sort," chap. 6; and Smith, "Poverty and Economic Marginality," 96–100.

5. The Daily Occurrences Docket consists of fifty-six volumes covering the years from 1787 to 1888, with only a few short gaps. They are part of the records of the Guardians of the Poor, Philadelphia City Archives.

Table 1. Admissions to Philadelphia's Almshouse, 1800–1801

Reason for Admittance	Adult Men (%)	Adult Women (%)	Children (%)	All People (%)
Old	5.9	8.3	—	5.7
Sick	66.2	38.0	—	43.1
Venereal disease	9.0	16.1	—	10.2
Alcoholic	3.6	3.9	—	3.1
Deranged	9.0	2.4	—	4.8
Poor, destitute	3.2	8.8	—	4.8
Miscellaneous	3.2	2.9	8.4	4.0
Pregnant	—	13.7	—	5.4
Physically abused	—	1.0	2.1	0.8
Deserted by husband	—	4.9	—	1.9
Deserted by parents	—	—	12.6	2.3
Orphaned	—	—	10.5	1.9
To be bound out	—	—	2.1	0.4
Parents could not support	—	—	14.7	2.7
Commited with parents	—	—	32.6	5.9
Parents in jail	—	—	16.8	3.1
Total	100.1	100.0	99.8	100.1

SOURCE: Daily Occurrence Docket, June 20, 1800, to June 20, 1801, Guardians of the Poor, Philadelphia City Archives, City Hall Annex.

NOTE: These tabulations include 895 individuals (380 adult men, 352 adult women, and 163 children) who entered the almshouse between June 20, 1800, and June 20, 1801.

cases that illustrate these statistics. Eighty-five-year-old William Wooten, for example, was "feeble and unable to contribute towards his support" (see the entry for July 17). Illness and disease were common among all Philadelphians (see Chapters 7 and 8), and John Morris (September 29), like many other inmates, suffered from poor health that "totally rendered [him] incapable of rallying round the standard of Labour for a Living." When their parents died or abandoned them, Margaret Dillmore (October 3) and Frederick Robertson (December 9), both about five years old, were taken to the almshouse.[6]

Women in eighteenth-century Philadelphia, as in late twentieth-century America, endured poverty more often than men. Because their

6. Daniel Blair (November 14) and Present Toss (November 22) numbered among other inmates included in the excerpts who received assistance because of their advanced age.

employment opportunities were limited, their marketable skills were few, and their wages were low, women generally earned only about half of the income of unskilled males (see Chapter 6). If their husband died, left, or became ill, married women and widows usually carried enormous economic burdens, especially if they had young children. When abandoned by her husband, Mariah Rawling and her three children (December 26) sought admission to the almshouse, as did Sarah Hamilton (August 31) when her husband eloped while she was pregnant. Unmarried women sometimes fared little better. Mary Berry (October 6) entered the house when "far advanced in her pregnancy and says the Father of the Child that she now bears is Named Matthias Clay, a Member of [the U.S.] Congress."[7] Elizabeth Deford (August 28) and Sarah Ferguson (July 9) numbered among the many prostitutes who earned their living among the city's sailors and other itinerant males and who frequently required public assistance, especially when badly afflicted with venereal disease.

African Americans also appeared in the Docket in significant numbers. Many slaves in the Mid-Atlantic region and the Upper South gained their freedom during the last quarter of the eighteenth century by fighting in the Revolutionary War, fleeing their master, or being manumitted by their owner. As former slaves flooded into Philadelphia during the 1790s, its African American population grew rapidly. While some were able to establish economic independence, others encountered financial difficulties in a society that limited their opportunities because of their race. Cato (July 11), James Breahere (November 6), and Sarah Bordley (December 2) were all manumitted slaves who entered the almshouse because of illness.[8]

Some indigents, lacking food, clothing, and shelter, sought immediate aid out of sheer desperation. Thomas Peters (November 20) appeared at the almshouse "in a Naked, starved and ragged condition, and running away with Vermin." Lydia Landram (December 30) was "brought in a

7. For married women, see also entries for the following: Rhodah Coombes (September 3), Mary Hyland (October 4), Mary Wright (October 7), the mother of Jeremiah Goolin (November 24), and Bridget Edward (November 29). Among the single women included in the excerpts are Elizabeth Fitzpatrick (July 13) and Abigail Penrose (September 16).

8. African Americans in Philadelphia are studied by Nash, *Forging Freedom*. African Americans appearing in the excerpts below include Thomas Lippincott (June 20), Aaron Larkins (July 3), Rebeccah Williams (September 13), John Perkins (September 15), Joseph Green (September 22), Mary Berry (October 6), Thomas Peters (November 20), Present Toss (November 22), Jeremiah Goolin (November 24), and Precilla (January 5).

Cart . . . being so extremely numb with cold, that she was entirely help-less." Other homeless people continued to live on the streets and to ask alms from passersby, even though begging was illegal.[9]

Poverty not only increased in Philadelphia during the eighteenth cen-tury but also affected new groups, including "respectable" working folk. As problems of unemployment, irregular employment, and low wages intensified during the century's second half, the city's relief system gradu-ally assumed the burden of assisting ordinary laboring people who simply could not make ends meet.[10] When she broke her thigh, Mary McNeal (June 29) became an inmate because her husband, "a poor labouring man," was not "able to support himself and her." And when Ignatius Waterman (July 12) fell ill and could not work, he had little choice but to move his entire family to the almshouse. To qualify for assistance, many applicants feigned sickness, because officials usually did not accept lack of employment as sufficient grounds for admission. In times of economic depression, "sore legs" thus reached near epidemic proportions among able-bodied people who could not find work.[11]

The poor devised ingenious ways to use the welfare system to their own advantage. Like many other indigents admitted when the weather cooled and discharged when it warmed, Philip and Sarah Haines (No-vember 24 and 27) entered "as usual to be fed and kept warm during the Winter and [they] jump the [almshouse] fence in the Spring." John Doug-lass (November 29) was blown into the almshouse by "Cold Boreas," while James Barry (November 15) likewise was a "frequent Autumnal Customer."[12]

More than 1,100 people entered the almshouse in 1800. Eligibility for admission required legal residency, generally defined as the payment of rent or taxes in an area for at least one year, in Philadelphia or its suburbs—Southwark and the Northern Liberties. Applicants also had to obtain a signed order from one of the Guardians of the Poor attesting to their impoverished circumstances and their "deserving character." In

9. See also George Lowerman (December 30) and John Hazless (January 2).

10. The considerable financial difficulties that laboring people encountered, and the economic reasons for those problems, are discussed in Smith, The "Lower Sort," chaps. 3 and 4.

11. The almshouse clerk was well aware of this charade. Robert Nesbit Jr. (November 18), for example, was admitted with the "usual" complaint of "sore legs."

12. Boreas is the Greek god of the wind from the north. See also Oliver Lynch (July 1), Peter Conner (July 14), John Howell (July 14), Robert Nesbit Jr. (November 18), John Douglass (November 29), John Collins (January 9), and Matthew and Sarah Morin (January 15).

each Docket entry, the clerk noted which official had signed the admission order. The clerk also debited or credited the admission or discharge of inmates to their place of legal residence.[13]

The destitute usually applied for admission to the almshouse only after appealing for help from all other sources. Many indigents avoided the institution because it functioned less as a refuge and more as a prison where officials tried to control the poor and to shape their morals. Locked gates and a brick wall confined inmates to the grounds (see Figure 6), and the steward's permission was required to enter or leave the house. Life inside was regimented as well. Inmates rose when a bell rang, retired at nine o'clock in the summer and an hour earlier in the winter, and ate together according to elaborate regulations. The possession or consumption of liquor was strictly forbidden; Richard Crosby (June 25), Ann Wallace (July 15), and James McGroty (October 5) were disciplined for violating that policy. The rules further enjoined the poor not only to "behave soberly, decently, and Courteously to each other," but also to act "submissively to their superiors & Governors." Anthony Muff (October 21) thus was banished to the "black hole," and William Wilson (July 17) was "confined in one of the Cells" for not displaying proper deference to the steward.[14]

Impoverished people also shied away from the almshouse because of the possibility that the authorities might sell them or their children into servitude. Officials frequently apprenticed the children of inmates— with or without their parents' consent—until the boys reached twenty-one years of age and the girls reached eighteen. The mother of Isabella Johnson (August 16) struggled in vain to keep her child from being "bound out," while the brother of Mary Ann Landram (January 2) helped her escape from the almshouse in order to prevent her being

13. The number of people admitted to the almshouse is from the Treasurer, General Ledger, vol. 1789–1803, Guardians of the Poor, Philadelphia City Archives. The identity of the official who signed the order of admission has been deleted from the entries dated after August 16 below.

14. The east wing of the "bettering house" contained the almshouse portion, in which paupers unable to work resided. Inmates capable of working occupied the west wing, or the "house of employment" section. The terms "almshouse" and "house of employment" were used interchangeably, and the entire institution also was referred to as the "bettering house." Chapter 1 contains a brief description of the almshouse. For a more detailed description of the institution and its regulations, see Alexander, *Render Them Submissive*, chaps. 5 and 6, regulations quoted on 95; and Alexander, "Institutional Imperialism and the Sick Poor in Late Eighteenth-Century Philadelphia: The House of Employment vs. The Pennsylvania Hospital," *Pennsylvania History* 51 (1984): 101–17.

apprenticed. Although it occurred less frequently, single adults who had not yet reached forty years old were also liable to be indentured as servants for up to three years.[15]

All able-bodied inmates were required to work "as well to inure them to Labour, as to contribute to their support." Workers faced punishment if they "neglect[ed] to repair to their proper places for work, or being there, shall refuse to work or shall tatter, be idle, or shall not well perform the task of Work set them." Most picked oakum, which involved untwisting old ropes into loose fibers, which then were sold for ship's caulking material. Men with shoemaking or tailoring skills made and repaired footwear and clothing, while women commonly spun yarn and labored as cooks, washers, seamstresses, and attendants in the house. In the excerpts below, the clerk noted weekly the amount of goods produced by this labor. Because so many inmates evaded or were incapable of working, officials failed to achieve their goal that the labor of the poor would pay the cost of their care.[16]

The institutional poor resisted the regimentation of their lives in other ways as well. Some fled the almshouse briefly or permanently without the steward's permission. Matthew Richards (July 3), "notwithstanding his being seventy years of age, scaled the fence" one morning, presumably in search of liquor. Later that day, after being "brought back in a Cart," he climbed the fence again.[17] Officials pressured each unmarried pregnant woman to identify the man who had impregnated her so he could be held financially responsible for the cost of raising the child. Some demurred. Charlotte Britton (December 31) "says she will suffer death sooner than she will expose the Man who is father of the Child she now bears," while Margaret Saffern (November 14) suffered imprisonment rather than disclose "who the Father of the Child is."

The excerpts below include some of the clerk's entries between June 20, 1800, and January 17, 1801. These were selected because they reveal

15. Alexander, *Render Them Submissive*, 106–7; and Smith, "Poverty and Economic Marginality," 85–86. In the excerpts below, other children were bound out on June 23, August 23, October 3, November 1, and December 2.

16. Alexander, *Render Them Submissive*, 98, regulations quoted on 95. The clerk's weekly notations of the goods produced by the inmates are not included in the excerpts after July 19.

17. Others who eloped include Catherine Bedient (June 25), Aaron Larkins (July 3), James Loddo (July 6), Sarah Lackey (September 18), Robert Nesbit Jr. (November 18), and Mary Ann Landram (January 2).

important information about the people admitted to the institution and about the daily operation of the almshouse. Unless otherwise indicated, the additional information included in brackets about a few of the inmates is from the almshouse clerk's entries at other times or from the Prisoners for Trial Docket (see Chapter 3).

Daily Occurrence Docket

June 20, 1800: Admitted Thomas Lippincott a Negro man highly venereal, his Master Benjamin Button of this City, Board Merchant, has engaged to pay for Board and expences of said Negro during his stay here, or till such time he shall be cured and taken away.[18] Per Order of Admission signed Thomas Hockley. Debit City.

June 21: Took in the Weeks Work: Spinning: twelve pounds flaxen yarn, seventeen pounds tow yarn, and two pounds woolen yarn. Shoemaking: two pair Mens Shoes and two pair Womens Shoes per John Gavin. Oakum: About four hundred weight picked this week.

June 23: Admitted Ann Nebecker, was admitted per Order Isaac Tatem Hopper for the purpose of being immediately bound out, which was accordingly done as per annexed entry. [See the next entry.] Debit City.

Bound Ann Nebecker to Henry Hawkins of this City, Mariner, to serve him eleven years, four months and twenty four days as per Indenture of this date. Admitted as above. Credit City.

June 25: Discharged Sophia Fitzpatrick and her daughter Catherine Morrow. Said Sophia was admitted the 6th last May, pregnant with said child and delivered of it the 3rd instant[19] June following. Credit City.

Eloped Catherine Bedient a Mulatto woman who was admitted the 10th instant June in a most distressing condition, being very sick and almost blind and not able to help herself till now. She has taken this

---

18. Room and board were paid for by the town of legal residence (usually the city of Philadelphia or one of its suburbs) for most almshouse inmates. Only rarely, as in this case of a master paying for his slave or servant, did private individuals pay for the care of an inmate.

19. Instant: of this month.

method of returning or acknowledging her gratitude to her benefactors. Credit City.

Sent to Jail Richard Crosby, having in a clandestine manner and derogatory to the rules and good order of this institution, introduced spiritous liquor among some of the women particularly Cate Levman, the consequence of which was, disorderly and quarrelsome behavior. He was accordingly committed yesterday in the evening under warranty of William Jones Esquire.

June 28th: Took in the Week's Work: Weaving: One piece, 800 Shirting 55 yards by John Story, this piece took 18 pounds flaxen yarn for chain and 25 pounds Tow yarn for filling.[20] Spinning: Twelve pounds flaxen yarn, sixteen pounds tow yarn and two pounds Woolen yarn 6 Hanks.[21] Shoemaking: One pair Mens Shoes and Two pair Womens Shoes by John Gavin. One pair Mens Shoes by Morris Dickinson. Mending and Cobbling as usual. Oakum: About four hundred weight picked this week.

June 29: Admitted Mary McNeal an Irish Woman, and hath legal residence, this poor creature had the Misfortune of breaking one of her thighs, last Wednesday, by falling down a pair of Stairs; her Husband John McNeal is a poor labouring man and not being able to support himself and her in the situation she is in, he obtained an Order of Admission from James Collings and Henry Molier to bring her in here. Debit Southwark.

June 30: Materials issued to be Manufactured: Twelve pounds flax, sixteen pounds Tow, and two pounds Wool to be spun, and about four hundred weight of Junk to be picked into Oakum.

Paid Lydia McCulloch fifteen shillings in full for Nursing Child Bridget Nugent . . . $2.[22]

Paid Mary Dixon eighteen shillings and nine pence in full for Nursing Child Elizabeth Dawson, two weeks . . . $2.50.

July 1: Admitted Joseph and Christiana, alias Harriet, Arriet. Joseph is Three years and seven months old, Harriet One year and seven months old. These Children were discharged the 1st last April with their

---

20. "Shirting" is a kind of stout cotton cloth suitable for shirts; the "chain" is the horizontal threads crossing the warp in a woven fabric; and the "filling" is usually an inferior cloth used primarily to occupy space.

21. A "hank" of worsted yarn contains 560 yards.

22. The almshouse officials paid Lydia to care for Bridget in Lydia's home because Bridget was too young to be apprenticed. In 1800, 7 shillings and 6 pence equaled 1 dollar, 12 pence equaled 1 shilling, and 20 shillings equaled 1 pound.

Father and Mother, the latter of whom is now dead, and the Father not being able to support them, has obtained an Order of Admission from Mr. Thomas Hockley and brought them here. Debit City.

Discharged Oliver Lynch, and notwithstanding his non-residency; has been a very troublesome to and fro Customer, too lazy to work out doors, or in doors, although he can eat two mens allowance and was punished with two days confinement for his idleness, but all to no purpose. Admitted the 15th May last. Credit Southwark.

July 2: Sent in per the Clerk of High street Market five quarts pickled Oysters, sent for being offered for Sale contrary to Laws, which was distributed [to the inmates].[23]

July 3: Eloped Matthew Richards, and notwithstanding his being seventy years of age, scaled the fence this Morning, by break of day. He had been out but a short time, when he was brought back in a Cart, and he has now jumped it again; said Old man is much addicted to liquor for which reason and the disturbance he makes in the streets when in that condition, has been often put into prison; he has been here often, and always took this method in getting out; his Wife who is a striving industrious body, but cannot live with him on account of his frequent intoxications and abuse—but rather than he should expose himself, and his family too, in the manner he does, she obtained an Order of Admission for him the 31st last May from James McGlathery and James Collings on promising them at the same time, that she would call at this house every week and pay One dollar for his board, which she has done. Credit Southwark.

Eloped Aaron Larkins a Mulatto Man who was admitted the 7th Ultimo[24] with a very highly venereal complaint, and for being made sound again has taken this ungratefull method of acknowledging Thanks to his benefactors. Credit Northern Liberties.

July 5: Took in the Week's Work: Weaving: One piece 1000 Sheeting 53 yards by William Wilson. This piece took thirty six pounds of flaxen yarn. Spinning: Twelve pounds flaxen yarn, thirteen pounds tow yarn and Two pounds Woolen yarn 7 Hanks. Shoemaking: Four pair Womens Shoes per [John] Gavin—two pair Mens Shoes per [Morris] Dickinson and two pair Mens Shoes per John Chatham—Mending and Cobbling as usual. Oakum: About four hundred weight picked this week.

---

23. By law, the clerk of the market could seize food sold illegally and turn it over to the almshouse. See the description of this process in Chapter 1.

24. Ultimo: of or occurring in the month preceding the present.

Provisions issued this Week:

Meat 1456 lbs	Flour 1960 lbs
Indian Meal [cornmeal] 300 lbs	Rice 104 lbs
Sugar 218 lbs	Tea 33 lbs
Coffee 15.5 lbs	Chocolate 2 lbs
Milk 140 gallons	Molasses 29 gallons
Shells [beans] 5 bushels	Indian Corn 12 bushels
Potatoes 20 bushels	Pease 0 bushels

Hogs: 55 Large and small, consisting of Boars, Sows, Barrows, Shoats and small pigs, were brought in at Seven different periods of the day by the Constables, in a Cart.[25] Some of them are remarkably fine.

July 6: Eloped James Loddo the little english Cockney, who was admitted the 30th last January very sick, and a bad swelling in his Groin, and much distressed. This makes three times that he has scaled the fence, being the most ready and easiest way of getting his liberty. Credit Northern Liberties.

July 7: Materials issued to be Manufactured: Twelve pounds flax, eleven pounds tow, and two pounds wool to be spun, also three pounds flax for sewing thread and about four hundred weight of Junk to be picked into Oakum.

July 8: Admitted Catherine McCoy who was brought here this day by a Constable from the Jail where she had been confined better than a Week for being frequently intoxicated, abusive and troublesome to the people in the neighbourhood she lived in. She, her husband, and son James were all discharged the 10th of April last. He seems to be an Orderly well-disposed Man, and is well settled, and would make her life comfortable only for her own imprudence and bad temper. Order of admission signed Isaac Tatem Hopper. Debit City.

July 9: Admitted Sarah Ferguson of legal residence, has the venereal disease and dont appear to be more than seventeen or eighteen years of age. She says her parents came to this City, from Ireland when she was but a suckling Baby, that they never bound her out, or took any care of her education, that they have been dead three years and upwards, and that ever since, she has been a wanderer through the streets, having no

25. A "barrow" is a castrated hog, and a "shoat" is a young hog. Hogs that roamed the streets uncontrolled by their owners were confiscated by the constables and turned over to the almshouse.

place wherewith to lay her head, by which means she has been exposed to every vile temptations being thus situated. . . . Debit Southwark.

July 10: Admitted Jane McAllister and her Child Margaret, who is four months Old, said Jane has a Husband but on account of his drunkeness, frequent intoxication and abuse, she cannot live with him, neither is it in his power to support them, in the situation and condition he continually is in. . . . Debit City.

July 11: Admitted Cato a Mulatto man, was formerly a Slave to Charles Pettit and says he was manumitted in the time of the revolutionary war, his complaint is weakness in his knees that renders him unable to contribute to his own support by labour . . . . Debit City.

July 12: Took in the Weeks Work: Weaving: One piece 800 Shirting 59 yards by John Story, this piece took nineteen pounds flaxen yarn for Chain and twenty six pounds tow yarn for filling. Spinning: Twelve pounds flaxen yarn, twenty pounds tow yarn and two pounds woolen yarn 6 Hanks. Shoemaking: Five pair womens Shoes per John Gavin. Five pair Mens Shoes per John Chatham. Two pair Mens shoes per Morris Dickenson. Mending and Cobbling as usual. Oakum: perhaps four hundred weight picked this week.

Provisions issued this Week:

Meat 1424 lbs	Flour 1960 lbs
Indian Meal 300 lbs	Rice 114 lbs
Sugar 220 lbs	Tea 33.2 lbs
Coffee 6.5 lbs	Milk 140 gallons
Molasses 29 gallons	Shells 4 bushels
Indian Corn 20 bushels	Potatoes 20 bushels
Chocolate 2.5 lbs	Pease 0 bushels

Admitted Ignatius Waterman, his wife Elizabeth and two Children William and Elizabeth Waterman. William is between five and six years of age, Elizabeth near seven months Old, they were all here last winter, and Elizabeth born then, and all discharged in the spring following. Said Ignatius is much afflicted with the rheumatism and has a violent pain in his breast, which renders him incapable of following his business, and being poor, needy and destitute of friendly assistance, had no other alternative for relief and support of himself and family than by applying to Isaac Tatem Hopper for an Order to come here, which he granted. Debit City.

July 13: Admitted Elizabeth Fitzpatrick who hath no legal residence, it being only six days since she left her Father, who lives about one Mile on the Road from Woodbury, New Jersey, and Came to Philadelphia and lived with Doctor Parcallas the above time of six days; she is a young woman and dont appear to be more than seventeen or eighteen years of age, and from the outrageous and desperate attempts she has made in being accessary to her own death, having taken a poisonous draft and plunging herself into the river off South street Wharf, it is presumed that she has been guilty of some imprudent conduct or other, that has rendered life a burden to her, and rather than survive a lost reputation, would sooner put an end to her own existance. Ebenezer Ferguson Esquire and two Constables conducted her here with an Order signed James McGlathery and James Collings. Debit Southwark.

July 14: Admitted Peter Conner who hath legal residence, is an old and frequent customer and is come in now with his old complaint of Rheumatism, lameness, and sore legs; his Wife and two Children are here also, he was discharged the 14th April last. . . . Debit City. [In 1793 Peter and his wife, Elizabeth, entered the almshouse, both afflicted with yellow fever, from which Peter suffered permanent lameness. Between 1800 and 1803, they were admitted to the almshouse an additional five times. The almshouse managers bound out their daughters Mary and Margaret in 1801 and 1803, respectively, and their son, Peter, was born in the almshouse in July 1802 and died there a year later. Peter and Elizabeth entered the almshouse again in 1808, at which time Peter was fifty years old and Elizabeth forty-seven; the clerk described both as "old customers" and natives of Ireland.]

Admitted John Howell, known by the name of crazy Jack The Sailor, who has been forty days confined [in jail] for (as he says) "having a brush with the Mayor in the publick Market"; he is an old customer, and brought . . . per Order Isaac Tatem Hopper. Debit City. [John, "a singing sailor who when sobered is very quiet," initially entered the almshouse in 1788.]

Bound Mary Johnson to William Hill of Kingsessing Township, Philadelphia County, Farmer, to serve him thirteen years one month and fifteen days as per Indenture of this date. Admitted September 1st 1798. Credit City.

July 15: Admitted Ann Wallace of legal residence, was here in June 1797 very bad with the Venereal disease and for clamorous and disorderly conduct was sent to Jail on the 19th of July succeeding for ten days and returned on the 29th and behaved as bad as before, and for the support of Order and peace of others, she was turned out of the building. Her name then was Mary Ann Kelly, but has been married since to One Wallace, and is now no more than twenty years of age. She is now afflicted with a Cancer in her nose, and is not able to contribute towards her own support, at the same time being poor and destitute of friends is sent here per Order David Lapsley. Debit City.

July 16: Admitted Susannah Kirk who has legal residence, she came from Ireland about seventeen years ago and served her time[26] with Abner Lukens of Upper Dublin Township, Philadelphia County then, now Montgomery County, and since her freedom has worked out at service for six years past with different families in this City, and is now come in here very sick with a bad lax,[27] which causes a coming down of the body, whereby she is rendered incapable of helping herself and is sent in per Order James Collings and James McGlathery. Debit Southwark. [Susannah was arrested for theft in 1799.]

July 17: Admitted William Wooten an Old Man aged eighty five years, born in Old England, and came to this City about seven years ago, and has lived in and about it ever since, striving to make a living by picking and gathering of rags, but now being feeble and unable to contribute towards his support by that or any other way of employment, and at the same time destitute of friends, is sent here with an Order signed Isaac Tatem Hopper. Credit City.

William Wilson, one of the hired Weavers, went out yesterday and returned in the evening of same day, in his old accustomed state of intoxication, jealous and in provoking language and abuse, so much so that it was absolutely necessary, as well as a duty incumbent on Mr. Cummings (for the support of the rules and good order of the institution) to have him confined in one of the Cells. But some time in the night, he effected an escape by forcibly breaking through three appartments, and being fearfull of returning again after such conduct, he went first to William Jones, Esquire, President of the Board, who wrote a letter to Mr. Cummings to receive him, and let matters rest untill Monday next, when the board will meet and determine the same.

July 18: Admitted Hannah McFurle, a Child two years Old, and very sick with a fever and lax. The Mother Elizabeth McFurle who brought the Child is not able to maintain it herself and another one that she has and obtained an Order from Abel Evans and Frederick Hockley. Debit City.

26. Susannah had been indentured or apprenticed to Abner.
27. Diarrhea.

July 19: Took in the Weeks Work: Weaving: One piece of 800 Shirting 55 yards of William Wilson. This piece took 19 lb flaxen yarn for chain and 26 lb tow yarn for filling. Spinning: Ten pounds flaxen yarn and Twenty pounds Tow yarn. Shoemaking: Three pair womens Shoes per John Gavin. Two pair Mens Shoes per John Chatham. Mending and Cobbling as usual. Oakum: Perhaps four hundred weight picked this Week.

Died George Syses an Old German who was admitted the 30th December 1799 in a weak and distressed condition and expired this morning. Credit City.

Birth Jane Craig has been in labour these two weeks past and was last night delivered of a still born Child.

Admitted Elizabeth Campbell who hath legal residence, and is very sick with a pain and dissiness in her head. Her husband Charles Campbell and who is a labourer was in the Country, and no person to take care of her, she was sent here to be provided for by Order Isaac Tatem Hopper. Debit City.

August 16: Admitted Isabella Johnson. This Child was bound by the Managers the 2nd June last to John C. Schneeds of this City and the Mother of said Child, finding to who it was bound, went and took her away by force. She is now in Jail and the child was brought from there to this House by a Constable with an Order signed Isaac Tatem Hopper. Debit City. [On November 17, Isabella was bound for fourteen years and one month to a farmer in Delaware.]

August 23: Admitted Mary Duffey a Girl about eleven years of age, of Legal residence. She was under Indenture to One Elizabeth Cathers of this City who lives in Carters Alley and keeps a boardinghouse, and has beat, and otherwise abused said Child Mary that complaint thereof was made to the Mayor who obliged the Mistress to give up the Indenture, and sent her here. Debit City. [Mary was bound again at the end of August.]

August 28: Admitted Elizabeth Deford, alias Aarons, is an Old Polishing Room Customer,[28] was here the 1st January last highly Venereal and discharged the 1st April following, and is not only returning now in the former Condition but with the addition of sore legs and an almost deprivation of the Use of her limbs, by being exposed to a Street lodging in the Night, not having wherewith to lay her head. Debit Southwark. [Elizabeth died in the almshouse in November.]

August 31: Admitted Sarah Hamilton Pregnant, and who has not

28. Women with venereal disease, especially prostitutes, were confined to the "Polishing Room."

Legal residence, she was committed to the Work-house[29] for thirty days as a Vagrant, and was brought here by Abel Evans on account of the situation she is in, her Husband John Hamilton who is a Taylor by trade has abandoned her about three months ago, at which time, and for several years previous to it, they had lived in Wilmington, Delaware State, and she seems to express an anxious desire or wish to go there, having hopes of being better provided for there, as she says, than here. . . . Debit Northern Liberties.

September 1: Admitted Mary Allen was born in Old England and came to this Country in the year 1776 with her Parents, and at which time she was but two years of age, says they landed at Wilmington, Delaware State and from thence they proceeded to Pittsburg. Her Father died, and in coming to this City in July 1799 with her husband and Mother, both of whom she had the Misfortune to bury on the Road, she arrived in it last fall just after the [yellow fever] sickness—of course she has not gained a legal residence, but very sick and weak indeed, with the companion poverty, and no friends. . . . Debit Southwark. [Mary was discharged in November, readmitted in November 1802, and discharged again in April 1804.]

September 3: Admitted Rhodah Coombes of Legal residence, she was born at Cape May [New Jersey], is twenty four years of age, and is married to William Coombes a Shoemaker by trade, with whom she has lived in this City two years and has now abandoned her and gone to Sea, without giving her the least notice of it. Being thus left destitute and friendless, and being violently afflicted with a pain in her head to such a degree that she has lost the sight of one of her eyes, that she is rendered entirely incapable of contributing towards a living by her work. . . . Debit City. [Rhodah was discharged in May 1801.]

September 13: Admitted Rebeccah Williams a Black Woman Twenty four years of age, has been in Jail these six months past, four of her toes on the right foot are cut off, she has legal residence and was brought in here from Jail by Jacob Facundus, Constable. . . . Debit City. [Rebecca appeared in the Vagrancy Docket on October 6, 1795, charged with disorderly conduct; see Chapter 3, case 163. She was jailed in 1798 and 1800 on suspicion of burglary, and she was sentenced for larceny in 1795, 1797, and 1799.]

September 15: Admitted John Perkins a Black who hath no Legal resi-

29. The city's workhouse was the same as its jail, to which vagrants usually were sent for thirty days. See Chapter 3.

dence, twenty eight years of age, was born in Dorset County, Maryland and was a Slave to One Thomas Vincent of said County, emancipated him about a Year ago (as he says) when he came to this City and resided ever since, and is now sent here in highly Venereal Condition. . . . Until he can be removed to his Legal place of Residence. Debit City.

September 16: Admitted Abigail Penrose a Young Woman of nonresidence, but being under the influence of a dose of Opium, with a view to destroy herself—is sent here. This is the third (and it has proved the most effectual attempt) time that she has endeavored to put end to her life. She lived with Thomas Moore, Sadler, the Northeast Corner of Front and Market Streets. The reason of this unhappy Young woman laying such violence on herself could not be ascertained. . . . Debit City. [See the following entry.]

September 17: Died Abigail Penrose expired about two hours after her admission yesterday, word of which was sent to Thomas Moore from whose house she was brought in a Carriage, and they desired word to be sent in case of her death, which was expected in a short time after she was brought. Word was accordingly sent and Moore did not take the slightest Notice or regard whatsoever of the Notice which was sent him by M. Lang informing of her death and she was this day buried at the expense of the institution. . . . Credit City.

September 18: Admitted Sarah Lackey. She had liberty of the Matron to go out on Saturday last, for the purpose of swearing the Child with which she is now pregnant to Isaac Hanson, Brother to Samuel Hanson our Baker, and promising Mrs. Marshall that she would return again in time, and sober, neither of which did she do, except the swearing said Isaac before John Jennings, Esquire, to be the Father of it. And was now brought in by a Constable in a most shamefully drunken and beastly condition, who says the [?] that measures are pursuing to find said Isaac Hanson, and make him give security for the maintainance of said Bastardy.[30] Note, said Sarah was a pauper in the House, and Isaac came back and forward to assist his Brother Samuel in the Bake house, but if he had heated one Oven only, it would have been better for him. Debit City. [See the entry for November 9.]

September 22: Admitted Joseph Green a Black man is deranged, was here once before in June Last of the 10th, and made his escape out of the Cell the 13th July, and is now brought in again by a Constable. . . . Debit

---

30. Hanson would be required to post a bond, which would be forfeited if he failed to help maintain the child.

City. [Joseph appeared in the Vagrancy Docket on February 24, 1792, charged with threatening the city's residents and with being a "Lunatick"; see Chapter 3, case 127. He was arrested on suspicion of petty theft in 1792 and 1798 and for breaking and entering in 1800.]

September 29: Admitted John Morris an Old German hath Legal residence, he served his time in this City, with old Mr. Gorman, Sugar Baker, many years ago; he was a Soldier in our revolutionary War from the beginning to the ending, he is now poor, sick and palsied,[31] and totally rendered incapable of rallying round the standard of Labour for a Living. . . . Debit City.

October 3: Admitted Margaret Dillmore a Child between four and five years of age, her mother died in the [yellow] fever of 1798, the Father Thomas Dillmore is a Seaman and hath deserted his Child ever since the death of his Wife, and the child has been taken care of ever since, till now, by its aunt, who is Wife to Robert Brown, and lives near the Playhouse in South Street. She says that said Dillmore sailed out of New York, but cannot tell in whose employ, and likewise that he has been in this very City lately, never came near his Child, neither could she learn or find out his hidden place. Margaret is a fine Child, and her aunt would still have taken care of it if her Husband had been in a way that would support it and his own family, and this not being the case She brought the child here. . . . Debit City. [On December 8, Margaret was apprenticed for fourteen years to Griffith Jones, a farmer in Chester County, Pennsylvania.]

October 4: Admitted Mary Hyland and her Child Rosannah fifteen Months old, she's also pregnant with another. Her Husband James Hyland is gone to Sea in the Ship George Washington, and left a Power of Attorney with Jacob Edwards, Taylor, in Water Street between Market and Chestnut streets, to receive for her use, of the Owner of said ship, seven dollars monthly, and said power, she says, is put into the hands of A. Musgrave who sent her here by a Watchman accompanied with his Order of Admission. Debit City. [See the entry for December 3.]

October 5: Admitted James McGroty. This artful chap gave his Surname to A. Musgrave as McTrosty, no doubt with intent to avoid a punishment which he anticipated, not only on account of his elopement on the 23rd August last but an aggravation of his fault by coming the next day after, tantalising his Ward mates by holding a bottle of Rum and shaking and putting it to his Mouth by way of contempt and defiance to Mr.

31. Paralyzed in some part of the body.

Cummings who at the juncture was standing at the Corner of the fence, looking at him. . . . Debit City. [James was jailed for assault in 1798 and for suspicious behavior in 1800.]

October 6: Admitted Mary Berry a Mulatto young Woman twenty three years of age, of legal residence, is far advanced in her pregnancy and says the Father of the Child that she now bears is Named Matthias Clay, a Member of [the U.S.] Congress and to whom she has swore it before Gunning Bedford, Esquire. Said Mary lived with the Widow Sadie in Arch street (and at the same time Clay boarded there) between seventh and eighth streets. . . . Debit City.

October 7: Admitted Mary Wright, hath Legal residence, is twenty years of age, born in this City. Her Husband Dominick Wright twelve months ago went to sea in the Ship Jane Brown to London (the Owner nor Captains Name she cannot tell) and heard only once from him since, and as she says, never received one farthing of his Monthly pay. (The reason is obvious, he neither gave Power of Attorney or Orders for her to receive any part thereof.) However, unfortunate it is that she was taken with a Fit and contiguous to the fire place, she fell into the Flames and got burnt in a most distressing manner. . . . Debit Southwark.

October 10: Admitted Sarah Baker, Pregnant, she was born in New England is thirty years of age, came to Philadelphia very young, and was bound to one James Hanniker of said City, Gardener, who in about three months after, moved down to the Neck [New Jersey], where she stayed and served her time out, which was nine years of Indenture. After she was free, went to Lancaster [Pennsylvania] and hired herself out as maid, to different families in said Town for the space of eighteen months, when she got married and moved to Hanover, York County [Pennsylvania] where she continued seventeen months, when her Husband died. After which she went to Baltimore and hired herself out in different families at least for the space of four years and seven months, as it was in November 1795 when she went there, and came to this City from there the 1st July last. The Father of the child she now bears is Named Jacob Adams, of Baltimore, Merchant, and with whom she hired herself as a Maid, and she says he went to sea last May, and thinks to the East Indies. However, she has never swore the Child. . . . Debit City. [Sarah was discharged in April 1801.]

October 21: Admitted Anthony Muff an Old Gardener and very worthless former Customer, much in liquor when he came in, and went and laid himself on one of the beds in the [illegible] Ward, and being desired to get off it he made use of very impertinent language and persisted in lying on it, till Mr. Cummings was informed of it, who ordered him into the black hole. . . . Debit Northern Liberties.

November 1: Sent to Jail Margaret Saffern admitted the 14th April 1797, is far advanced in her pregnancy. And for obstinately persisting in not giving satisfaction to the Manager by informing where the reputed Father of the Child she now bears is or liveth, they thought this procedure was the best, or would be the only means of getting satisfactory information from her. [See the entry for November 14.]

Admitted Sarah Campbell and her three Children, James Campbell eight years of age, Elizabeth Campbell six years of age, and Sarah Campbell aged fourteen months. The Husband and Father of those Children died of the [yellow] fever in 1798—and the Mother not being able to support herself and the Children. . . . Debit Northern Liberties. [On December 8, Elizabeth was bound for twelve years to Esther Creaton in Northern Liberties, and James was apprenticed for thirteen years to Josiah Claypoole, a shoemaker in the same suburb. Sarah and her daughter, Sarah, were discharged on December 16, readmitted in September 1803, then released in December of that year. According to the city directory, Sarah Campbell worked as a washerwoman in 1800.]

Admitted Rebeccah Carter, born in New Castle, Delaware State, was seventeen years of age last May. Says her Parents moved to this City three years ago, and she came with them, that they both died in 1798, and she has continued in it ever since, and is now come in here in a highly Venereal Condition. . . . Debit City. [Rebeccah was jailed for theft in 1800.]

November 3: Admitted John Barry, came to this City from Ireland seventeen years ago and says he has taught school in it ever since, and now come in here with a highly Venereal complaint, and running away with bodily Vermin. . . . Debit Southwark. [John was discharged on December 8.]

Admitted Rebeccah Jones who hath no Legal residence, is a Young Woman between eighteen and nineteen years of age, was born at Cross Roads, Delaware State; has been in this City six weeks, four of which has been in the Workhouse, being put there as a vagrant and was brought from there. . . . Has a bad sore leg. Debit City. [Rebeccah was jailed in 1799 for disturbing the peace.]

November 6: Admitted James Breahere a Black man, was born at Marcus Hook. His Master Joseph Marshall Manumitted him in the Year 1783, and says he has worked in this City as a Labourer for these twelve years past. And by hard work, and frequent colds, which has fell into his limbs, he is rendered unable to support himself by any kind of Work, and is sent here. . . . Debit Southwark. [James died in the almshouse on December 6.]

November 9: Birth: Sarah Lackey was last night delivered of a Mulatto Child whom she calls Charlott Marborough (notwithstanding said Sarah swore before John Jennings, Esquire, that Isaac Hanson was Father of the Child she is now brought to bed with; see Occurences of the 18th September last. Thomas Marborough, the real Father of the Child, is the Black Man who eloped the 26th May, last, on account of having Criminal Contact with Rachael Ward, another pauper at that time in the House.) Debit City. [See also the entry for September 18.]

November 14: Returned from Jail Margaret Saffern. This Woman, notwithstanding the punishment she has undergone, will not [disclose] to the Managers who the Father of the Child is. She was ordered by the Managers to be enlarged from prison, which was done on Tuesday last and instead of returning here, she went to see one Elizabeth Davis, an acquaintance of hers and wife of Francis Davis who lives at the Corner of New fourth street; in a House belonging to Henry Apple between the Old fourth street road and third street near poplar lane. And said Elizabeth came here the ensuing day to inform that said Margaret had not been in the House two hours when she was delivered of a female infant whom she names Mary Ann Long. Quere: Whether Margaret has or not divulged to her friend Davis some matters by which the Managers may find out Who the real Father of the Child is. Debit City. [See the entry for November 1.]

Admitted Daniel Blair an Old Irish-man, upwards of eighty years old, he landed in this City fifty seven or eight years ago, and listed as a Soldier in the Kings service; was in Braddocks Army when they were defeated.[32] He has been now about two years in this City, has a Complication of disorders such as the Gravel, Phthisick[33] and Rheumatism; thus being helpless and poor withall is sent here. . . . Debit City.

November 15: Admitted James Barry a Noted, worthless, and frequent Autumnal Customer, has come in as usual with sore legs and the addition of a broken head, to be nursed, doctered and kept warm all Winter and when cured, he will procure a discharge and go out in the spring as usually. . . . Debit City. [James first entered the almshouse in October 1789, and he was readmitted at least ten times during the 1790s

---

32. In the Seven Years' War, British troops commanded by General Edward Braddock, including a number of colonial militiamen under George Washington, were defeated in 1755 by a French and Indian force in western Pennsylvania.

33. Any type of debilitating affliction.

and six more times between 1800 and 1803. An invalid who had been injured as a soldier during the Revolutionary War, Barry drew an annual pension from the federal government, part of which he paid to the almshouse to help defray the cost of his maintenance. When he left the almshouse in 1790, the clerk noted that he took Elizabeth McGee, a "Noted Strumpet," with him as his wife. Both they and their three children, described as "former and constant winter customers," were admitted in November 1793. The Managers of the Almshouse bound one child in 1793 and another in 1796. James was arrested for larceny and for burglary in 1798 and was confined for vagrancy in 1799.]

November 17: Admitted Catharine Groves and her two Children, Nancy Groves One year and seven months Old, John Groves five weeks Old—her husband, John Groves, is in Jail and she says is sentenced to fourteen years imprisonment for killing a Horse and skinning it. Having these young children and no friends to assist her, she was advised to make application to the Guardians of the Poor, which she did and is come here. . . . Debit Northern Liberties.

November 18: Admitted Robert Nesbit Jr. a notorious, worthless chap, is a common nuisance to the institution, has been here repeatedly and has often eloped; not long since he was discharged from the Pennsylvania Hospital where he had been some considerable time a burthensome charge to this House, and has now come in as usual with sore legs. . . . Debit City.

November 20: Admitted Thomas Peters a black-Man, hath legal residence, is afflicted with the Rheumatism; came here in a Naked, starved and ragged condition, and running away with Vermin, insomuch that they stript him and shaved his head, and put clean cloathes on him. . . . Debit City.

November 22: Admitted Present Toss a Black-woman has been here before, says she's upwards of eighty years Old, is lame, and a very bad sore leg so that she was brought in a Cart; being poor, destitute and incapable of supporting herself by labour, is sent here. . . . Debit Southwark.

November 24: Admitted Jeremiah Goolin an Illegitimate Mulatto Child about three years of age, his Mother being poor, and not able to support it and herself, having no other means to live but by hiring herself out at service as a Maid in a family, which she could not do with the child. Harry Goolin the reputed Father has run off and left her two years ago. . . . Debit City. [Jeremiah was bound in August 1801.]

Admitted Stephen alias Philip Haines a very worthless, troublesome in and out Customer . . . is now come in as usual to be fed and kept warm during the Winter and jump the fence in the Spring, as was the case April 24th, 1799. . . . Debit City. [See the following entry.]

November 27: Admitted Sarah Philips alias Haines, Wife of Philip Haines who came in the 24th instant (November). A worthless troublesome couple, she's as good at fence jumping as he is. What reason could this Woman have in telling the Guardian her name was Philips? There could be no other than to deceive, as he was the same who sent her Husband here, and her being of a notorious drunken character, thought that if she told her right name he would not have granted an Order for her admission, and is come in very sick as she says with the fever and Augue.[34] . . . Debit City.

November 28: Admitted George Crouse, he dont appear to have gained any legal residence, is a German and landed in New York and continued in that City three years, constantly in the capacity of an Hostler,[35] and for seven or eight years since has been backwards and forwards from that City to this, likewise to and from Charleston, South Carolina as a Gentleman Waitingman,[36] is now been about three weeks in this City, is sick and much swelled in his Body and legs—twenty seven years of age. . . . Debit City.

November 29: Admitted Bridget Edward and her four Children (nine weeks ago arrived at this Port from Wales in England, her Husband who also came with them died three weeks after their arrival). Margaret and Martha Edwards (Twins) are four years Old—Catharine between three and four years old, and Malia three months Old, all of them fine hearty Children. The Mother being destitute of the means of supporting herself and them, they are sent here. . . . Debit City. [In January 1801 the twins were bound to a farmer outside Philadelphia, and Catharine died in the almshouse. Bridget and Malia were discharged in July 1801.]

Admitted John Douglass an Ordinary Chap, has been in and out several times before this. He is not sick but Poor and ragged and is come in at this time as usual for Winter quarter to be cloathed and kept Warm, and in the Spring go out and continue till autumn, when cold Boreas perhaps will blow him here again. . . . Debit Southwark. [John was arrested twice in 1801 on the charge of burglary.]

Admitted Elizabeth Smith hath legal residence, was born in Maryland, came to this City ten years ago, has continued in it ever since at service as

34. An acute fever marked by regularly recurring chills.
35. A person who took care of horses, generally at an inn or stable.
36. A personal servant.

maid in different families, and is afflicted with a complication of diseases, such as the Arthritis, rheumatick pains and swelling in all her limbs; not being able to walk was brought in a Cart at 9 O'Clock PM. . . . A Mulatto Woman. Debit City.

December 2: Admitted William Bell a Native of Chester County [Pennsylvania], is fifty five years of age, has lived and worked as a Labourer in this City these fifteen or sixteen years past and paid taxes during the whole time. He has frosted feet, a bad scalled, and pain in all his limbs, which renders him unable to support himself by his labour and being poor and friendless is sent here. . . . Debit Southwark. [William was discharged on January 1, 1801, then entered the almshouse three more times during that year. The entry for May 3, 1801, notes that he had lost his eyesight and could not support himself. William died and was buried in St. Peter's churchyard in 1808.]

Admitted Sarah Bordley and her Child Ann Boardly, Black, (the Child is five years of age), have no legal residence. She was born in Cecil County, Maryland. One Robert Thompson was her Master who, as she says at his death Manumitted her, and it dont appear from her own account that she has gained any legal residence in any other place since. She has been in this City near two years and has maintained herself and Child in the line or business of a Washerwoman ever since, and she has come here much afflicted with pains through all her limbs that she cannot labour for her support. . . . Sarah and her child were in a perishing condition. Debit City. [In December, Ann was bound for thirteen years. Sarah was released in March 1801.]

December 3: Admitted Mary Hyland and her Child Rosannah Hyland seventeen months Old, she's now pregnant with another. Her Husband James Hyland is now on board the United States Ship Washington, and she not likely to receive any pecuniary aid at present from her Husbands employ, and her present situation renders her incapable of supporting herself and Child. . . . Note this Woman and Child was here before, see Occurrences of October 4th, 1800. Debit City. [See October 4 entry.]

December 9: Admitted Frederick Robertson a Child about five years old, its Father went to Sea and supposed to have been taken.[37] The Mother has deserted it and taken up with another Man and gone to New York. Being thus left destitute and no one to take care of it, he is sent here. . . . Debit Southwark.

December 26: Admitted Mariah Rawling and her three Children, of legal residence. Mariah, six years old, Charles four years old, and John

37. Robertson's father probably was captured by the French or English navy.

six months old. The Mother is sick, and unable to support herself. Their Father George Rawling who is a Farrier or Horse Doctor by Profession, deserted them four or five months [ago] and supposed to have gone to New York, and this unfortunate family being in the utmost distress are sent here. . . . Debit City.

December 30: Admitted Lydia Landram and her Child Mary Ann Landram, of Legal residence, the Child is four years of age. They were in a state of starvation and Nakedness, and brought in a Cart; the Mother being so extremely numb with cold, that she was entirely helpless, and at the same time seems to be in a Consumption.[38] She has a Husband, William Landram who works at Henry Kinsley's Brick Yard. The dreadfull situation of this poor Woman and Child was such that an Order of admission was obtained, signed Selby Hickin and Isaac Tatem Hopper and another friend came with them. Debit City. [On January 11, 1801, Lydia died in the almshouse. Mary Ann eloped on January 2, 1801; see entry for that date. William was jailed in 1800 for not supporting his family.]

Admitted George Lowerman of Legal residence, and formerly a reputable industrious Taylor but having of late years given himself up to hard drinking; is reduced to that situation which totally renders him unable of taking care, and providing for a livelihood, and is come here, in a naked and perishing condition. The Steward, as soon as he saw him, immediately ordered some cloaths to be given him. . . . Debit City.

December 31: Admitted Charlotte Britton (Pregnant), was born about two miles from Crosswicks, New Jersey, says she lived and hired herself out as Maid with different families in this City, is twenty years of age, and says she will suffer death sooner than she will expose the Man who is father of the Child she now bears. The last place she hired at was William French in Laurel Court. . . . Debit Southwark. [Charlotte was discharged by an order of the court on January 5, 1801.]

January 2, 1801: Eloped Mary Ann Landram the Child who was admitted with its Mother the 30th December. The Brother of this Child, a Lad fifteen or sixteen years of age came to see his Mother, and must have seized a favorable opportunity in escaping the vigilance of the Gatekeeper, and thus bore away his Sister. . . . Credit City. [Mary Ann's brother probably took his sister away to prevent the Managers from indenturing her. See the entry for December 30.]

Admitted John Hazless and Christian Frederick Onazorga two Vagrants very ragged and swarming with Bodily Vermin brought from Jail

---

38. A progressive wasting away of the body, particularly by tuberculosis.

by Jacob Facundus, Constable. Hazless is an Englishman, landed in Boston thirty five years ago, and continued in it upwards of four years, and in Cambridge eighteen months, and has been a wanderer ever since he left the last mentioned place; Onazorga is a German and has been in this Country thirteen years and it dont appear that he has gained legal residence anywhere. These poor Creatures were taken up by the night Watch and put into duress for thirty days. Hazless has very bad sore legs, Onazorga is hearty and Stout. Debit City.

January 5, 1801: Admitted Jeremiah Connel who hath legal residence, he came from Ireland and landed in this City seventeen years ago, has followed labouring ever since for a livelihood, and is now afflicted with a bad Cough and violent pains in all his Limbs that totally renders [him] unable to work. . . . Debit City. [Jeremiah died in the almshouse in March 1801.]

Admitted Precilla a Negro Girl eleven or twelve years of age, was born at a place called Milford about six miles from Dover, Delaware state, and belonged to one Purdon of that place, and says that he sold her to Captain John Earle, in Queen street, Southwark. This girl has been in Prison these four months past. Debit City.

January 9, 1801: Admitted John Collins a old Customer and ordinary sort of a Chap, has lost the use of his right hand occasioned by a bad gathering.[39] He was discharged the 25th last March and has been in the Country ever since spunging upon the Farmers, for he is not able to work on account of his lame hand. . . . Debit City. [John was discharged in March 1801, readmitted in November 1801, and released in February 1802.]

January 15, 1801: Admitted Matthew Morin and his Wife Sarah Morin, Old Customers. They were both Discharged the 11th March 1800. He is a Gardener, and goes out in the Spring to follow Gardening all Summer and autumn, then comes here to Garden and keep himself warm all winter and get Cloathed, then take a trip in the Spring again. They have some household furniture which is pretty good, and is now in the Hall, and to mend the matter she is Pregnant. . . . Debit Northern Liberties.

January 17, 1801: Admitted Rose Kennedy a Child two years and seven months Old, her Father is dead and Catharine Kennedy, the Mother, lives in Locust street between Walnut and Spruce and eleventh and twelfth streets; [she] is poor and unable to Support herself and Children and this [child] being too young to bind out, she obtained an Order of Admission. . . . Debit City.

39. A festering abscess.

CHAPTER 3

Prisoners

The Prisoners for Trial Docket and the Vagrancy Docket

G. S. ROWE AND BILLY G. SMITH

Crime has reached crisis proportions in the United States today. Americans kill one another with much greater frequency than in any other industrialized nation, and cases of robbery, rape, drug violations, and domestic violence have become national preoccupations. Between 1980 and 1990 as officials struggled to bring crime under control, the number of incarcerated Americans doubled. As a result, the United States now has one of the highest prison populations per capita in the world. And more than ever, Americans are afraid they will be victims of crime or violence.[1]

1. The problem of crime in contemporary America is cogently discussed in Andrew Hacker, *Two Nations: Black and White, Separate, Hostile, Unequal* (New York: Ballantine Books, 1992).

The nature of both the crimes and the criminals can reveal a good deal about the character of a society. Which activities are defined as "criminal," the manner in which lawbreakers are treated, and how vigorously or lightly certain infractions are prosecuted indicate what a community values most or least. Crimes against property (such as burglary), for example, suggest something different about a society than do crimes against people (such as assault). In addition, criminal behavior is generally associated with poverty. A lack of life's necessities impels some individuals to commit crimes in order to feed themselves or their families. Furthermore, law enforcement officials tend to arrest the poor and the powerless more often than the wealthy and the influential, which means that a disproportionately large number of prisoners come from the former group.

Registers of detentions of alleged and real criminals can therefore serve as an important window into the world of the lower classes—the "inarticulate"—who left very few firsthand accounts of their lives and who appear infrequently in the types of records and documents traditionally examined by scholars. Historians have only recently begun to appreciate that early legal records contain many details about the behavior, lives, and values of the lower classes and the impoverished. Dismissed previously as mere lists of mundane criminal offenses and offenders, and thus as of no real interest to future generations, these sources now are prized for their information about social and legal history in general and for the history of the inarticulate in particular.[2]

The Prisoners for Trial Docket (1790–1948) and the Vagrancy Docket (1790–1932) from Philadelphia County, both of which are excerpted below, are excellent examples of court records rich in information about the lower and middle classes.[3] Both dockets came into existence as a result of penal reform. Colonial Pennsylvania required a variety of court records. Clerks wrote county dockets for both civil (Common Pleas) trials and criminal (Quarter Sessions) trials, while Justices of the Peace maintained their own ledgers. The Pennsylvania Supreme Court likewise kept accounts of its civil (Supreme Court) and criminal (Oyer and Terminer) proceedings. After the Revolution, the Pennsylvania legislature began to enact a series of reforms designed to ease the lot of people accused of crimes and to humanize the treatment of prisoners. New records, such as

2. See, for example, G. S. Rowe, "Women's Crime and Criminal Administration in Pennsylvania, 1763–1790," *Pennsylvania Magazine of History and Biography* 109 (1985): 335–68.

3. Prisoners for Trial Docket, 1790–1948, 164 vols.; Vagrancy Docket, 1790–1932, 36 vols. Both dockets are at the Philadelphia City Archives.

the Prisoners for Trial Docket and the Vagrancy Docket, became necessary to identify, track, and record the fate of the incarcerated. When the
new national government passed laws defining federal offenses in 1789,
Pennsylvania agreed to record the presence and fate of federal prisoners. (This explains why federal offenders Edward Wright and William
Thompson, cases 30 and 69, appear in the Prisoners for Trial Docket.)[4]

Both the Prisoners for Trial Docket and the Vagrancy Docket contain
the clerk's comments about people jailed for actual or alleged criminal
activity. While these notations usually are terse, they provide details otherwise unavailable about the lives of criminals as well as ordinary Philadelphians. The Prisoners for Trial Docket contains information about
people accused of a crime but awaiting trial, while the Vagrancy Docket
describes individuals who were already convicted of an offense. Suspects
listed on the former were apprehended in either of two ways. The first
was on complaint of a justice of the peace or by a constable or sheriff on
orders from a justice of the peace or judge. Such individuals generally
were listed simply as "committed." The second means was by complaint
(or by "oath," "affirmation," or "information") of another citizen. Apprentice Charles McConnel (case 9) was committed "upon Oath" of his
master, Samuel Carpenter, for leaving his service and for stealing cash
and other items. Alexander McDonald (case 40) was implicated for passing a counterfeit check "on affirmation" by Sarah Clare.[5] According to
law, the city's mayor, an alderman, or a justice of the peace could "commit any vagrant or idle and disorderly person (being thereof legally
convicted before him)" to hard labor in jail for a maximum of one month
(see Figure 7). The clerk then recorded these prisoners on the Vagrancy
Docket and noted their crimes.[6]

Obviously, justices of the peace enjoyed considerable discretion in judging criminal activities and in taking people into custody, especially in the

4. Marylynn Salmon surveyed early Pennsylvania courts and their records in "The
Court Records of Philadelphia, Bucks, and Berks Counties in the Seventeenth and Eighteenth Century," *Pennsylvania Magazine of History and Biography* 107 (1983): 249–62. The
Pennsylvania Supreme Court records are available in the Supreme Court Appearance and
Continuance Dockets, 1740–1953, Record Group 33, Supreme Court, Eastern District;
and Dockets of the Courts of Oyer and Terminer and General Gaol Delivery, 1778–1828;
both in the Pennsylvania Historical and Museum Commission, Harrisburg.

5. Because of their religious beliefs, Quakers refused to take traditional oaths, which
contained (and thus corrupted) God's name; they preferred "affirmations," which merely
proclaimed they would be honest and would tell the truth.

6. *Collection of the Penal Laws of the Commonwealth of Pennsylvania* [1790–1794] (Philadelphia, 1794), 10.

Fig. 7. "Gaol, in Walnut Street, Philadelphia," 1794. The Walnut Street jail is in the background, and Richard Allen's Bethel Church, which became the heart of the city's African American community, is in the foreground as it was being moved to its new location. From W. Birch and Son, *The City of Philadelphia . . . As It Appeared in 1800*. Courtesy of the Historical Society of Pennsylvania.

matter of low-level offenses. Because these infractions seldom appear on Quarter Sessions Docket, the Prisoners for Trial Docket and the Vagrancy Docket remind us that there was a range of criminal behavior of concern to the community that heretofore escaped the attention of historians. Few of the city's records other than these two dockets offer glimpses of these types of offenses. The flexibility justices of the peace had in assessing the "bad conduct" of individuals raises the possibility that they could have been swayed in their decisions by matters of age, gender, condition, or race. A close examination of these dockets can help to identify such biases.

One way to analyze these two dockets is to tabulate the various characteristics of the imprisoned and to correlate those traits with the types of crimes with which the accused were charged. This technique can reveal similarities and differences in the lives of various ethnic, racial, and gender groups. Tracking seasonal variations in crime is another approach that can disclose much about the conditions of the lower classes, the poor, and criminals in particular.

Approximately 1,000 Philadelphians were inscribed each year during the 1790s on the Prisoners for Trial Dockets for various illegal deeds. Some infractions were domestic in nature. Patrick Howley (case 2) was jailed for "assaulting and beating his Wife," while Elizabeth Sturois (case 25) claimed that her husband, James, "deserted her and utterly refuses to contribute towards the support of her & their son." A handful of cases involved murder; five men (case 14) were accused "of having Killed or caused the death" of William Humphries. Unruly conduct was also common. The neighbors of Joseph Hines and Mary Hines (case 36) complained that the couple were "disorderly people" who kept "a house for admitting Street Walking women." Burglary likewise was widespread. Charles Addy (case 12), suspected of "having committed Robberies in New York & Baltimore," was charged with stealing "sundry articles" in Philadelphia as well.

Three general levels of criminal activity are represented in the Prisoners for Trial Docket. The first level consisted of very minor offenses handled summarily by justices of the peace. The offenders either spent time in jail or made arrangements to provide for their future good conduct. A second, more serious level of misdemeanors and felonies, such as those associated with Charles Addy (case 12), James Sturois (case 25), and Bob (case 33), were dealt with in courts of Quarter Sessions or the Mayor's Court (which had Quarter Sessions functions for the city of Philadelphia). The names of the accused were registered on the "Convicts Dockett," as occurred in nine cases below. A third level of crime involving serious felonies was viewed as sufficiently important to go either to the State Supreme Court justices in their oyer and terminer capacity or to a federal district court. Edward Wright (case 30) is an example of such a case.

The names of about 400 people appeared on the Vagrancy Docket in the early 1790s, and their number grew rapidly to more than 900 by the middle of the decade. Ann Drain (case 91), Joseph Kelly (case 93), and Catherine Hays (case 102) all were committed as vagrants, although many other criminals were picked up by constables and entered into the docket.[7] Prostitutes were numerous in a city filled with mariners and other transient men. Sarah Evans (case 119) was condemned at least a dozen times for prostitution. Evans also took refuge in the almshouse, and when she eloped on March 13, 1796, the clerk described her as "a young venereal Hussy, off to Innoculate, but not for the [small]pox."[8] Margaret Britton (case 148) admitted that "to get money," she "wished to have carnal Intercourse with" farmers who had brought their goods to market. Masters often charged their servants and slaves—both white and black—with misbehaving and running away, and the owners paid the city to punish their workers with hard labor (see information on runaways in Chapter 4). Wilhelmina Tyser and Martin Cline (cases 153 and 154), two of President George Washington's servants, thus were confined, Tyser for "being a disorderly Servant," and Cline for "being frequently Drunk, neglecting his duty, and otherwise misbehaving." Andrew Pettit (case 137) grumbled that Charles, "a Negro," had fled five times in five months. The living conditions of some people when they were arrested indicates the daily difficulties many poorer Philadelphians endured. Nancy (case 168), "a negroe," was charged "with having no place of abode & having for some time past slept in the Stable's."

As was typical of eighteenth-century criminal procedures, the designation of criminal infractions sometimes was not precise. John Porter (case 11) was accused of "having again absconded from his Master John McElwee and of behaving himself in a disorderly Manner." Margaret Rogers (case 23) allegedly was a "common & intolerable nuissance etc." Lewis (case 26), "a Negroe," was charged "by his Master with running away and for other bad conduct," while Eswoix (cases 43 and 67) was accused of "being a disorderly vagabond and of being guilty of dishonest Practices" as well as with "being a Noted Thief." James Henry (case 64) was arrested for being "concealed under a Shed . . . & not giving a Satisfactory Account of himself."

The excerpts below were selected because they contain interesting details about crime, criminals, and the lower classes. A more systematic sample from the two dockets indicates that crimes ranged from adultery to treason, and from fornication to piracy (see Table 2). Of the individuals on the Prisoners for Trial Docket, 38 percent were indicted for burglary, 22 percent for assault, 10 percent for disorderly conduct, and 5

7. See James Mease's description of this process in Chapter 1.
8. Daily Occurrence Docket, March 13, 1796, Guardians of the Poor, Philadelphia City Archives.

percent for running an illegal establishment such as a brothel or an unlicensed tavern. Not surprisingly, 40 percent of individuals on the Vagrancy Docket were charged with vagrancy. But disorderly and drunken individuals accounted for another 27 percent, and unruly servants and slaves made up 24 percent of those on the docket.

The two dockets can be studied profitably in conjunction with other legal records. For instance, comparison of these dockets with other criminal court dockets reveals that Ann Winter (case 29) was a habitual criminal. Considered "a Notorious Thief," Winter (who used the alias Mary Flood) was arrested two dozen times in three decades. Although she promised authorities in 1779 that they "should never after this time hear of the least blemish against her character," and that she was "retiring into the country to endeavour for an honest livelihood," she was arrested and convicted numerous times thereafter.[9] Recently, the accessibility of computer and statistical programs has enabled scholars to examine legal records more systematically and to identify patterns such as those involving Ann Winter's criminal career.[10]

The names on the two dockets have been compared with each other and also with the Almshouse Docket (see Chapter 2) and the information on individuals that appear on two or more of these dockets is included in brackets in the excerpts below. The presence or absence of substantial numbers of a particular ethnic or racial group on numerous lists could prove significant. By the same token, if a high percentage of African Americans and women appeared on the Vagrancy Docket but not on the Prisoners for Trial Docket, that too might have significance for legal and social historians. These types of patterns are of special interest in interpreting crime and criminality in past societies.[11]

The length of time each prisoner was confined is also worth noting

9. See Rowe, "Women's Crime and Criminal Administration," 335–36.

10. Crime in early Pennsylvania was studied half a century ago by Lawrence H. Gipson, *Crime and Its Punishment in Provincial Pennsylvania* (Bethlehem, Pa.: Lehigh University Press, 1935); and Herbert W. K. Fitzroy, "The Punishment of Crime in Provincial Pennsylvania," *Pennsylvania Magazine of History and Biography* 60 (1936): 242–69. The most recent analysis for Pennsylvania is Rowe, "Women's Crime and Criminal Administration"; and Rowe, "*Femes Covert* and Criminal Prosecution in Eighteenth-Century Pennsylvania," *American Journal of Legal History* 32 (1988): 138–56. For an overview of crime in colonial America, see Peter Charles Hoffer, "Crime and Law Enforcement: The British Colonies," in *Encyclopedia of the North American Colonies*, 1:391–402.

11. For another list of names against which the Prisoners for Trial Docket and the Vagrancy Docket might be matched, see Leslie Patrick-Stamp, "The Prison Sentence Dockets for 1795," *Pennsylvania History* 60 (1993): 353–82.

How long individuals remained incarcerated depended in some instances on the law and in other cases on their personal circumstances. Many faced a predetermined sentence, which constituted full punishment. In those cases, the law established a set period of incarceration for a crime, or permitted a justice of the peace to set the time to be spent in jail. Thus, when L'Amitie (case 57) became intoxicated, broke windows, and "was very disorderly & Disobedient," he was to be "kept untill discharged by due course of law." Others, like George (case 28), faced indeterminate terms; he remained in jail "untill his plea of Freedom [could] be legally determined." James Sutter (case 1), Alexander Adams (case 44), and Mary Johnson (case 52) were confined until the next court term, when they would be tried. A few, like John Fagan (case 53), gained their freedom as soon as they posted bail, although they were still re-

Table 2. Alleged Crimes of People in Prisoners for Trial Docket and Vagrancy Docket for Philadelphia County

Crime	% of People in Prisoners for Trial Docket	% of People in Vagrancy Docket
Adultery	0.6	
Assault		1.5
On nonfamily member	16.6	
On family member	5.4	
Arson	0.3	
Begging		0.9
Bigamy	0.2	
Burglary or larceny	37.9	
Desertion		
From military	1.1	
From ship	3.5	
Of wife	1.8	
Disobedient servants, slaves, apprentices, mariners		
Ran away	1.0	16.1
Misbehaved	0.2	8.1
Disorderly or drunken conduct	9.7	27.0
Escape from jail	0.3	
Forgery	1.4	
Fornication	2.6	
Gambling	0.2	
Kidnapping	0.2	
Miscellaneous	3.6	3.0
Murder	0.6	
Perjury	0.2	
Piracy	0.1	

Table 2.   (Continued)

Crime	% of People in Prisoners for Trial Docket	% of People in Vagrancy Docket
Prostitution[a]	0.2	3.8
Quarantine violations	0.1	
Rape	0.1	
Receiving stolen goods	1.0	
Running an illegal establishment		
Brothel	0.8	
Disorderly house	4.0	
Gambling house	0.1	
Tippling house	0.2	
Suspicious or threatening behavior	3.4	
Swearing or blasphemy	0.4	
Treason	0.4	
Vagrancy	1.8	39.6
Totals	100.0	100.0
Number of people in samples	4,379	533

SOURCE: Prisoners for Trial Docket, 1790–1948, 164 vols.; Vagrancy Docket, 1790–1932, 36 vols. Both dockets are at the Philadelphia City Archives.

NOTE: This table is based on a sample of names drawn from the Prisoners for Trial Docket for 1791, 1792, and 1798–1802 and a sample of names taken from the Vagrancy Docket for 1790, 1791, and 1804. When a person was accused of multiple crimes, only the initial one noted by the clerk was counted in the tabulations in this table.

[a]The proportion who were prostitutes is a minimum figure because many were charged with other crimes too.

quired to return later for trial. Some, like Margaret Rogers (case 23) and Elizabeth Williams (case 24), secured their freedom as soon as they arranged to put up money (called "sureties") to guarantee their future good behavior.[12] There were also individuals like John Greer (case 14) who had to wait until they could be questioned by one of the judges of the Court of Common Pleas or the Supreme Court to learn whether they would stand trial for their alleged crime.

Although Pennsylvania reformed and humanized its prisons after the Revolution, prisoners still experienced appalling conditions and lived under rigid controls. The 1790 law specified that convicts were to

12. These were also called "peace bonds." See Paul Lermack, "Peace Bonds and Criminal Justice in Colonial Philadelphia," *Pennsylvania Magazine of History and Biography* 100 (1976): 173–90.

be "clothed in habits of coarse material," "sustained upon bread, indian meal [cornmeal], or other inferior food," and "allowed one meal of coarse meat in each week." The notations in the Vagrancy Docket that Henry (case 87) was to receive "no Bread" and that Billy (case 88) was "to be fed upon Bread & Water only for the space of 36 Hours" indicates that jail keepers sometimes limited prisoners to even more minimal rations. The accused were also forced to "work every day in the year, except Sundays" for between eight and ten hours daily, not counting "an interval of half an hour for breakfast, and an hour for dinner."[13]

The excerpts below include most of the clerk's entries in the Prisoners for Trial Docket between January 1 and September 5, 1795, and selected entries from the Vagrancy Docket from May 31, 1790, through October 30, 1797.

Prisoners for Trial Docket

Case 1. James D. Sutter, committed Jan. 3, 1795. Charged with having frequently absconded from his Master Abraham Morrow, to be kept untill the next Mayors Court.[14] Discharged Jan. 7.[15] [Sutter appeared in the Prisoners for Trial Docket in 1800 and 1801 for theft. He was sentenced for horse stealing in 1801, at which time the notation in the Sentence Docket indicated that Sutter was a white, twenty-three year old gunsmith.]

Case 2. Patrick Howley, committed Jan. 5, 1795. Charged on Oath with violently assaulting and beating his Wife. Discharged Dec. 12.

Case 3. Francis McHenry, committed Jan. 24, 1795. Charged with having threatened his Master Richard Babe and his Family in a very

13. *Collection of the Penal Laws,* 11–12.

14. The Philadelphia's Mayor's Court, consisting of the mayor, the recorder, and two of the City's aldermen, sat quarterly and had jurisdiction over the offenses usually tried in a county court of general quarter sessions—that is, it tried all felonies (except capital cases), misdemeanors, and nuisances committed within the city.

15. The year for all dates of discharge is the same as the year for admission unless otherwise indicated.

unjustifiable Manner. To be Kept untill he find security for his future good behaviour.[16] Discharged Feb. 5.

Case 4. Mary French, committed Jan. 27, 1795. Charged with breaking the Windows of Hugh McConnell and Ann Kean and assaulting and beating one of her Children. Discharged Mar. 5.

Case 5. Martin Hice, committed Jan. 28, 1795. Charged on Oath by Mary Hice his Wife with a breach of the peace and threatening the life of Said Mary, and also with profane swearing in the Office of William Coats, Esquire. Discharged Feb. 3.

Case 6. John Jackson, committed Jan. 31, 1795. Charged on Oath of John Fisher with committing an Assault & Battery on the person of his Wife Elizabeth Fisher, to be kept untill discharged by due course of Law. Discharged Feb. 3. [Jackson appeared on the Prisoners for Trial Docket in 1801 for assault.]

Case 7. David Ten Eyk, Robert Ten Eyk, committed Feb. 4, 1795. Charged on the Oath of John Prince with having in the night between the 2nd & 3rd Instant[17] feloniously entered the Cabin of the Snow[18] Antonio in the City and there stole & carried away divers Goods and Chattells,[19] the Property of the said John Prince to the value of eleven pounds and five shillings.[20] And the said David Ten Eyk also stands charged on the oath of the said John Prince with having on the evening of the 3rd Instant (with a Man whose name is unknown) did feloniously enter the vessel aforesaid at the place aforesaid with an intention to steal the Goods and chattells of the said John Prince—to keep them both untill they give good security to appear at the next Court of general quarter Sessions—and the said David Ten Eyk to be kept for the second offense to answer the same at the next Mayors Court—and both kept untill legally discharged. Discharged Feb. 9.

Case 8. Delphin a Negroe Woman, committed Feb. 7, 1795. Charged by her Master Fiette La Garde with taking from his house sundry articles of cloathing—to be kept untill she be discharged by due course of Law. Discharged Oct. 6.

Case 9. Charles McConnel, committed Feb. 9, 1795. Charged upon

16. McHenry needed to put up a bond, which would be forfeited if he misbehaved in the future.
17. Instant: of this month.
18. A small ship.
19. Movable personal property.
20. In 1795, 7 shillings and 6 pence was the equivalent of 1 dollar.

Oath by Samuel Carpenter whose apprentice he is—of leaving his service for nine Weeks and stealing Money & other Articles to the value of seven dollars—to be kept untill discharged by due course of Law. Discharged Mar. 5.

Case 10. John Stewart a negroe, committed Feb. 15, 1795. Charged with having on the 7th Instant stole a Surtout Coat[21] the property of Michael Shanahan of the value of Two Dollars—to be kept untill he find surety for his appearance at the next Mayors Court, or otherwise legally discharged. To Convicts Dockett.

Case 11. John Porter, committed Feb. 17, 1795. Charged with having again absconded from his Master John McElwee and of behaving himself in a disorderly Manner, to be kept to answer the Complaints of his said Master at the next Mayors Court. Discharged Feb. 27.

Case 12. Charles Addy, alias Jean Pierre Du Roche, committed Feb. 19, 1795. Charged by Lewis Thierry of having robbed him of sundry articles such as Silver Buckles, Shirts, Hat fiddles,[22] etc. & also charged of having committed Robberies in New York & Baltimore. To be kept untill the next Court of Quarter Sessions or discharged by due course of Law. Discharged Mar. 5.

Case 13. Tom a negro, committed Feb. 23, 1795. Charged with being a runaway from William Phillpot of Celam County State of New Jersey, his Master . . . to be kept untill Legally discharged. Discharged Mar. 3.

Case 14. John Greer, John Fleming, William Wilson, Archibald Kerr, William Platt, committed Feb. 24, 1795. Charged on suspicion of having Killed or caused the death of a certain William Humphries who was this day found dead in the River Delaware; to be kept untill further examined before one of the Judges of the Court of Common Pleas or of the Supreme Court. Discharged [all five] Mar. 2. [Greer appeared on the Prisoners for Trial Docket in 1792 for assaulting his wife.]

Case 15. Florence Rose, Lewis Moraro, Peter Bordenave, committed Feb. 27, 1795. Charged with conspiring to Cheat & defraud Charles deVille of one hundred & 10 French Pinch-beck Washed Watches[23] of the value of 2200 Dollars and for having actually deceitfully & fraudulently got possession of the same watches—to be kept for further examination or severally discharged by due course of Law. [Ross] Discharged Mar. 5, [Moraro] June 5, [Bordenave] Sept. 24.

21. A man's large overcoat.
22. Ornaments on hats.
23. A "Pinchbeck" watch was a toy watch, or one made of cheap alloy resembling gold.

Case 16. Jaine Dunn, committed Feb. 17, 1795. Charged with having received from some person unknown a pocket Book containing a Check on the Bank of Pennsylvania for 6 Dollars & 39 Cents the property of John Moore, well knowing the same to have been Stolen—to be kept untill she gives security to appear at the next Mayors Court. Discharged May 2.

Case 17. Richard ODaniel, committed Mar. 3, 1795. Charged on Oath, that on the 26th of Feb. last he did steal & carry away from Aron Mundenhall a Black Mare, saddle and Bridle and did swop or sell the said Mare, saddle & Bridle, to be kept till tryed at the next Mayors Court for the said felony. To Convicts Dockett.

Case 18. John Lapp, committed Mar. 5, 1795. Charged on oath by Thomas Reed with being a disorderly, idle Vagrant, & on the information of Captain Christian Hubbish of receiving his bounty as a substitute[24] in the Militia and deserting—to be kept untill the next Court of Quarter Sessions—or discharged by due course of Law. Discharged May 20.

Case 19. William Stoltz, committed Mar. 6, 1795. Charged on oath with having on or about the 16th Ultimo[25] and at divers other times violently assaulted, beat & otherwise ill treated his wife Catharine & refuses to bring before me sureties for his future good behaviour—to be kept to answer the said charges at the next Mayors Court or find security to keep the peace. Discharged Mar. 12.

Case 20. John Bergenhof, George Wirtz, Elias Boyer, committed Mar. 20, 1795. Charged with having on Sunday the 15th Instant on the oath of Elizabeth Bemper aged about 12 years & 4 Months with having assaulted Her the said Elizabeth by throwing her down by force & Violence, and the said John Committing a Rape in presence of the said George & Elias who aided and abetted by refusing her assistance altho she called & begged them. [Boyer] Discharged Mar. 25, [Wirtz] June 2, [Bergenhof] June 9. [Bergenhof appeared on the Prisoners for Trial Docket in 1802 for assault.]

Case 21. James Amies, Roger McCoy, Francis Johnson, committed Mar. 21, 1795. Charged with making a Riot and of violently assaulting & Beating Robert Harrison & Thomas Harrison of the said City—to be kept to answer the said charge at the next Mayors Court or be otherwise legally discharged. [Amies] Discharged Mar. 29, [McCoy] Mar. 25, [Johnson] Mar. 27.

24. The bonus for signing up for the militia.
25. Ultimo: of or occurring in the month preceding the present.

Case 22. Daniel Baugh, committed Mar. 21, 1795. Charged upon oath with being concerned in an attempt to defraud Thomas Marley of his property & occasioning a riot in the Street—to be kept untill discharged by due course of Law. Discharged Mar. 23.

Case 23. Margaret Rogers, committed Mar. 26, 1795. Charged with being very disorderly, common & intolerable nuisance etc.; to be kept untill the Mayors Court, or find security for her good behaviour or otherwise legally discharged. Discharged June 19.

Case 24. Elizabeth Williams, committed Mar. 27, 1795. Charged on the Oath of James Wilson & his Wife with violent assaults & Threatenings against their persons, to be kept untill she find Security or otherwise legally discharged. Discharged Apr. 4.

Case 25. James Sturois, committed Apr. 1, 1795. Charged by his Wife Elizabeth with having for upwards of 13 Months past without reasonable cause deserted her and utterly refuses to contribute towards the support of her & their son Thomas—to be kept to answer the said Charge at the next Mayors Court or otherwise Legally Discharged. Discharged Apr. 4.

Case 26. Lewis a Negroe, committed Apr. 3, 1795. Charged by his Master Thomas Cuthbert with running away and other bad conduct—to be kept untill Legally discharged. Discharged [date unknown].

Case 27. Jamacai a negroe, committed Apr. 13, 1795. Charged with having absconded from his Master John Harrison, Lumber Merchant, & of deserting his service and misbehaving. To be kept untill legally discharged. Discharged May [date unknown].

Case 28. George a negroe, committed Apr. 21, 1795. Charged with being a runaway Slave the property of John Woods, Esquire of Pittsburg; to be kept untill his plea of Freedom be legally determined. Discharged May 22.

Case 29. Ann Winter, committed May 1, 1795. Charged with stealing 2 loaves of sugar the property of M. Muhallon, is to be kept till discharged by due course of Law. To Convicts Dockett.

Case 30. Edward Wright, committed May 11, 1795. Charged with Treason against the Laws and Constitution of the United States. Discharged Oct. 8.

Case 31. John D. Mulhollen, committed May 14, 1795. Charged with violently assaulting & wounding on the evening of the 13th Instant a certain John Christie through the affects of insanity as is supposed—to be kept untill further orders. Discharged June 2.

Case 32. James a negroe, committed May 15, 1795. Charged with entering on board the Schooner[26] Charming Betsy by William Lark the master without his knowledge in the Island of Grenada—to be kept at the proper [illegible] and Charges of the said William Lark for the purpose of transporting him back again to the Island of Grenada or otherwise legally discharged. Discharged June 15.

Case 33. Bob a negroe, committed May 18, 1795. Charged by George Plumstead, Esquire with being the Property of William Pennock of Norfolk in Virginia & of having absconded from his service—to be kept untill the next Mayors Court or otherwise legally discharged. Discharged May 19.

Case 34. Joseph Bruden, committed May 18, 1795. Charged with being an apprentice to John Murray and of absconding from his service & refuses to return to his Duty—to be kept till discharged by due course of Law. Discharged May 25.

Case 35. William Till, committed May 20, 1795. Charged with others of committing a riot in this City and with assaulting & beating James McClutchon, Mariner, & William McClutchon—to answer the said Charges at the next Mayors Court.

Case 36. Joseph Hines & Mary Hines, committed May 21, 1795. Charged on the oath of their Neighbours with being disorderly people and keeping a house for admitting Street Walking women, and of assaulting John Lewis & threatening to beat him—to be kept till they provide security to keep the peace, or legally discharged. Discharged May 22.

Case 37. Henry Higgart, committed May 29, 1795. Charged with having on the night of the 28th Instant and frequently theretofore by violent ill treatment in beating his Wife Ann greatly indangered her life—to Answer the same at the next Mayors Court. Discharged June 18.

Case 38. William Feren, committed June 1, 1795. Charged with being found drunk in the house of Robert Morris about 2 O'Clock in the morning, supposed with an intent to take something from thence—to be kept untill legally discharged. Discharged June 13.

Case 39. Aaron Morris, committed June 2, 1795. Charged on the Oath of Henrietta Johnson with being the father of her Bastard Child with which she is now Pregnant—to be kept untill legally discharged. Discharged Aug. 13.

Case 40. Alexander McDonald, committed June 5, 1795. Charged by Sarah Clare on affirmation with passing a Counterfeit Check of Britton

26. A vessel with two or more masts.

& Massy on the Bank of Pennsylvania—to be kept untill discharged by due course of Law. Discharged Dec. 11.

Case 41. Louise Beuller, committed June 6, 1795. Charged with being a bound servant[27] to Doctor Massy and of absconding from his Service & refuses to return—to be kept untill discharged by due course of Law. Discharged June 8.

Case 42. Ann Albert, committed June 9, 1795. Charged by Leonard Keemly with being a disorderly woman and of having absconded from her infant about three months old—to answer the same at the Next Mayors Court. Discharged Sept. 24.

Case 43. Eswoix [see case 67], a spanish negroe, alias John, committed June 9, 1795. Charged with being divers times Committed for being a disorderly vagabond and of being guilty of dishonest Practices—to be kept 'till the next Mayors Court—to abide the order of the said Court. Discharged July 14.

Case 44. Alexander Adams, committed June 16, 1795. Charged on the Oath of his Master Michael Dictrick with assaulting & beating his said Master & of threatening to take his said Masters Life, & on the same day knocked down his Mistress Mary the Wife of the said Michael & otherwise misbehaved himself in a disorderly manner at divers times— Answer at Mayors Court. Discharged June 18.

Case 45. Peter Reimler, committed June 19, 1795. Charged on suspicion of having in a felonious manner broke open a Box of Irish Linnens on board the ship Washington and secreted a part thereof with an intent to steal & carry away the same, 28 pieces of which has been found with him this morning. Discharged July 7.

Case 46. Andrew O'Neil, committed June 20, 1795. Charged by the Guardians of the Poor with deserting his Wife & Child and leaving them a charge on the City; to be kept untill discharged by due course of Law. Discharged June 25.

Case 47. Antoine, a negroe, committed June 24, 1795. Charged with having concealed himself on board the Schooner Minerva in Hispaniole[28]—and of having run away from his owner in that place; till discharged by due course of Law. Discharged Aug. 15.

---

27. Most "bound servants" were Europeans who sold themselves into servitude for three or four years in return for food, shelter, clothing, and passage to North America. A few Americans also indentured themselves as bound servants for several years. Occasionally, when defendants could not pay court fees, even when they were exonerated, the court sold them into servitude to recover costs.

28. Hispaniola is an island in the West Indies.

Case 48. Mary Pate & Jane Kearney, committed June 25, 1795. Charged on the Oaths of sundry Persons with keeping a disorderly House[29]—till the next Court of Quarter Sessions. Discharged [Pate] Sept. 24—said to be gone & a discharge on file. Jane Kearney discharged July 21.

Case 49. Thomas Devine, committed June 25, 1795. Charged with being drunk and of throwing himself into the River & was saved from drowning by some of the Citizens; till discharged by due course of Law. Discharged July 27.

Case 50. Molly a negroe Girl about 16 years old, committed June 25, 1795. Charged on her own confession with being the property of the Reverend W. Wharton of Prospect Hill, Brandywine Hundred, New Castle County [Delaware] & of having eloped from him—till discharged by due course of Law. Discharged July 8.

Case 51. Catharine Carr, committed July 4, 1795. Charged with committing an Assault & Battery on the person of her own Mother—to be kept untill she find Bail or be otherwise legally discharged. Discharged Sept. 23.

Case 52. Mary Johnson, committed July 6, 1795. Charged by divers of her Neighbours with being a common Scold & intolerable Nuisance, who by continually scolding, cursing & swearing terrifies & disturbs their peace; to answer the same at the next Mayors Court. Discharged July 8.

Case 53. John Fagan, committed July 11, 1795. Committed [originally on] 30 of June 1795, charged with beating & Assaulting Violently and of biting off a Piece of the left Ear of George Carson. On the 2nd July following, Security was given for His appearance at the next Mayors Court—& this day delivered into Jail by his Securitys Brannan & Molineaux.[30] Discharged July 13.

Case 54. Catharine Louisa Figge, committed July 10, 1795. Charged by her Master Peter Blight with committing divers Larcenys of his Goods & Chattells, hath absconded & been guilty of other Misdemenors; to be kept at reasonable Labour untill the next Mayors Court. Discharged Sept. 5.

Case 55. Jacob Wirms & [?] Hutchings, committed July 11, 1795. Charged with having some time heretofore Conducted themselves in a very notorious disorderly manner to the great terror, Danger & disturbance of their neighbourhood; to be kept untill they provide good secu-

29. A brothel or an illegal tavern.
30. Brannan and Molineaux had loaned bail to Fagan.

rity for their future good behavior. Discharged Hutchings July 13 and Wirms July 14.

Case 56. Francoise, a negroe, committed July 20, 1795. Charged with being a Slave to William Penton of Pensecola & of absconding from the Schooner Shear Water, Captain Nicholas Cook, on the 29th May last; to be kept untill discharged by due Course of Law. Discharged Aug. 31.

Case 57. L'Amitie, a negroe, committed July 21, 1795. Charged with being Servant to Angelica Jujuste and of getting Drunk, breaks Windows and is otherwise very disorderly & Disobedient—to be kept untill legally discharged by due course of Law. Discharged Aug. 11.

Case 58. Matthew Austin, committed July 20, 1795. Charged on the Oath of Ester Eastburne with stealing one Gold Watch, one Silk Shawl & 1 pair of Silver Buckles—to be kept untill the next Mayors Court. Discharged Oct. 21.

Case 59. Mary Davis & Margaret Smith, committed July 24, 1795. Charged with having on the 23rd Instant stolen & Carried away from the Dwelling House of William Shippen three Casimer Westcoats[31]—to be kept till next Mayors Court. Discharged July 30.

Case 60. John James Farre, committed July 28, 1795. Charged with breaking down the fence between him & John Lauch & with having violently assaulted, beaten & with an ax attempted to kill the said John Lauch and also of threatening to do further injury to the said John; to answer at the next Mayors Court. Discharged Aug. 10.

Case 61. James Wear, committed July 29, 1795. Charged with keeping a disorderly ill governed house to the great Disturbance of the neighbours; is to be kept untill legally discharged. Discharged Sept. 8.

Case 62. Margaret Magill, committed July 29, 1795. Charged on suspicion of opening the House of Frederick Foy in the dead of the night whereby said Foy suffered injury. To be kept till legally discharged. Discharged Sept. 22.

Case 63. Stephen Dominick, committed July 30, 1795. Charged on the Oath of Hannah Johnson with begetting her with the Child whereof she is now Pregnant & of frequently promising her marriage & refusing to do the same; to be kept untill legally discharged. Discharged Aug. 3.

Case 64. James Henry, committed Aug. 3, 1795. Charged with being taken up by the High Constables concealed under a Shed between 4th & 5th Streets & Chestnut & Walnut Streets & not giving a Satisfactory Account of himself, till discharged by due course of Law. Discharged Sept. 6.

---

31. A "waistcoat" was an underjacket or a vest.

Case 65. John Cramsay, committed Aug. 8, 1795. Charged on Oath with violently Assaulting and beating his Wife & threatening to beat her to death—to be kept till discharged by due course of Law. Discharged Aug. 12.

Case 66. Marianne, a negress, committed Aug. 13, 1795. Charged with having in her possession a quantity of goods the property of Elizabeth Le Garde which were Stolen and refuseing to give satisfactory information how she got them—till discharged by due Course of Law. To Convicts Dockett.

Case 67. Eswoix [see case 43], committed Aug. 13, 1795. Charged by Thomas Durnell with being a Noted Thief—to be kept till legally discharged.

Case 68. William Thompson [see case 69], committed Aug. 16, 1795. Charged on suspicion of Stealing & carrying away from the Store of T. Shreve & M. West a silver Watch, some Money and other property—to be kept untill he be further dealt with according to law. To Convicts Dockett.

Case 69. William Thompson [see case 68], committed Aug. 19, 1795. Charged with being a Deserter from the Army of the United States—to be kept till due Notice be given to the Secretary of War—or otherwise legally discharged.

Case 70. Peter Cunningham, committed Aug. 17, 1795. Charged with being an imposter, pretending that he hath lost the use of his arm & hand, which upon examination appeared to be false to be kept untill discharged by due course of Law. Discharged Aug. 28.

Case 71. Figaro, committed Aug. 19, 1795. Charged on Oath with selling a watch to Henry Henron, which was stolen, & not giving any account how he came by it—to be kept untill discharged by due course of Law. Discharged Oct. 5.

Case 72. Mary Maloney, committed Aug. 22, 1795. Charged with being a drunken, disorderly Vagrant having no place of abode, & with being a nusance to the City—to be kept to abide the Judgment of the Mayors Court. Discharged Sept. 7.

Case 73. John Billins, John Davis, & Alexander Gardner, committed Aug. 23, 1795. Charged on the Oath of John Ferredy with Robbing him on the High Way—'till discharged by due course of Law. [All three] to Convicts Dockett.

Case 74. Jacob Hendrick, committed Aug. 25, 1795. Charged on the Affirmation of Abram Mitchell with having at a late hour last night behaved in High Street in a very disorderly manner, and with violently assaulting him and divers other Watchmen—till the next Mayors Court. Discharged Aug. 29.

Case 75. Cato Williams, committed Aug. 26, 1795. Charged on the Oath of Thomas Cash with taking off his Barr Room a pair of Saddle Baggs Containing 60 or 70 dollars, & 2 shirts, etc. which he confesses he did take & throw into a necessary[32]—till next Court of Quarter Sessions. To Convicts Dockett.

Case 76. Matthew Dowdle Reardon alias John Young, committed Aug. 28, 1795. Charged with giving a very contradictory and unsatisfactory account of himself and said to be Matthew Reardon who has divers times been Convicted of Felonies in this City—to be kept untill legally discharged. Discharged Jan. 7, 1796.

Case 77. Ann Young, committed Sept. 1, 1795. Charged on the Oath of her husband John Young with assaulting & beating him, & with threatening to take his life, of which he swears that he believes himself in danger—Next Mayors Court. Discharged Sept. 22.

Case 78. Cuff alias Jack Smith, committed Sept. 1, 1795. Charged on the oath of Toby White with stealing out of his Pockett 2 Silver dollars & about a half, which he confesses. Same Charged on the Oath of Jane Gray that a Gold Watch which had been in her charge was Stolen from her dwelling on 30 Ultimo which is found in his possession—and he confesses that he did take the same—to be kept untill he be dealt with according to Law. To Convicts Dockett.

Case 79. John Barry, committed Sept. 3, 1795. Charged with having without cause deserted his Wife and Infant Daughter without having made any provision for their Support—till he provide Security or is otherwise legally discharged. Discharged Sept. 7.

Case 80. Catherine Stealy, committed Sept. 3, 1795. Charged on the Oath of George Fox with having aided & assisted, as he believes, a certain George Stealy in making his escape from the Debtors apartment[33]—to be kept untill she be legally discharged. Discharged Aug. 4.

Case 81. Charles Johnson, committed Sept. 5, 1795. Charged on Oath by Sarah Amey with having begotten her with Child, which Child is likely to be born a Bastard & become Charge able to the City—till discharged by due course of Law. Discharged Sept. 8.

Case 82. LaViolette [see case 175], a negroe, committed Sept. 7, 1795.

---

32. A toilet.
33. The part of the prison where debtors were incarcerated.

Charged on Oath with having stolen a puppy of Danish Breed, the property of M. Morris. Discharged Sept. 24.

Case 83. Frederick, a negroe, committed Sept. 5, 1795. Charged on the Oath of Marie Dennis LaPoule on Suspicion of entering her dwelling last night & stealing a quantity of Wearing aparel—till further examination. To Convicts Dockett.

Vagrancy Docket

Case 84. William Smith, confined May 31, 1790. Charged with Running away from his Master Henry Ritter. Discharged June 1st.

Case 85. Joe (Negro), confined May 31, 1790. Charged with being a Slave & Running away from his Master Alexander Bayley. Discharged Aug. 31.

Case 86. Faramong (Negro), confined June 1, 1790. Charged with Refusing to be removed from the Work House and be employed in his Masters Service. Discharged July 13.

Case 87. Henry (Negro), no Bread, confined June 14, 1790. Charged with Misbehaving himself toward his Master John Lawrence, Esquire, to be kept to Labour ten Hours. Discharged June 15.

Case 88. Billy (Negro), confined June 14, 1790. Charged with Drunkness, to be kept at hard Labour & to be fed upon Bread & Water only for the space of 36 Hours. Discharged June 16.

Case 89. Toney, alias Tom (Negro), confined June 17, 1790. Charged with concealing himself on Board the Sloop[34] Prince William Henry, Captain Jones, from St. Kitt,[35] and being a Runaway. Discharged June 24.

Case 90. Sarah Harrington, confined June 21, 1790. Charged with being a Vagrant, to be kept at hard Labour for the space of Thirty days. Discharged July 21.

Case 91. Ann Drain [see cases 110, 112, 114, 117, 161, and 162], confined June 21, 1790. Charged with being a disorderly Vagrant Person, to be kept at hard Labour One Month. Discharged July 21.

---

34. A small, one-masted vessel.
35. St. Kitts is a British island in the West Indies.

[Drain appeared in the Prisoners for Trial Docket in 1800, charged with theft.]

Case 92. Dick (Negro), confined June 23, 1790. Charged with Conducting himself very disorderly & absenting himself from his Master Edward Burd, Esquire, to be kept at hard Labour for the space of thirty days. Discharged June 28.

Case 93. Joseph Kelly, confined June 24, 1790. Charged with being found lurking about the market & giving contradictory Accounts of himself, etc., to be put at hard Labour 20 days. Discharged July 14.

Case 94. John Stuart, confined June 25, 1790. Charged with lurking about the City & refusing Employ when offered him; to be kept at hard Labour Thirty days as a Vagrant. Discharged July 25.

Case 95. Elizabeth Johnson, Mullato, confined July 7, 1790. Charged with very bad behaviour to her Master Hugh McCollough. Discharged Aug. 3.

Case 96. Sarah Ilson, confined July 9, 1790. Charged with keeping a disorderly Riotous and Ill famed House, to be kept at hard Labour for the space of Thirty days. Discharged Aug. 7.

Case 97. Thomas Roberts, confined July 12, 1790. Charged with Neglecting to obey the lawfull commands of his Master. Discharged July 24.

Case 98. Ann Moor, confined July 15, 1790. Charged with Assault & Battery on the Body of Andrew Murray, to be kept at hard Labour. Discharged July 17.

Case 99. George Escher, no Bread, confined July 16, 1790. Charged with being an Idle drunken Vagrant & with a violent assault & Battery on his Wife, to be kept confined five days. Discharged July 19.

Case 100. Elizabeth McCoy, no Bread, confined July 16, 1790. Charged with obstinately refusing to obey the Lawfull commands of her Mistress Mary Robinson. Discharged July 19.

Case 101. Jacob Drummer, no Bread, confined July 21, 1790. Charged with being a disobedient disorderly apprentice & of absconding from his said Master Richard Allen, to be kept at hard Labour Thirty days. Discharged July 29.

Case 102. Catherine Hays, confined July 23, 1790. Charged with being a Vagrant lewd drunken disorderly person, to be kept at hard Labour one month. Discharged Aug. 21.

Case 103. Nancy (Negress), confined July 26, 1790. Charged with disobeying the lawfull commands of her Mistress, to be kept at hard Labour. Discharged Aug. 30.

Case 104. Peter (Negro), confined July 28, 1790. Charged with being guilty of disorderly and turbulent conduct towards his Mistress, to be kept at hard Labour Thirty days. Discharged Aug. 26.

Case 105. Sarah Thompson, confined July 29, 1790. Charged with being an Idle disolute & Notorious Prostitute, to Labour One month. Discharged Aug. 27.

Case 106. Emilia Otter, no Bread, confined July 29, 1790. Charged with being an Idle disolute and Notorious Prostitute, to Labour one month. Discharged Aug. 29.

Case 107. Martha Patterson, confined July 31, 1790. Charged with being an Idle disolute Person and common Street Walker, to be kept at hard Labour one month. Discharged Aug. 9.

Case 108. Charles (Negro), confined July 31, 1790. Charged with absconding from his Master John Goslin, to be kept at hard Labour Untill he be legally discharged. Discharged Aug. 25.

Case 109. John Hazlehurst, confined Aug. 3, 1790. Charged with Stroling & beging in the Streets contrary to Laws,[36] to be kept at hard Labour Thirty days. Discharged Sept. 1.

Case 110. Ann Drain [see case 91], confined Aug. 9, 1790. Charged with being a disorderly Vagrant Person, to be kept at hard Labour for the space of Thirty days. Discharged Sept. 7.

Case 111. Tevia Disetwey, Negress, confined Aug. 10, 1790. Charged with disobeying her Master William McMatrey, to be kept at hard Labour. Discharged Sept. 20.

Case 112. Ann Drain [see case 91], confined Sept. 27, 1790. Charged with being a disorderly Vagrant person, to be kept at hard Labour for the space of Thirty days. Discharged Oct. 26.

Case 113. Jesse Cooper, confined Oct. 25, 1790. Charged with being a disorderly Vagrant person, to be kept at hard Labour for the space of Thirty days. Discharged Oct. 26. [Cooper was inscribed on the Prisoners for Trial Docket in 1798 for stealing three hogs and in 1801 for physically abusing his wife.]

Case 114. Ann Drain [see case 91], confined Nov. 3, 1790. Charged with being a Prostitute, to be kept at hard Labour for the space of One Month. Discharged Dec. 2.

Case 115. Harry [see cases 116, 118, and 120], Negro, confined Feb. 28, 1791. Charged with disorderly behaviour, getting drunk and absent-

36. Begging was against the law.

ing himself day and Night from the service of his Master William Lewis, Esquire, to be kept at hard Labour Thirty days. Discharged Mar. 29.

Case 116. Harry [see cases 115, 118, and 120], Negro, confined Mar. 30, 1791. Guilty of disorderly behaviour and getting drunk & Absenting himself from the service of his Master William Lewis, Esquire, to be kept at hard Labour 30 days. Discharged May 8.

Case 117. Ann Drain [see case 91], confined Apr. 5, 1791. Charged with being a vagabond, to be kept at hard Labour for 10 days. Discharged Apr. 14.

Case 118. Harry [see cases 115, 116, and 120], Negro, confined May 9, 1791. Charged with getting drunk and Misbehaving himself towards his Master William Lewis, Esquire, to be kept at hard Labour 30 days. Discharged Aug. 19.

Case 119. Sarah Evans, confined May 9, 1991. Charged with being a vagrant, to be kept at labour 30 days. Discharged June 7. [Evans appeared thirteen more times in the Vagrancy Dockets (see cases 121 through 124, 133, 135, 136, 150, 152, 157, 161, and 162). She was enrolled in the Prisoners for Trial Docket in 1792 for "having a disorderly house." The clerk of the almshouse noted that Evans, "a young venereal Hussy," eloped from the institution on March 13, 1796, "off to Innoculate, but not for the pox."]

Case 120. Harry [see cases 115, 116, and 118], confined June 23, 1791. Charged by Master William Lewis with having much misbehaved and also absconded from his service. Discharged July 6.

Case 121. Sarah Evans [see case 119], confined June 24, 1791. Charged with being a vagrant and an abandoned Prostitute, to be kept at labour 30 days. Discharged July 23.

Case 122. Sarah Evans [see case 119], confined July 26, 1791. Charged with being a vagrant, to be kept at labour 30 days. Discharged Aug. 24.

Case 123. Sarah Evans [see case 119], confined Oct. 16, 1791. Charged with being a vagabond and disorderly person, to be kept at labour 30 days. Discharged Nov. 16.

Case 124. Sarah Evans [see case 119], confined Nov. 17, 1791. Charged by the watch[man] as being drunk and behaving in a disorderly manner in the streets, to be kept at labour 30 days. Discharged Dec. 16, 1791.

Case 125. Crispin [see cases 143 and 149], no Bread, confined Dec. 5, 1791. Charged with having absconded from Master Monsieur D. Artis of this City on the Second Instant and refused to return to his duty, to be kept at Labour 30 days. Discharged Dec. 20.

Case 126. Solomon Ryan, No Bread, confined Feb. 16, 1792. Charged with having absconded from the Ship Euphrasia after having signed articles to proceed [on] the Voyage with Capt. McFaddin.[37] Discharged Mar. 1.

Case 127. Joseph Green, confined Feb. 24, 1792. Charged with having yesterday, this day and at divers times heretofore been roving about the City insulting and violently treating the Inhabitence. Sent to [the Pennsylvania] Hospital, he being a Lunatick. [Green entered the almshouse in June 1799, escaped the following month, was admitted in June 1800 and was released the following month. He was readmitted on September 22, 1800 (see Chapter 2), when the clerk indicated that Green was a "deranged" black man. He appeared in the Prisoners for Trial Docket on suspicion of petty theft in 1792 and 1798 and for breaking and entering in 1800.]

Case 128. Richard Hill, confined Mar. 2, 1792. Charged with leading a lewd and disorderly life, associating [and] cohabiting with Lewd Women, particularly with Elizabeth Buskin [see case 129] & Elizabeth Hunter [see case 130]. To be kept at labour Thirty Days. Discharged Mar. 5. [Hill was registered in the Prisoners for Trial Docket earlier in 1792 for assaulting his wife.]

Case 129. Elizabeth Buskin [see case 128], confined Mar. 2, 1792. Charged with being a Woman of a disorderly Character, to be kept at Hard Labour for the Space of Thirty Days. Discharged Mar. 9. [Buskin appeared in the Prisoners for Trial Docket in the same year for petty theft.]

Case 130. Elizabeth Hunter [see case 128], confined Mar. 2, 1792. Charged with being a Woman of a disorderly Character, to be kept at Hard Labour for the Space of Thirty Days. Discharged Mar. 13.

Case 131. L'ville, no bread, confined Mar. 28, 1792. Charged by Monsieur Lufferest [see case 132], Consul General of France, with behaving in a very insolent and unbecoming manner to his Mistress. Discharged Mar. 31.

Case 132. Caesar, no bread, confined Mar. 28, 1792. Charged by Monsieur Lafferest [see case 131], Consul General of France, with behaving in a very insolent and unbecoming manner to his Mistress. Discharged Mar. 31.

Case 133. Sarah Evans [see case 119], confined Apr. 7, 1792. Charged with behaving in a Disorderly manner in the Streets and being of bad character, to be kept at labour 30 days. Discharged May 6.

---

37. Sailors customarily received a month's wages when they signed on to work on a ship, but some men, like Ryan, absconded after collecting their pay.

Case 134. Philipina Deiterick, confined June 16, 1792. Charged by her Master Lewis Farmer with being a disorderly Servant and having frequently gone out of the House after the family had retired to rest, and remaining out during the Night in Company with disorderly Men. Discharged and delivered to her Master Aug. 18.

Case 135. Sarah Evans [see case 119], confined July 5, 1792. Charged with being a vagabond and having no place of abode, to be kept at labour 30 days. Discharged Nov. 22, 1792.

Case 136. Sarah Evans [see case 119], confined Jan. 2, 1793. Charged with being a vagrant, to be kept at labour 30 days. Discharged Feb. 2, 1793.

Case 137. Charles a Negro, confined Feb. 5, 1793. Charged by Mr. Andrew Pettit with being a very disobedient and disorderly Servant, who since October last Runaway five times without any Reasonable cause of complaint. To be kept at hard labour thirty days. Delivered to his master Feb. 11.

Case 138. Amy a Negress, confined Feb. 9, 1793. Charged by her Master George Davis, Esquire with absconding from him Eight times in the Course of this Week. To be kept untill her Master finds Suitable persons to dispose of her, to which he Expects to effect in a few days. Discharged Feb. 12.

Case 139. Will a Negro, confined Feb. 11, 1793. Charged by his Master Edward Dunant with absenting himself from his Service and refusing to return to his duty. To be kept untill next Mayors Court or untill legally discharged. Delivered to his Master Feb. 22.

Case 140. Mary Yard, confined Feb. 18, 1793. Charged on Oath by Catharine Mooney & others with assaulting, and beating said Catharine and with Getting drunk & keeping a Disorderly House. To be kept at hard labour 30 days as an Idle disorderly Vagrant. Discharged Mar. 20.

Case 141. Anthony de Banger [see cases 142 and 151] of the Sun Moon & Twin Stars, a Negro, confined Feb. 20, 1793. Charged by Thomas Cumpston & Jonathan Gostelow with being a Vagrant Vagabond, and under pretence of Insanity, ill treats the Citizens in the Streets. To labour ten days. Discharged Mar. 2.

Case 142. Anthony DeBanger [see cases 141 and 151], confined Apr. 19, 1793. Charged with throwing a Stone and wounding a certain John McGuire, and also with being an Idle Vagabond, to labour thirty days or untill Legally discharged. Discharged May 18.

Case 143. Crispin [see cases 125 and 149], confined Apr. 20, 1793.

Charged by his Master Monsieur D'Artis with absconding the 14th instant. Discharged Apr. 28.

Case 144. Richard Ball, confined June 25, 1793. Charged with behaving himself in a very Riotous, Outrageous, Ungovernable manner on Board the Sloop Betsey, Refusing to perform his duty, and attempting to desert the said Vessel. To be Kept untill call'd for by Benjamin Weeks the Master of said Vessel. Discharged July 26, Captain Weeks having sailed from Port and left him in Custody.

Case 145. Susannah Johnson, confined Aug. 16, 1793. Says she served her time with William Keyser of Germantown,[38] but by her appearence and the Company in which she was found, appears to be a Strolling Vagrant or a Servant to some person. To be Kept untill Legally Discharged. Discharged Sept. 2.

Case 146. Sarah Mortan [see case 147], confined Sept. 23, 1793. Charged by her Master Henry Harper with getting drunk and embezzling his property. To be Kept at hard labour thirty days. Discharged Dec. 6.

Case 147. Sarah Mortan [see case 146], confined Dec. 10, 1793. Charged with again getting drunk and beating her Mistress and otherwise misbehaving, to be kept at hard labour thirty days unless sooner discharged. Discharged Jan. 4, 1794.

Case 148. Margaret Britton & [?], confined Jan. 16, 1794. Charged by [Constables] Gibbons and Durnal with skulking about Country Waggons in High Street at a late Hour of the night and acknowledges that they wished to have carnal Intercourse with them to get money.[39] To labour 30 days. Discharged Feb. 16.

Case 149. Crispin [see cases 125 and 143], confined Mar. 17, 1794. Charged by his Master Monsieur D'Artois with having frequently absconded from his Service, to be kept at Labour 30 days. Discharged Apr. 17.

Case 150. Sarah Evans [see case 119], confined Apr. 23, 1794. Charged with being a Lewd Girl, taken by the watch[man] at night, to be kept at labour 30 days. Discharged May 3.

Case 151. Anthony DeBanger [see cases 141 and 142], confined May

---

38. Johnson claimed that she had served her apprenticeship in Germantown, several miles north of Philadelphia.

39. Using their wagons to cart their produce to the city's main market twice a week, farmers often arrived the evening before the market opened and spent the night in their wagons.

17, 1794. Charged with going about the streets disturbing the citizens. Discharged May 17.

Case 152. Sarah Evans [see case 119], confined June 13, 1794. Charged with being Lewd & Disorderly and suspected of concealing money brought into jail by Theodora, a negress, to be kept at labour 30 days. Discharged July 19.

Case 153. Wilhelmina Tyser, confined July 2, 1794. Charged with being a disorderly Servant belonging to the president of the United States.[40] To be kept at hard labour thirty days, unless sooner discharged by her Mistress. Discharged July 7.

Case 154. Martin Cline, confined Aug. 6, 1794. Charged on Oath of James Germain, Steward to the President of the United States (and done by desire of the President), with being frequently Drunk, neglecting his duty, and otherwise misbehaving. To be Kept untill legally discharged. Discharged Aug. 22.

Case 155. Peter Christensen, Christian Haln, Hans Ueale, Johan Peter Hirman, & Thomas Brock, confined Oct. 11, 1794. Charged on Oath by James George Capinger with having on the 10th Instant absented themselves from the Ship Henrietta without permission from the Said J. G. Capinger, Master, the Voyage not being yet ended.[41] To be Kept untill said Vessel shall be ready to proceed to Sea. Discharged Oct. 14.

Case 156. Lewis Mengis, Christopher Miller & Frederick Elmer, confined Oct. 11, 1794. Charged on Oath with threatening to Desert the Service of their Master Jonathan Meredith, and refusing to Obey his lawful commands—To be kept at hard labour thirty days each. Discharged [all three] Oct. 30.

Case 157. Sarah Evans [see case 119], confined Dec. 6, 1794. Charged with being a vagrant, to be kept at labour 20 days. Discharged Dec. 26.

Case 158. London Derry, Francis Williams, Cato Williams, Jack Copeland, all Negroes, confined Feb. 26, 1795. Charged by George Faganda with being idle vagrants, 30 days. Discharged [all four] Mar. 26.

Case 159. John, Spanish Negroe, confined Apr. 30, 1795. Charged with the appearance of being a vagabond and of being guilty (probably through necessity) of some pilfering, to be kept at hard Labour for the space of thirty days. Discharged June 1.

40. President Washington lived in Philadelphia, the country's temporary capital during the 1790s. Note also the next entry on Martin Cline.

41. Mariners normally were obligated to help unload the ship's cargo at the voyage's conclusion.

Case 160. Will, Negroe, confined May 20, 1795. Charged on his own voluntary confession of having absconded from Master Benjamin Wells of Baltimore. Discharged June 6.

Case 161. Sarah Evans [see case 119], Ann Gallagher [see case 163], Ann Draine [see case 91], and Milley Wheeler, confined June 19, 1795. Charged with being vagrants and old offenders, to be kept at labour 30 days. [All four] discharged July 20.

Case 162. Sarah Evans [see case 119], Mary Cope, Hannah Bond, Mary Carlisle, and Ann Draine [see case 91], confined Aug. 4, 1795. Charged with being idle, lewd & disorderly women, to be kept at labour 30 days. Discharged Sept. 4.

Case 163. Ann Gallagher [see case 161] & Rebecca Williams, confined Oct. 6, 1795. Charged with being two very disorderly girls who were apprehended strolling about the Streets at a very late hour last night—to be kept at hard Labour for the space of 30 days. Discharged Nov. 6. [When Williams entered the almshouse on September 13, 1800 (see Chapter 2), the clerk described her as being twenty-four years old, black, missing four toes on her right foot, and having spent the previous six months in jail. The Prisoners for Trial Docket listed Williams in 1798 and in 1800 on suspicion of burglary, and she was sentenced for larceny in 1795, 1797, and 1799.]

Case 164. Patience, confined Nov. 26, 1795. Disorderly negroe Woman who refuses to perform any kind of Labour for her subsistance. Discharged Dec. 31.

Case 165. Margaret Malowney & Elizabeth Jones, confined Feb. 25, 1796. Charged with having come to this City some Weeks since from Albany [New York] with intention of begging, and who are vagrants—to be kept untill the Middle of May next at which season of the year they can doubtless get employment in the Country[42]—and to be kept at some useful labour till then, or that they provide such satisfactory security for their good behaviour as may be deemed sufficient. Discharged [date unknown].

Case 166. Joseph Berry, confined Dec. 21, 1796. Charged with going about the Streets begging money from the Inhabitants, etc., to be kept at such labour as he is able to perform—15 days. Discharged Jan. 5, 1797.

Case 167. William Matthews, confined Dec. 28, 1796. Charged with

42. Employment generally was plentiful in the countryside during the spring planting season.

being found by the Patrole[43] stealing wood and also with being accustomed to Pilfer in the neighbourhood—to be kept at hard Labour at least 30 days. Discharged [date unknown].

Case 168. Nancy a negroe, confined Dec. 30, 1796. Charged with having no place of abode & having for some time past slept in the Stable's of Thomas Ryerson, etc.—to be kept at Labour 30 days. M. Baker has no objections to her being discharged in [illegible] time, provided a place in the Country can be got for her. Discharged Jan. 30, 1797.

Case 169. Marselin a Negroe, confined Dec. 31, 1796. Charged on the Oath of his Master Monsieur Arnauld, with refusing to do his duty as a Servant & also behaves impudent & saucey; to be kept for one month unless he will return to his duty before the time expires. Discharged Jan. 28, 1797.

Case 170. William Dempsey, confined Jan. 14, 1797. Charged with beating & Abusing his wife & threatening her in such a manner that she conceives herself in danger, & being a drunken disorderly person—to be kept at hard labour for Thirty days. Discharged [date unknown].

Case 171. Sally, negress, confined Feb. 19, 1797. Charged with being a woman of a very turbulent ungovernable Temper & disposition & refuses to obey her Master Charles William Whitlock—to be kept at hard labour 30 days unless sooner discharged by her said master. Discharged Feb. 25.

Case 172. Frank, Negro, Apr. 9, 1797. Charged by his master David McCormick with positively refusing to return to his Masters house or to serve him. Delivered to Mrs. Weed by his Master May 15.

Case 173. Bob, Negro, July 9, 1797. Charged with being taken up as a Vagrant, and from circumstances he is strongly suspected of being a Runaway Slave, the property of some person unknown—to be further examined or otherwise legally discharged. Discharged Aug. 9.

Case 174. Tobias, negro boy, confined Aug. 4, 1797. Charged with having at divers times eloped from the service of his Master Andrew Brown & refuses to promise better behaviour. Discharged Sept. 7.

Case 175. LaViolette [see case 82], confined Oct. 30, 1797. Charged with absconding from her master Mr. Vanden Busche. Discharged Nov. 22.

---

43. The city's night watchmen.

CHAPTER 4

Fugitives

Newspaper Advertisements for
Runaway Slaves, Indentured Servants,
and Apprentices

RICHARD WOJTOWICZ AND
BILLY G. SMITH

Eighteenth-century America contained numerous transients. Many Native Americans were retreating westward to evade the European invasion, some immigrants were fleeing persecution and deprivation in the Old World, and countless impoverished Americans roamed from place to place in search of a livelihood. At the same time, people of various racial and ethnic origins who were slaves, indentured servants, and apprentices often tried desperately to escape bondage in the New World. When they made a break for freedom, they sometimes encountered citizens who were willing to apprehend them for the rewards their masters offered. Benjamin Franklin, for example, recounted how he was questioned while absconding from his apprenticeship, noting that he "was suspected to be some runaway servant, and in danger of being taken up on that suspicion." Adult white males routinely challenged blacks, mulattoes, Indians, and young whites, who, if unable to produce papers certifying that they were freed, were liable to be jailed until authorities were satisfied about their status. (See the Vagrancy Docket in Chapter 3 for suspected runaways who were detained.) Just as the perceived threat of crime and physical violence contributes to the tensions and alienation in modern American cities, the extreme suspicion and scrutiny of strangers in eighteenth-century America may have created peculiar problems for that society as well.[1]

Many early Americans served in some sort of bondage for part or all of their lives, as apprentices, indentured servants, or slaves. Youngsters acquired vocational skills principally through apprenticeships, whereby most young men and some young women learned "the art and mystery" of a specific craft from a master artisan. By contract, youngsters generally lived and worked for approximately seven years (until their twenty-first birthday for males or their eighteenth birthday for females) with their master (or mistress), who also usually served as their surrogate father (or mother). Indentured servants were mostly European migrants who signed a contract called an indenture. According to this agreement, an immigrant labored as a servant for a designated master for a number of years—normally three or four—in return for the cost of the Atlantic voyage, daily maintenance, and perhaps "freedom dues," consisting of cash, new clothing, or occasionally land at the conclusion of their service. At least half of European migrants ventured to America during the eighteenth century as indentured servants. Although still popular, both apprenticeship and indentured servitude began a slow decline in late eighteenth-century Philadelphia as the city's work force shifted from bound laborers to wage workers.[2]

1. On the wandering poor in early America, see Douglas Lamar Jones, "The Strolling Poor: Transiency in Eighteenth-Century Massachusetts," *Journal of Social History* 8 (1975): 28–54; and Gary B. Nash, "Urban Wealth and Poverty in Pre-Revolutionary America," *Journal of Interdisciplinary History* 6 (1976): 545–84. Descriptions of the predicaments of impoverished Philadelphians are available in the Almshouse Daily Occurrence Docket in Chapter 2. The quote from Franklin is in Jesse Lemisch, ed., *Benjamin Franklin: The Autobiography and Other Writings* (New York: New American Library, 1961), 37. See the advertisements in this chapter by officials who had apprehended individuals suspected of being fugitives; similar cases appear in the Vagrancy Docket in Chapter 3.

2. Indentured servitude and other forms of bound labor are discussed by Philip D. Morgan, "Bound Labor: The British and Dutch Colonies," in *Encyclopedia of the North American Colonies*, 2:17–31. On the decline of indentured servitude in Philadelphia, see Sharon Salinger, "Colonial Labor in Transition: The Decline of Indentured Servitude in Late Eighteenth-Century Philadelphia," *Labor History* 22 (1981): 165–91. The apprentice

Slaves were Africans or African Americans perpetually owned by another person; they inherited their unfree condition from the status of their mother. Like apprenticeship and indentured servitude, racially based bondage subsided in the Mid-Atlantic region beginning in the post-Revolutionary decades. In 1780 Pennsylvania became the first state to guarantee by legislative act that slavery would end. Inspired in part by their own struggle for independence from Great Britain, the state assembly abolished slavery out of a desire "to extend a portion of that freedom to others, which hath been extended to us, and a release from that state of thraldom, to which we ourselves were tyrannically doomed." But the legislators brought the institution to a gradual rather than abrupt end: children born to slaves after March 1, 1780, would gain their freedom only after serving their mother's master as an indentured servant until their twenty-eighth birthday, if they were male, or their twenty-first birthday, if they were female. The status of all slaves born before that date remained unaltered, and their struggle for freedom—including absconding—continued. Still, the gradual emancipation of slaves encouraged the growth of a sizable free black community in Philadelphia, and thus provided a haven where runaways might find refuge among other African Americans.[3]

The colonies and new American states established elaborate regulations to discourage people held in bondage from taking flight. In Pennsylvania, indentured servants who absconded could legally have their terms of servitude extended by five days for every day of their absence, to compensate their masters for the lost time and expense of recovering their human property. The regulations for slaves were even harsher. Statutes required slaves to carry a pass from their owner when away from home. If detected without a written permit more than ten miles from their master, slaves, according to the law, "shall be whipped by order of any justice of the peace on the bare back at the owner's charge not exceeding ten lashes." Authorities and masters voiced particular concern about people who harbored fugitives and advocated stiff penalties to discourage such activities. Free

---

system is treated by W. J. Rorabaugh, *The Craft Apprentice from Franklin to the Machine Age in America* (New York: Oxford University Press, 1986).

3. The 1780 law is in James T. Mitchell and Henry Flanders, comps., *The Statutes at Large of Pennsylvania from 1682 to 1801*, 18 vols. (Harrisburg, 1896–1911); quote from 10:67. On the growth of the black community, see Nash, *Forging Freedom*. Slavery in the colonies is discussed by Robert McColley, "Slavery: The British Colonies," in *Encyclopedia of the North American Colonies*, 2:67–86.

blacks who aided a runaway suffered a fine of five shillings for the first hour and one shilling for each succeeding hour; those unable to pay the fine were themselves liable to be sold into servitude. The law assessed whites thirty shillings for each day they abetted a black runaway, to discourage them too from hiring or enslaving escapees for their own use.[4]

Despite these legal threats, thousands of people fled their apprenticeship, servitude, or enslavement. Masters frequently responded by placing advertisements in newspapers offering rewards for their capture and return. These published notices, eighty-seven of which are reprinted below, provide a valuable cache of information about the physical and personal characteristics of escapees. Designed to identify as precisely as possible the men, women, and children who had absconded, the advertisements disclose a great deal about the lives of a group of people who left few personal records. Some notices offer extensive vignettes of individual runaways, sketching their fortunes, revealing their perceived idiosyncrasies, and suggesting the complexity of their relationships with other laboring people as well as with their owners. The advertisements also delineate many particulars about people who fled that make it possible for scholars to analyze many of those traits systematically. For example, the physical aspects of runaways—including age, sex, height, color, scars, and body marks—as well as the type of apparel they wore are sometimes included in exquisite detail. The depiction of "Bet" in Figure 8 illustrates the type of detail that researchers can reconstruct from the information contained in many of the advertisements. Various features of the daily lives of bound people—from the kind of work they performed to the type of chains that shackled some—occasionally accompany reports of their birthplaces, musical and linguistic talents, speech difficulties, number of previous owners, and frequency of escape attempts. The runaway's name, principal language, hobbies, religion, literacy, and connections to friends and family offer additional clues about the culture and values of many escapees.[5]

Constables, jailers, and private citizens also published newspaper an-

4. The law on runaway indentured servants is discussed in Abbot Emerson Smith, *Colonists in Bondage: White Servitude and Convict Labor in America, 1607–1776* (New York: Norton, 1947), 257. The law on runaway slaves is in *Statutes at Large of Pennsylvania*, 4:63. On runaway slaves, see also Edward Raymond Turner, *The Negro in Pennsylvania: Slavery—Servitude—Freedom, 1639–1861* (Washington, D.C.: American Historical Association, 1911), 109–13; and Edgar J. McManus, *Black Bondage in the North* (Syracuse, N.Y.: Syracuse University Press, 1973), 108–24.

5. Three hundred advertisements for runaway slaves published in the *Pennsylvania Gazette* are reproduced in Billy G. Smith and Richard Wojtowicz, eds., *Blacks Who Stole Themselves: Advertisements for Runaways in the Pennsylvania Gazette, 1728–1790* (Philadelphia: University of Pennsylvania Press, 1989).

Fig. 8. "Bet," an escaped slave. In an advertisement for his runaway slave, Bet's Maryland master described her as wearing "black leather high-heeled shoes, silver buckles, and blue worsted stockings, with clocks." He believed that she had fled to Philadelphia. *Pennsylvania Gazette* (Philadelphia), October 9, 1776. Drawing by Adrienne Mayor.

nouncements, some of which are reprinted below. These contain abbreviated descriptions of suspected fugitives who had been apprehended and identify their owners, if prisoners had specified any. Legally, constables did not need a warrant to incarcerate any black person suspected of being a runaway. If no one claimed the captives after advertisements appeared in the newspapers, sheriffs sometimes sold them (even those who were not slaves) as servants for weeks or months, to pay the cost of their detention. Under such conditions, even free blacks, once arrested, encountered considerable difficulty regaining their freedom.[6]

The advertisement for Peter (case 54 below) is an example of a notice that includes a great deal of information about the nature of racial bondage and the lives of slaves. Peter's escape attempt is initially reported, with a reward of ten dollars offered. He absconded while supposedly visiting friends at Christmas in 1795, a time of year when slaves traditionally were given a holiday. The notice also provides a physical description of Peter and his occupational skills. He was approximately forty years old, "about 5 feet 6 or 7 inches" tall (average height for an adult male slave at the time), "square and well built, [and] a little bow-legged." When he fled, he wore a new coat, trousers, and shoes and an old jacket, and he took money (most likely to aid in his escape) and a fiddle (indicating that he probably liked playing music). Peter had worked on a farm and as a sailor in a host of places, including New Jersey, Philadelphia, and several other Pennsylvania counties. References to Peter's personality, behavior, and values help round out the details of his identity. Peter is described as a "smooth tongued artful fellow, a noted liar, a great villain, and fond of liquor." But we should not accept this assessment by a frustrated master uncritically. It suggests that Peter was intelligent and often used his verbal abilities to outwit and confound his owner. It is significant that Peter resisted slavery for a great part of his life—he fled again and again, for two decades, "almost ever since he was 20 years of age." Apparently he was apprehended each time, but during his travels he not only lived with "an Indian wife," but also fathered "children by four black women, to all of whom he says he is lawfully married." Peter's marital behavior parallels that of many of his African ancestors who practiced polygamy. Finally, Elisha Price promised to free Peter after four more years of service. Such pledges came to be common in the Philadelphia region during this time, as support for racial bondage in the North weakened and as slaves pressured their owners in various ways—including absconding—to gain their liberty.[7]

The advertisements for runaways, like all historical records, exhibit a certain set of biases and limitations that we must consider when using

6. *Statutes at Large of Pennsylvania*, 4:63. On the dangers posed to the liberty of free blacks, see Billy G. Smith and Richard Wojtowicz, "The Precarious Freedom of Blacks: Excerpts from the *Pennsylvania Gazette*, 1728–1776," *Pennsylvania Magazine of History and Biography* 113 (1989): 237–64.

7. How slaves bargained for their freedom is discussed in Gary B. Nash and Jean R. Soderlund, *Freedom by Degrees: Emancipation in Eighteenth-Century Pennsylvania* (New York: Oxford University Press, 1991).

them to interpret the past. Most important, they reflect the perspective of the masters rather than the fugitives. Although we can generally rely on reported objective traits of escapees such as their sex, height, and occupation, we must be more wary about how the personalities of fugitives, or their motivations for escape, are described. The latter characteristics may reflect how the owners perceive the runaway, rather than reality. Masters tended to envision their bondspeople in certain ways— for example, docility might justify their bondage, and deviousness would explain their escape. And some bound people undoubtedly found it personally advantageous to play on the misconceptions of masters, to behave outwardly in ways that reinforced those images. Still, in the Mid-Atlantic region most masters worked alongside their apprentices, servants, and slaves in shops or on small farms, so they probably knew their bondspeople well.

Even though these records demand judicious interpretation, scholars have employed this evidence profitably. Many historians have relied on notices for runaway blacks to help interpret slave culture and to draw composite portraits of fugitives. Most of these studies, however, have focused on the southern colonies and states, and few scholars have examined these sources of information for apprentices and indentured servants.[8]

All the advertisements for runaway slaves, servants, and apprentices that appeared in the *Pennsylvania Gazette* in 1795 and 1796 are reproduced below. The eighty-seven ads make it possible for readers both to analyze a significant number of runaways and to decipher the conditions of a few escapees where the notices offer particularly rich detail. Originally owned by Benjamin Franklin, the *Gazette* was Philadelphia's foremost newspaper throughout the eighteenth century and enjoyed wide

8. Among the studies of eighteenth-century slavery and fugitives that have used advertisements for runaways are Gerald W. Mullin, *Flight and Rebellion: Slave Resistance in Eighteenth-Century Virginia* (New York: Oxford University Press, 1972); McManus, *Black Bondage in the North*; Daniel E. Meaders, "South Carolina Fugitives as Viewed Through Local Colonial Newspapers with Emphasis on Runaway Notices, 1732–1801," *Journal of Negro History* 60 (1975): 288–319; Lorenzo J. Greene, "The New England Negro as Seen in Advertisements for Runaway Slaves," *Journal of Negro History* 29 (1944): 125–46; Philip D. Morgan, "Colonial South Carolina Runaways: Their Significance for Slave Culture," *Slavery and Abolition* 6 (1985): 57–78; and Lathan Algerna Windley, "A Profile of Runaway Slaves in Virginia and South Carolina from 1730 through 1787" (Ph.D. diss., University of Iowa, 1974). Windley also compiled advertisements from southern newspapers in *Runaway Slave Advertisements: A Documentary History from the 1730s to 1790*, 4 vols. (Westport, Conn.: Greenwood Press, 1983). Studies that have used advertisements for runaway servants and apprentices include Salinger, "Colonial Labor in Transition"; and Rorabaugh, *The Craft Apprentice*.

circulation in the Mid-Atlantic region.[9] Some ads appeared several times; we included the repeated ones only in the few cases when they provided significant additional information. The date of the newspaper's publication appears after the case number at the top of the advertisement and the date of submission appears at the end.

These notices include runaways from throughout the Mid-Atlantic region (see Map 2), the region in which the *Gazette* circulated, but they by no means represent *all* the escape attempts by bound people living in the Philadelphia region during 1795 and 1796. Many fugitives went unadvertised. Owners sometimes expected, quite correctly, that their bondspeople would voluntarily return after taking a "holiday" for a few days and that advertising would merely be a waste of money. And the low value of some runaways, especially older slaves, did not justify the expense of advertising and a reward. Masters also often hesitated to advertise for troublesome apprentices. Occasionally they offered token rewards for apprentices, not in hopes of recovering them, but as a means of notifying other masters and thereby preventing their apprentices from obtaining employment. In addition, notices placed exclusively in any of the city's dozen newspapers other than the *Gazette* are not included in these selections.[10]

Advertisements for Runaways
in the *Pennsylvania Gazette*

1. January 7, 1795

Eight Dollars Reward.

RAN AWAY from the subscriber, living in Pixton township, Dauphin county, about 6 miles from Harrisburg, on Friday, the 19th instant,[11] a

---

9. The title of the newspaper, originally *The Universal instructor in all arts and sciences; and Pennsylvania Gazette*, was changed to the *Pennsylvania Gazette* when Franklin assumed ownership in 1729. The newspaper's name changed several more times during the next nine decades of its existence but always maintained *Pennsylvania Gazette* as part of its title. All issues of the weekly newspaper are extant for 1795 and 1796 except for a few weeks after December 14, 1796.

10. The names and dates of publication of Philadelphia's newspapers are contained in Edward Connery Lathem, comp., *Chronological Tables of American Newspapers, 1690–1820* (Barre, Mass.: American Antiquarian Society, 1972).

11. Instant: of the current calendar month.

Negro BOY, named SAM, 17 years of age, 5 feet 9 or 10 inches high, well made, has very large feet, large featured, and thick lips, much pitted with the small-pox;[12] had on when he went away, a brown coloured hunting-shirt, under jacket with strings to it, and trowsers of the same, a pair of coarse tow[13] trowsers, and a linen shirt. It is probable he will change his name and clothes. Whoever takes up said Negro, and secures him in any gaol,[14] so that his master may get him again, shall have the above reward, and reasonable charges.   BENJAMIN DUNCAN.
December 26, 1794.

2. January 7, 1795

Eight Dollars Reward.

RAN AWAY, on the night of the 28th of November last, from the house of JAMES MARTIN, in the Falls township, Bucks county, state of Pennsylvania, an Apprentice BOY, named WILLIAM STARKEY, between 17 and 18 years of age, about 5 feet 7 or 8 inches high, a little stoop shouldered; and brown complexion; took with him, one dark brown fulled linsey[15] coat, one light coloured broadcloth ditto[16] and one green ditto, three under vests, one of which was spotted velvet, one brown linsey, and one green ditto and a pair of old leather breeches, with a patch on the right knee, a pair of footed woolen stockings, with old shoes and large plated buckles, and a white hat. Any person taking up and securing said Apprentice in gaol, or otherwise, so that his master may get him again, shall receive the above Reward, and all reasonable charges paid, by applying to the subscriber, in the township aforesaid.
December 15, 1794.   JOHN HULME.

3. January 7, 1795

Six Dollars Reward.

RAN AWAY from the subscriber, Paper-Maker, in Lower-Merion township, Montgomery county, a German Servant MAN, named CONRAD HEIDI, about 22 years of age, about 5 feet 5 or 6 inches high, has redish hair, tied behind, a freckled face, down look, and slim; had on when he went away, a blue cloth surtout[17] coat, a blue cloth sailor's jacket, a grey

---

12. Smallpox often left its victims "pitted" with marks.

13. Coarse broken flax or hemp fiber prepared for spinning.

14. Jail.

15. Linsey or Linsey-wolsey: coarse woolen material first made at Linsey in Suffolk, England, and very popular in early America.

16. Ditto: the same as the aforesaid, meaning "coat" in this instance.

17. An outer covering or garment.

cloth under jacket, a pair of black velvet, and a pair of corduroy breeches, and shoes tied with strings. Whoever takes up the said Servant, and secures him in any gaol, so that his master may have him again, shall receive the above Reward, and reasonable charges, paid by FREDERICK BICKING.

N.B.[18] All masters of vessels, and others, are forbid to harbour or carry him off, at their peril.

4. January 7, 1795
Four Dollars Reward.

RAN-AWAY from the subscriber, living in Stow creek township, Cumberland county, state of New-Jersey, on the 26th of November last, an Apprentice LAD, named DAVID STOGDIN, about 18 years of age, is streight built, well grown, has thick brown hair, which he sometimes wears tied behind; had on and took with him, a lead coloured thick cloth homespun coattee, almost new, very large in the sleeves, an out-side jacket of the same colour, much worn, a deep blue waistcoat, with two rows of metal buttons, one old lead coloured ditto, a new tow and linen shirt, one other ditto a little worn, a pair of redish coloured striped linsey trowsers, one pair of tow and linen ditto, one pair of woolen stockings, of a mixed blue and white colour, broken in the feet, neats leather[19] shoes, with yellow metal buckles, a round small brim wool hat, almost new, a silk handkerchief, red, checked large with narrow stripes. Whoever takes up and secures said Apprentice, so that I get him again, shall have the above reward, and reasonable charges if brought home, paid by DAVID AYARS.

December 6, 1794.

5. January 14, 1795
Eight Dollars Reward.

RAN-AWAY on Sunday, the 4th instant, an Apprentice BOY, named JOSEPH WHITE, by trade a Blacksmith, between 17 and 18 years of age, about 5 feet 7 or 8 inches high, of a dark complexion, with black streight hair; had on and took with him, a dark olive coloured cloth coat and vest, two pair of trowsers, the one fustian,[20] the other milled linsey, a new, high crowned, wool hat, two pair of pale blue coloured

18. N.B.: The abbreviation for the Latin *nota bene*, meaning to mark well and pay particular attention to what follows.

19. Neat's leather: made from the hide of a bovine animal.

20. A type of cloth originally manufactured at Fusht on the Nile; it contained a warp of linen thread and a woof of thick cotton.

stockings, two homespun linen shirts, almost new, and a pair of strong leather shoes with old buckles in them. Whoever takes up and brings home said Apprentice, or lodges him in gaol in the States, shall be entitled to the above reward, and reasonable charges, paid by me, WALTER LILLY, junr.

East-Caln, Chester county, January 5, 1795.

6. January 14, 1795

Four Dollars Reward.

RAN AWAY from the subscriber, on Thursday the 25th of December, living in Lower-Salford township, Montgomery county, a Negro MAN, named JOE, about 5 feet 5 inches high, was 23 years of age last May, walks lame, has a piece of his little finger cut off; had on and took with him, a new mixture linsey coat, and under jacket of the same, a striped jacket of linen, blue and white stripes, two pair of trowsers, a pair of yellow linsey, and a pair of striped cassimer, two pair of stockings, one pair of pale blue yarn, ribbed, the other black woolen yarn, a new pair of shoes, a new high crowned hat, bound with black tape. Whoever takes up said Negro, and secures him in any gaol, so that his master may get him again, shall have the above reward, and reasonable charges if brought home, paid by   JACOB REIFF, Senior.

January 8, 1795.

7. January 21, 1795

Twenty Dollars Reward.

RAN away from the subscriber, living near Nottingham, on Patuxent river, Prince George's county, Maryland, a likely, active Mulatto slave, called HARRY, who since his departure has assumed the name of FLEET. He is about 22 or 23 years of age, and 5 feet 10 inches high; has grey eyes and sandy coloured hair, which he wears turned up before, and very short and straight behind. He appears confused when spoken to, but when closely examined, much embarrassed. His cloathing cannot be particularly described, as he has been gone ever since July. By a letter from him to his father, dated the 17th of Sept. last, it appears that he was then in Philadelphia, and he says he expected to sail for London in about two months. All masters of vessels are hereby cautioned against carrying off the said slave at their peril. Whoever takes him up, and secures him in gaol, so that I get him again shall receive the above reward, and all reasonable charges for bringing him home.

MATHEW EVERSFIELD.

8. January 28, 1795

WAS committed to the gaol of Chester county, on the 13th of this instant, a negro man, who calls himself JOE JENKINS, and acknowledges to be a slave to Mr. JAMES CLEGETT, of George-Town, state of Maryland, his master is hereby desired to come, pay the charges, and take him away, in 4 weeks from the date hereof, other-wise he will be discharged on paying his fees.

Jan. 20, 1795.   THOMAS TAYLOR, Gaoler.

9. February 25, 1795

Half a Dollar Reward.

Ran away from the subscriber, living in Bridgeton, West-Jersey, an Apprentice LAD, named EZRA WESTCOT, about 14 years of age, has worked some time at the taylor's trade, is small of his age, and has a mole on his right cheek, near his mouth; had on, when he went away, a brown cloth coat and trowsers, a spotted swanskin[21] vest, wool hat, muslin[22] shirt, and some other cloaths. Whoever takes up said apprentice, and secures him, so that his master may get him again, shall have the above reward, but no charges paid by   ZACHARIAH LAWRENCE.

February 16, 1795.

N.B. All persons are forewarned against harbouring said Boy.

10. February 25, 1795

Half a Cent Reward.

RAN-AWAY from the subscriber, on the 16th instant, a certain indented Apprentice, named JOHN CLERK; he is about 16 years of age; had on when he went away, a bottle green coloured cloth coat, a velvet waistcoat, a pair of cloth overalls, and a roram hat,[23] all nearly new; he is very much given to drinking, has, lately, been often observed groggy in the store, and consequently so rude as to throw his shoes through the windows; he was corrected for taking money out of the drawer and getting drunk on Sundays, at an infamous cake and beer-house, after which he absconded. Any person who will bring him back to his master, shall have the above reward but no charges; for although he has activity to be useful, his habits are such as to render him unsafe to be trusted where goods are easily embezzled.

Princeton, New-Jersey, Feb. 17, 1795.   JOHN M'CLELLEN.

21. Swanskin: a fleecy cloth like Canton flannel used especially for linings.
22. Generally a delicately woven cotton fabric.
23. A hat made of a woolen cloth with a fur face.

11. March 4, 1795

Six pence Reward.

Ran away on the 9th instant from the subscriber, living in East-Bradford township, Chester county, a Servant GIRL, named RACHAEL REECE, had two years and seven months to serve; she is very talkative, bold, and fond of the men; had on and took with her, a chip hat with a broad striped green, blue and yellow ribbon, three shifts, four short gowns, of different kinds, a yard and a half of striped linen, to make up into a short gown, 4 stockings, two of which were blue, and the other white, and a pair of good leather shoes. Whoever brings her home to her master shall receive the above reward.

February 27.   JOSEPH GEST.

12. March 11, 1795

WE the subscribers became bound, by an obligation, about the latter end of the year 1791, in a certain penalty, to deliver up a certain Mulatto, or Black MAN, named WILLIAM LEWIS, if he should be proved a slave; and as the Black Man hath, for the most part, resided since the security was given, in Chester county, Pennsylvania, and no one having appeared to claim him: Therefore these are to give public Notice, that if he hath a master, or owner, he is desired to come within 30 days after the date hereof, and prove property, according to law, otherwise we shall hold our-selves free from the said obligation.

WILLIAM TINSLEY, JOSEPH PENNOCK.

West-Marlborough, Chester county, Feb. 20, 1795.

13. March 11, 1795

Five Pounds Reward.

Ran away on Sunday, the 1st instant, from the subscriber, an apprentice boy named JONATHAN PAUL, by trade a blacksmith, between 19 and 20 years of age, about 5 feet 7 or 8 inches high, stoop shouldered, brownish hair, and commonly wears it tied behind, grey eyes, pug nose, surly look, subject to very sore shins, has been lately cured, which may be easily seen, very heavy walk, took with him one dark blue cloth coatee, one short light coating jacket, with sleeves, two under vests, one of which was olive corduroy, the other Washington's rib, olive coloured, with metal buttons on each, three pair trowsers, one pair coating almost new, one ditto olive fustian, one ditto striped cotton, two pair grey woolen ribbed stockings, two pair shoes, one pair almost new, three shirts two coarse, and one fine, one calf-skin apron, almost new. —Whoever takes up and brings home said apprentice, or lodges him in gaol in the states, shall be entitled to the above reward and reasonable charges by

Germantown, Feb. 9.   CHRISTOPHER HERGESHEIMER.

14. March 18, 1795

Twenty Dollars Reward.

RAN-AWAY on Sunday, the 15th instant, from the subscriber, living in Lower Merrion township, Montgomery county, a Negro LAD, about 16 years of age, and goes by the name of CALEB BROWN, about 5 feet 5 or 6 inches high, has a round face, and somewhat of a down look, a mark near one of his temples, speaks coarse, and leans forward in his walk; had on when he went away, a blue sailor jacket lined with white flannel, a linsey under jacket, striped brown linsey trowsers, Russia sheeting shirt, two pair of stockings, one pair blue, the other brown, calfskin shoes, and an old wool hat. Whoever secures said Negro in any gaol, so that his master gets him again, shall have the above reward, and reason-able charges, paid by Frederick Bicking.

March 15, 1795.

N.B. All masters of vessels, and others, are forbid to harbour or carry him off at their peril.

15. April 1, 1795

Twelve Dollars Reward.

RAN-AWAY from the subscriber, living in Moreland township, Philadel-phia county, on Sunday, the 22nd instant, an apprentice LAD, named *George Bamford*, between 18 and 19 years of age, was bred a farmer; light brown hair, pale countenance, slim made, wears his [hair] tied, grey eyes, slim legs, knock-kneed, and drinks to excess; had on and took with him, a roram hat, striped green cloth coattee, striped velvet vest, thick-set breeches, ribbed stockings, all new, two pair of shoes, a fulled linsey lead coloured coattee, linsey vest and trowsers, striped red and blue, one shirt ruffled at the bosom, one flax and tow ditto, both new, two ditto of flax, much worn, muslin neckcloth, a new wallet, marked J.S. with whiter thread. Any person apprehending said Apprentice, and securing him in any gaol, so that his master may get him again, shall receive the above reward, and reasonable charges.

All masters of vessels, and others, are forewarned, not to harbour or carry off said Apprentice.

March 25, 1795.   JACOB SHEARER.

16. April 22, 1795

Four Dollars Reward.

RAN away on the 24th of March last, an apprentice boy, named Daniel Creely, about 16 or 17 years of age, 5 feet 5 inches high, slim made, strait brownish hair, sometimes wears it tied; had on, and took with him, an old shirt, greyish cloth under jacket, a lightish lincey coattee, old buckskin breeches, a pair of striped corduroy ditto, pale blue yarn stockings, and half worn shoes, with plated buckles, also two felt hats, one nearly new. Whoever takes up and secures said apprentice, so as his master may get him again, shall have the above reward, paid by the subscriber, in Newtown, Bucks county, state of Pennsylvania.

STEPHEN TWINING.

N.B. The said apprentice took with him a likely young dog, of a greyish colour, belonging to his master.

April 4, 1795.

17. April 22, 1795

Thirty Dollars Reward.

RAN-AWAY, on the 12th instant, from the subscriber, living in Upper Dublin township, Montgomery county, an Apprentice LAD, named MATTHEW BARNHILL, between 18 and 19 years of age, better than 5 feet high, remarkably thick set, fair hair, tied, very coarse featured, with large nose and eye-brows, has a scar on the right cheek down to the chin, his left great toe apt to be sore with the nail, his beard appears as if he might be more than thirty years of age, has very hairy legs: Had on, when he went away, a high crown castor hat,[24] broadcloth mixt coloured coattee, very much worn, with plated sugar-loaf buttons, spotted velveret[25] vest, new cut and ribbed velvet breeches, with sugarloaf buttons, and silver knee-buckles, grey yarn stockings which have been soaled, half worn neats leather shoes, with double chaped plated buckles, and a fine homespun linen shirt; he had two neckcloths, one white, the other black, is a shoemaker by trade, has two years and seven months to serve; he may loiter about and try to get work, as he had not much money. It is supposed he will make toward Pittsburgh, as his mother lives there with her son-in-law—Finnemore. Whoever takes up said Apprentice, and secures him in any gaol so that his master may get

---

24. A hat originally either made of beaver's fur or intended to imitate such, but by the late eighteenth century it was often made of rabbit's fur.

25. Velveret: a variety of fustian with a velvet surface.

him again, shall have the above reward, and reasonable charges if brought home to his master, paid by HENRY TIMANUS.

N.B. All masters of vessels and others, are forbid to harbour, conceal, or carry off said Apprentice at their peril.

April 16, 1795.

18. April 29, 1795
Eight Dollars Reward.

RAN away, in the evening of the 30th of March, from the subscriber, an apprentice boy, named Joseph Couch, about eighteen years of age, 5 feet 3 or 4 inches high, slender built, dark eyes, brown hair, sometimes wears it tied; had on, and took with him, two upper short jackets, made of home spun thick cloth, lead coloured, one of them new, double breasted, with large white metal buttons on, and three large buttons to each sleeve, the other single breasted, pretty much worn, two home spun waist-coats, of the same cloth, single breasted, one of them nearly new, one new roram hat, another wool hat, half worn, and sundry other cloaths, which cannot be described. Whoever secures the said boy in any gaol, so his master may get him again, shall have the above reward, and reasonable charges paid if brought home by   JOSHUA THOMPSON.

Salem, New-Jersey, April 10th, 1795.

N.B. All masters of vessels and others are forbid to harbour, employ or take said apprentice away, at their peril.

19. April 29, 1795
Four Dollars Reward.

RAN away from the subscriber, in Oxford township, Chester county, in the night of the 24th of March last, an apprentice lad, named John Ferguson, about 19 years of age; had on, and took with him, a cloth coat, fulled lincey jacket and overalls, and a pair of nankeen[26] overalls, good shoes and stockings, and a good hat. Whoever takes up and secures said apprentice, so as his master may get him again, shall have the above reward and reasonable charges, paid by

April 3.   ALEXANDER RUSSEL.

20. May 6, 1795
WAS committed to the gaol of Chester county, some time ago, a Negro Man, who calls himself Sam. Roach, acknowledges to be a slave to Benja-

---

26. Nankeen: an imported yellow cotton cloth manufactured in Nanjing, China.

min Duncan, of Dauphin county, near Harrisburgh. His Master is hereby desired to come, pay charges and take him away, in four weeks from the date hereof, otherwise he will be discharged, on paying his fees.

    April 30, 1795.   THOMAS TAYLOR, Gaoler.

21. May 20, 1795
Four Dollars Reward.

RAN-AWAY from the subscriber, living in the town of Salem, on Saturday evening last, an Apprentice LAD, named *Nathan Long*, about 18 years of age, has black hair, which he commonly wears tied; had on and took with him, one fur and one felt hat, a jean coat, lapelled, and one light coating coattee, one fine and two coarse shirts, one pair blue cloth and two pair nankeen trowsers, and good shoes and stockings. Whoever will take up said Apprentice, and secure him in any gaol, so that his Master may get him again, shall receive the above reward and reasonable charges, paid by JACOB HUFTY.

    Salem, New-Jersey, May 7, 1795.

22. June 10, 1795
Ten Dollars Reward.

RAN-AWAY from the subscriber, in Chester, on the night of the 2d of June, instant, an Irish servant LAD, named JOHN BOYLE, about 15 or 16 year of age, 5 feet 6 inches high, stout built, rocks and stoops a little in his walk, round fair face and ruddy complexion, dark short curly hair, and when spoken to appears bashful or diffident; had on and took with him, three shirts, one of which was check, the others white, one forest cloth coat turned, of a brown and yellow mixed colour, lapelled, one short brown sailor jacket, lined with white flannels, one pair of old brown trowsers of the same cloth, one ditto old jean, one ditto new striped ticking,[27] one white waistcoat, one old blue surtout coat, a pretty good hat lined with white linen, with some other articles not easy to describe, among which is a piece of coarse napped cloth, the same as his jacket. Whoever will secure the above described Lad, shall receive the above reward. Should the said *John Boyle* incline to return, he shall be received as kindly as ever, and all former faults forgiven. Masters and owners of vessels are requested to attend to the above.

    Chester, June 4.   WM. R. ATLEE.

---

27. Ticking: a case or covering containing feathers, flocks, or the like to form a mattress or pillow; also the strong hard linen or cotton material used for making such cases.

23. June 10, 1795

Four Dollars Reward.

RAN-AWAY from the subscriber, living in the township of Lower Alloway's creek, county of Salem, state of New-Jersey, on Monday morning last, a servant MAN, named ABNER CARTWRIGHT, about 23 years of age, about 5 feet 7 or 8 inches high, long light hair, which he wears tied; had on when he went away, one striped nankeen coat, a spotted cotton jacket, a pair of stockings, half worn boots, a half worn roram hat, and what is very remarkable, he has lost his right ear. Whoever takes up said Runaway, and secures him in any gaol, so that his master may get him again, shall receive the above reward, and reasonable charges if brought home, paid by me,   JOHN BRIGGS.
    June 3, 1795.

24. June 24, 1795

Ten Dollars Reward.

RAN-AWAY from the subscriber, on the 29th of April last, an Apprentice BOY, named JAMES DUNBAR, about 18 years of age, 5 feet 7 or 8 inches high, down look, long dark hair, tied behind; had on and took with him a grey coloured short coat, with metal buttons, light coloured overalls, made of coating, one spotted velvet jacket, one ditto broad stripes, white and black, one ditto printed cotton, of a light colour, a round castor hat, a pair of neats leather shoes with buckles. Whoever takes up said Apprentice, and secures him in any gaol in this state, or the adjacent states, and will give information thereof to *Michael Roberts*, No. 92, Market-street, Philadelphia, or the subscriber, in Trenton, shall receive the above reward, and all reasonable charges.
    May 18, 1795.   JONATHAN DOAN.

25. July 1, 1795

Six-pence Reward.

RAN-AWAY on the 14th instant, from the subscriber, living in Horsham township, Montgomery county, a Servant GIRL, named ELIZABETH LIVINGSTON; had on a linsey petticoat and gown. Whoever takes up the said Servant, shall have the above reward, and no charges.
    June 26, 1795.   PHEBE JONES.

26. July 8, 1795

Ten Dollars Reward.

RAN-AWAY from the subscriber, on the 19th ultimo,[28] an indented Servant LAD, named JOHN CONNELL, lately from Cork, in Ireland, about 19 years of age, 5 feet 5 or 6 inches high, tolerably well set, brown hair, hazle eyes, his forehead and top of his head remarkably high, and of a parabolar form, speaks in the Irish dialect, and can converse in the Irish tongue, served some time to the cork making business before he came to America, in which, it is probable, he may endeavour to get encouragement: had on, when he went off, a shirt of white homespun linen, ticklenburg[29] trowsers, a lead coloured vest, round black hat, and a pair of heavy shoes tied with strings. Whoever secures said Servant in any gaol, so that his master gets him again, shall receive the above Reward. Masters of vessels, and others, are requested to attend to the above, and not to harbour or take him off at their peril.

Philadelphia, July 4, 1795.   JAMES HUNTER,
                                                No. 37, North Second-street.

27. July 8, 1795

Ten Dollars Reward.

RAN-AWAY from the subscriber, living in Pennsborough township, Chester county, on the night of the 28th instant, an Apprentice LAD to the shoemaking business, named JAMES MAXWELL, about 5 feet 6 or 7 inches high, well set, between 19 and 20 years of age, has a coarse dark complexion, long dark brown hair, which he commonly wore tied or quieued; had on and took with him, a new dark striped nankeen coat, stampt cotton waistcoat, red striped trowsers, a pair of striped linen ditto, a pair coloured tow ditto, 3 shirts, one of which was new, one roram and one wool hat, new shoes with plated buckles. Whoever secures the said Apprentice, so that his master may get him again, shall have the above Reward, and if brought home, reasonable charges paid by

June 28, 1795   JAMES PASSMORE.

N.B. The said Maxwell went off in company with a Lad of the name of Isaiah Hollingsworth, about 16 years of age, and it is supposed they will continue together.

28. Ultimo: in or of the month before the present one.
29. Ticklenburg(s): a kind of coarse linen cloth.

28. August 26, 1795

RAN-AWAY from the subscriber, on the night of the 10th instant, an indented Servant LAD, named JOHN JOHNSTON, a native of Ireland, about 17 years of age, about 5 feet 4 or 5 inches high, short red hair, sandy complexion, grey eyes, pitted with the smallpox; had on and took with him, an old felt hat, old jacket without sleeves, toilinet[30] stripe, with the back part of country made linen, striped also, with a remarkable piece up the middle, two shirts, one new tow linen, the trowsers, both coloured dark olive. Whoever secures said Servant in the gaol of this county, shall have SEVEN DOLLARS Reward, and reasonable expences if brought home, paid by JOHN MENOUGH, Junior.

New-London Cross Roads, Chester county, August 17, 1795.

N.B. It is supposed the above servant is gone toward Carlisle, as he has relations in that place; he is ill provided for travelling, it is hoped the different ferries will be careful to examine such, &c.

29. September 2, 1795

Eight Dollars Reward.

RAN-AWAY, on the 24th instant, from the subscriber, living in North-ampton township, Bucks county, a Negro MAN upwards of 40 years of age, goes by the name of BRAM, about 5 feet 5 or 6 inches high, leans forward in his walk, loves spirits, and is fond of a violin, one of which he took with him; had on when he went away, a light coloured cloth short coat, a striped pattern under jacket, a fine shirt, and a tow linen ditto, two pair of trowsers, one pair of black and white striped cotton, the other pair tow linen, a pair of black and white speckled cotton stockings, and a pair of light coloured worsted[31] ditto, coarse leather shoes, and an old fine hat. Whoever secures said Negro in any gaol, so that his master gets him again, shall have the above reward, and reasonable charges, paid by HUGH EDAMS.

N.B. All masters of vessels, and others, are forbid to harbour or carry him away.

August 26, 1795.

30. September 2, 1795

Forty Dollars Reward.

RAN-AWAY from the subscriber, living in Oxford township, Chester county, state of Pennsylvania, the beginning of last October, a Negro

---

30. A kind of fine woolen cloth.

31. Worsted: a woolen fabric or material made from well-twisted yarn spun of long-staple wool combed to lay the fibers parallel; first made at Worstead in England.

MAN, named JOE, about 24 years of age, near 6 feet high, of a tawney colour, much given to drink, playing on the fiddle, dancing and frolicking and his disposition is such, that it is expected he will continue so to do; it is thought unnecessary to describe his cloathing, being so long gone, it is supposed he has exchanged them with some of his associates; he has a large scar on his head, a little above his forehead, also a large scar on one of his feet, at the root of the great toe. Said fellow has a brother, named Abel Gibbens, who has worked in and about Philadelphia for some years, who is a freeman. I intended to set said slave free at a reasonable period, and still mean the same, in case he returns, or is brought to me. The above reward will be given to any person securing said fellow in any gaol, so that I get him again, and reasonable charges if brought home.

    August 24, 1795   ANDREW LOWREY.

    N.B. All masters of vessels, and others, are forbid harbouring or carrying him off, at their peril.

31. September 16, 1795

Six Dollars Reward.

RAN-AWAY, on the 7th instant, from the subscriber, an Irish servant LAD, calls himself ARTHUR O'NEIL, is stout and well built, about 16 years old, and 5 feet 5 or 6 inches high, fair complexion, short black hair lately cut square behind, has a scar on the side of his face near his eye, and has a heavy clumsy walk; had on an old high-crown'd wool hat, blue jacket, black home-made linsey under jacket, dyed tow trowsers, with a hole in the legs, old shoes with strings, and a leather apron tanned with allum. Who-ever takes up said servant, and secures him in any gaol in this state, and gives me information thereof, shall receive the above reward, paid by me, living in Kennet township near Kennet Square, Chester county.

    September 14th, 1795.   WILLIAM MANSELL.

32. September 16, 1795

Eight Dollars Reward.

RAN away from the subscriber, living in Salem county, New-Jersey, about three miles from the town of Salem, on the 13th instant, an indented servant lad, named JOHN TEST, about 14 years of age, slim made and tall, with black hair; had on, and took with him, two hats, part worn, and a thick coat, with sundry other cloaths. Whoever secures said boy in any gaol of this state, or in the gaol of Philadelphia, so that his master may get him again, shall receive the above reward.   JOSIAH MILLER

N.B. All masters of vessels and others are forewarned, at their peril, from taking off or harbouring said boy.

September 14th 1795.

33. September 30, 1795

Forty Dollars Reward.

RAN away from the subscriber last night, two Negroe men. One named PETER, about twenty-eight years of age, five feet four or five inches high. He took with him one dark brown homespun worsted coat, white cashmer waistcoat, jean olive coloured breeches, one fine and two coarse shirts, two light brown cloth coattees, one sagathy olive coloured coattee, one pair of old calfskin shoes, one pair of new shoes hob-nailed, two pair of stockings, one pair of large plated buckles, a new white hat, and one black hat. He is remarkably clear from swearing.

The other named POMPEY, about twenty-four years of age, five feet eight inches high, knock-kneed, and remarkably small legs. He took with him one clouded nankeen coat, fancy pattern'd jean striped waistcoat, nankeen trowsers, a homespun sagathy coatee olive coloured, a home-spun striped cloth coat half worn, one pair of cotton stockings, one pair of yarn ditto, one fine shirt, two coarse ditto, two pair of linen trowsers, two pair of hob-nailed shoes, a new black hat and an old hat, besides a variety of other cloaths not mentioned. Said POMPEY is very fond of strong drink, and when in liquor is very quarrelsome.

Whoever secures said run-aways in any gaol, so that the subscriber may get them again, shall receive the above reward, or twenty dollars for either of them paid by JOSEPH ELLIS.

Gloucester county, New-Jersey, September 23d, 1795.

34. October 7, 1795

RAN-AWAY on the 10th of last May, a young Negro MAN, who had 5 years and six months to serve, is short and thick, and has a down look, named CUFF, though he has changed his name at other times, and it is probable he may do so again; had on, when he went away, a white coattee and red waistcoat, olive coloured trowsers half worn, felt hat, and skipskin shoes. All masters of families are forbid to conceal, harbour or hire him, if they do they shall pay 3 quarters of a dollar per day, as I have to pay that to them I hire, and masters of vessels are forbid to hire or carry him away. Let every one act the honest part, and see a certificate of freedom before they employ a Negro. Whoever takes up said Runaway,

and secures him in the gaol of Philadelphia, shall have EIGHT DOL-
LARS REWARD and reasonable charges paid, by

REBECCA SANDHAM.

35. October 14, 1795

Eight Dollars Reward.

RAN-away from the subscriber, living in Fairfield township, Cumberland county, West New-Jersey, on the 15th of September last, an indented servant lad, between 17 and 18 years of age, had on, when he
went away, one pair of striped homespun trowsers, a shirt and a wool
hat; he is a well set lad, and has lost the fore finger of his left hand, at the
second joint. Whoever takes said lad, and secures him, so that the subscriber may get him again, shall have the above reward.

October 14.   PHILIP WESCOTT.

36. October 14, 1795

Eight Dollars Reward.

RAN AWAY from the subscriber, on or about the 2d day of August, an
apprentice boy, named PETTIT BRITTIN, about 20 years of age, five
feet nine or ten inches high, light complexion, his dress can't be described, as he took all his cloaths with him. Whoever takes him up, and
brings him to me shall receive the above reward, and all reasonable
charges paid, by JOHN GORDON,

No. 23, North Third-street, Philadelphia.

N.B. His parents live near Morristown, East-Jersey, and it is thought he
is gone that way.

37. October 21, 1795

Forty Dollars Reward.

RAN-AWAY from the subscriber, living at the head of Bohemia, Cecil
county, Maryland, on the 9th of August last, a Negroe man, named NED
about forty years of age, 5 feet 8 or 9 inches high, of a yellowish complexion, forward and impertinent; had on a coarse tow linen shirt and
trowsers, a high crown'd felt hat, and old corduroy or thickset waistcoat,
a greyish mix'd cloth coat, and carries a large cane with a brass head
carved, and wears a belt round his waist, on account of the rim of his
belly being broke. The above Negroe worked with Jesse Holt and Samuel
Torrance, in Horsham township, Montgomery county, near Mrs. Ball's
tavern these six weeks past, and calls himself *Jack*; it is likely he will leave

that neighbourhood and change his name again, as he was pursued in that neighbourhood on Thursday last, by one of his young masters, who got all his clothes except the above mentioned.

Whoever takes up the said Negroe, and secures him in Philadelphia gaol, shall have THIRTY DOLLARS, or if brought home, the above reward and reasonable charges, paid by ABIGAIL RYLAND.

October 19.

38. October 21, 1795

Six Dollars Reward.

RAN away from the subscriber, living in Allen-town, East New-Jersey, an apprentice lad, named John W. Jackson, by trade a weaver, about 17 years of age, of fair complexion, light strait hair, and blue eyes; had on, when he went away, a light bearskin coat, homespun linen jacket and trowsers, and a wool hat. Whoever takes up said lad, and brings him to his master, shall have the above reward and reasonable charges, paid by JAMES COLVIN.

June 26, 1795.

N.B. It is supposed he is lurking about Queen-street, as his parents live there. All persons are forbid to harbour him at their peril.

39. October 21, 1795

Twenty-five Dollars Reward.

RAN away from Millstone, on Saturday, the 3d instant, a Negroe lad, named NED [see December 9 advertisement], about 5 feet 7 inches high, well set, tolerable black, smooth skin, a small scar over one of his eyes, if attacked closely is apt to stammer in his answers, about 19 years old; had on, when he went away, a short blue lappell'd coat with metal buttons, a brown short cloth jacket, and tow shirt and trowsers. Also ran away with the above Negroe, from the subscriber, in Trenton, a Negroe man, named DICK, about 28 years old, 5 feet 5 inches high, tolerable black smooth skin, has a bunch of bushy hair behind, and had his fore-top lately cut off; has scars on his back, having been several times flogg'd at the whipping-post; if attacked closely will stammer in his answers; had on, and took with him, an old fur hat, with a remarkable high crown and narrow brim, a blue surtout, and homespun trowsers. Whoever apprehends the above Negroes, and delivers them to ABRAHAM HUNT, at Trenton, or HENRY DISBROW, at Millstone, Somerset county, New-Jersey, shall be entitled to the above reward, and all reasonable charges, or in proportion for either of them.

N.B. From information, it is evident that said Negroes, have crossed the Delaware into Bucks county, Pennsylvania.

October 12th, 1795.

40. October 28, 1795
One Dollar Reward.

RAN away from the subscriber, living in Waterford township, Gloucester county, state of New-Jersey, on Thursday the 8th day of October, an apprentice boy, named Elijah Toy, about nineteen years and ten months old, about five feet nine inches high; had on a suit of fustian clothes and a felt hat. Whoever takes up said run-away, and brings him home, shall receive the above reward.   ISAAC FISH.

41. November 11, 1795
Four Dollars Reward.

RAN away from the subscriber, living in Upper-Penn's-Neck, Salem county, a Lad, about 18 years of age, 5 feet 9 inches high; had on and took with him an old brown coat, of superfine cloth, an old fustian ditto, a good fur hat, a pair of shoes with hob-nails, and sundry other articles of cloathing unknown. Whoever takes up said run-away, and secures him in any gaol, so that his master may get him again, shall have the above reward, and all reasonable charges paid.

November 10, 1795.   HENRY STYNER.

42. December 9, 1795
Thirty Dollars Reward.

RAN-AWAY from the subscriber, at Milstone, Sommerset county, in the State of New-Jersey, on the 3d day of October, a Negro LAD, named NED [see October 21 advertisement], 19 years old, about 5 feet 6 or 7 inches high, smooth skin, tolerably black, with a small scar over one of his eyes, has likewise a small one on his upper lip; if attacked closely will stammer in his answer, and speaks quick; had on when he went away, a short lappelled blue coattee, with large metal buttons, a brown cloth jacket and trowsers; it is thought he will change his apparel; he went away with a Negro man belonging to Abraham Hunt, of Trenton, who since has been taken, and says he parted with the aforesaid Negro near Buckingham, in Bucks county, Pennsylvania. Any person taking up and securing the said Negro in any gaol, so that his master may get him again, shall have, by applying to *Lewis Bender*, innkeeper, at the sign of the Black Horse north Second-street, Philadelphia, the sum of *Twenty*

Dollars, with reasonable charges, or the above reward if brought home to the subscriber at Millstone.

December 4, 1795.   HENRY DISBRON.

43. December 9, 1795
Six Cents Reward.

RAN away, on the 24th of September last, from the subscriber, near Swedesborough, Woolwich township, Gloucester county, an apprentice lad, named William Elliott, about five feet ten inches high, stout built, long black hair, and very talkative, had on, and took with him, a clouded green coat, light coloured surtout, with metal buttons, and high crown hat. Any person securing said run-away, so that his master may get him again, shall have the above reward, but no charges, paid by SAMUEL OGDEN.

44. January 6, 1796
Twenty-four Dollars Reward.

RAN-away, last night, from the subscriber, in Concord township, Delaware county, two apprentices to the paper-making manufactory, one named HUGH GLENN, near 20 years of age, 5 feet 10 inches high, has light hair, fresh coloured, and slender made; had on, when he absconded, a London brown coattee, thickset jacket, spotted flannel under jacket, light cloth trowsers, and a half worn wool hat, and took with him a clouded nankeen coat and plain nankeen pantaloons. The other named THOMAS CARNY, 5 feet 7 inches high, dark complexion, black hair, and has lost one of the joints of his fore finger on the left hand; had on a London brown coattee, thickset jacket, light cloth trowsers, and a half worn wool hat, and took with him a clouded nankeen coat and trowsers. Whoever takes up and secures said apprentices, so that their master may get them again, shall have the above reward, or *Twelve Dollars*, and reasonable charges, for either of them.

Dec. 26, 1795.   MARK WILCOX.

45. January 13, 1796
RAN-AWAY from the subscriber, on the 19th of December last, an apprentice lad, named *Alexander Weldon*, aged 19 years, about 5 feet 8 inches high. Whoever secures said apprentice in any gaol, so that I may get him, shall receive a reward of *six pence halfpenny*, and if brought home reasonable charges will be paid by   JAMES COLEMAN.

Bristol Island, Bucks county,
January 7th, 1796.

46. March 2, 1796

Ten Dollars Reward.

RAN-AWAY from the subscriber, in Oxford township, Chester county, on the 13th day of this month, a Negro man, named ALE, he is a stout well set fellow, 24 years of age, about 5 feet 9 inches high, well acquainted with all kind of country work; Had on when he went away, a short coat and trowsers of grey coating, the trowsers tied with red tape, striped cotton jacket, blue stockings, shoes tied with thongs, an old high crown'd felt hat. The above reward will be paid on my receiving said Negro, and reasonable charges if brought home.

Oxford, Feb. 22, 1796.   WILLIAM PINKERTON.

47. March 16, 1796

Fifty Dollars Reward.

RAN-AWAY from the subscriber, at Three Mile Run, near New-Brunswick, Somerset county, New-Jersey, in July 1794, a MULATTO NEGRO MAN, named PETER, about 5 feet 6 inches high, 30 years old, slim built, narrow face and sharp chin, is very talkative, and has large glaring eyes, he has been owned by the following persons in Somerset county, viz. first by Mr. Beekman, of Griggstown, next by Squire Hoogland, afterwards by Captain Baird, both of the same place; he was afterwards owned by Mr. Brokaw, at Ricefield, from whom the subscriber purchased him. Any person taking up said Negro, securing him in gaol, and giving information to his master, shall have Forty Dollars, and if sent home, shall be intitled to the above reward of Fifty Dollars.

March 7, 1796.   REM GARRITSEN.

N.B. The above Negro was seen in Philadelphia in January last, and is supposed to be lurking thereabouts.

48. March 16, 1796

WAS committed to my custody, on the first day of February, 1796, a certain NEGRO MAN, who has went by different names, viz. MOSES WHITE, alias, DICK HATBAND, but says he is free, and was born of free parents in the county of Sommerset, state of Maryland, but says he left Maryland about four years since, and lived with Thomas Beason, butcher, near Wilmington, Brandywine, state of Delaware: he is about 5 feet 10 or 11 inches high, very black, and about 26 years of age. His master, if he has any, is requested to come and take him away, otherwise he will be sold in three weeks from this date, for his expences, by

Lancaster, March 8, 1796.   JOHN BURY, Jailer.

49. March 16, 1796

Six Cents Reward.

RAN away on the 22d instant, an apprentice boy, named Hubberd Baker, about nineteen years of age, about six feet high, of yellow complexion;—had on when he went away, a linsey coat, westcoat and overalls—a checked woolen shirt; it is not known what other cloaths he took with him. Whoever takes up said apprentice and delivers him to his master, or lodges him in any gaol, so that his master can have him again, shall receive the above reward, but no charges paid by PHILIP JACKSON.

Kingston, Luzerne county, Feb. 25, 1796.

50. March 23, 1796

EIGHT Dollars Reward.

RAN away from the subscriber, an indented servant boy, named James Hand, has dark bushy hair, about 16 years of age: Had on, and took with him, a jean coattee, a mixt cloth coattee, waistcoat and trowsers of the same, good felt hat and good shoes, besides other clothes. Whoever takes up said boy and brings him home, or secures him in any gaol, so that his master may get him again, shall receive the above reward, and reasonable charges, paid by   JOHN WARE.

Baken's neck, Cumberland county, West New-Jersey,
March 14, 1796.

51. March 23, 1796

EIGHT Dollars Reward.

RAN away from the subscriber, an indented servant boy, named Evans Scott, about 17 years of age, slender made, strait hair, sometimes wears it tied: Had on, and took with him, a snuff coloured coat, a mixed nankeen coattee, a pair of thick cloth trowsers, two pair of woollen stockings, two pair of shoes, three linen shirts, a half-worn fur hat, besides other clothes. Whoever takes up said boy, and brings him home, or confines him in any gaol, so as his master may get him again, shall have the above reward, and reasonable charges, paid by SMITH BOWEN.

Bridgetown, March 14, 1796.

52. April 6, 1796

COMMITTED to the gaol of the city and county of Philadelphia, a Negro man, who says his name is NED, and the same person who was advertised on the 19th October, 1795, by Abigail Ryland of Cecil county, in the state of Maryland. His owner is desired to pay charges and take him away, as he will be dealt with according to law.

Philadelphia Gaol, April 1, 1796.

53. April 6, 1796
Twenty Dollars Reward.

RAN away last night from their respective masters in this city, the three following indented German servants: 1. Christian Henry Malchowff, aged about 26 years, sandy hair, fair complexion, about 5 feet 9 inches high, rather slight built, shrill voice, very much addicted to pleasure, and a great gambler. He had with him an excellent dark brown mixed superfine cloth coat, a lead coloured short waisted cloth coat, and other articles of dress, and generally looks neat and makes a good appearance, a tailor by trade. 2. John Henry Matthias, aged about 28 years, a very great sloven, fond of smoaking, and very lazy, about 5 feet 10 inches high, boney and stout made, stoops, in-kneed and very clumsy in his manner, pockmarked, has lost a fore tooth, light, almost sandy hair, which he wears very full at the sides, and twisted and turned up behind; had on a blue superfine cloth coat with yellow buttons, a green twilled old silk waistcoat, fustian breeches with white buttons, on which are engraved a Griffin crest, a round hat almost new, shoes with ribbons, and blue ribbed stockings, by trade a hair-dresser. 3. Henry Daniel Matthias, brother of the last mentioned servant, aged 24 years, light hair, inclining to sandy, which he wears tied and remarkably bushy, ruddy complexion, blue eyes, in both which he has a remarkable cast, good teeth; he is about 5 feet 8 inches high, slender made, in-kneed, rather clean in his dress; had on a dark coloured surtout coat, buttons of the same, lead coloured corduroy breeches, a pair of fancy striped cotton stockings, and shoes tied with ribbons, very long quartered, round hat half worn. As these servants were treated with great kindness by their masters, it becomes the duty of every man to prevent their making off. The two last having very little craft about them, their desertion is imputed to the artifice of the first who has proved himself to be a very worthless, designing and ungrateful character. Whoever will apprehend the said three run away servants, and confine them in any prison, shall receive Twenty Dollars Reward or a proportion of that sum for each—by applying to the Printers hereof.

Philadelphia, March 28, 1796.

54. April 13, 1796

Ten Dollars Reward.

RAN-AWAY from the employ of the subscriber, living near Wilmington, on the 28th of December, 1795, a Negro man, named PETER, the property of Elisha Price, Esq; of Chester, who had bound himself and heirs to liberate him, on condition of his serving him faithfully four years from the 1st of October last. Said Peter is 39 or 40 years of age, about 5 feet 6 or 7 inches high, square and well built, a little bow-legged, a smooth tongued artful fellow, a noted liar, a great villain, and fond of liquor. He will probably change his name and endeavour to pass for a freeman. He had on when he went away, a new homespun cloth coattee and trowsers of a light colour, an old velvet jacket, and new strong shoes with strings. He understands farming and driving a team, can play on a fiddle, and took one with him belonging to his fellow-servant, and money belonging to another of his comrades. Said fellow has been a run away almost ever since he was 20 years of age; he has lived in New-Jersey, where he changed his name to Jeffery Homes; has been a voyage or two to sea; has lived in Philadelphia, in Bucks county, and almost every part of Chester county. In September last, he lived with Mr. John Crozer, in Delaware county, where he says he has an Indian wife; but as he has children by four black women, to all of whom he says he is lawfully married, it is not known to which (if to either of them) he will apply to conceal him. Said Peter had leave of absence for four days at the time he ran away, with a permit to pass and repass to and from Delaware county, to see his acquaintance there, and to deliver a letter to his master, Elisha Price, Esq; and to return on the 28th of December, 1795, but he has not delivered the letter, nor been seen in Chester since.

Whoever takes up and secures said fellow in any gaol, so that his master may get him again, shall receive the above reward, and if brought home, all reasonable charges paid by Elisha Price, Esq; in Chester, or by the subscriber, on his farm, near Wilmington.

Long-Hook, January 6, 1796.   PETER JAQUETT.

N.B. All persons are hereby forbid to employ or harbour said negro.

55. April 13, 1796

Twenty Dollars Reward.

RAN-away from the subscribers this day, a servant man, named *William Williams*, about six feet two inches high, very boney, walks stooping, about thirty-two years of age; had on when he went away, an old large brim round crowned hat, half cocked, an old light coloured cloth coat and trowsers, light plush vest, strings in his shoes, and is an indented servant to Richard Gibbs; likewise an indented servant man, named *Thomas Brown*, supposed to be about thirty years of age, straight short black hair, dark eyes, much pitted with the small pox, about five feet seven inches high, roman nose; had on when he ran-away, an old light brown sailor's jacket, new linen trowsers, good shoes with strings, square crowned fur hat, and is indented to Samuel Nicholson. Whoever takes up said servants, and secures them in any gaol, so that their masters may have them again, shall receive the above reward, and all reasonable charges paid, or ten dollars for either.

RICHARD GIBBS, SAMUEL NICHOLSON.

Salem county, West New-Jersey,
April 3, 1796.

56. April 20, 1796

RAN-away from the subscriber, living in Bensalem township, Bucks county, in the state of Pennsylvania, on the 12th instant, a negro slave, named ISHMEAL, well set, about five feet eight inches high, very sensible, and of a genteel behaviour, something of a scholar, about thirty-eight years of age, his sight somewhat bad, a blemish in one eye, if not both, but scarcely perceivable, the little finger on his right hand lays flat, the others on the same hand somewhat stiff, with a cut near his elbow, which left a scar; he is subject to drink; had on, when he went away, a led coloured full linsey coattee, trowsers of the same, a waistcoat near the same, with striped back, a new surtout coat near the same colour, a light cloth coat and waistcoat of the same, one brown coat, two pair of blue woolen footed stockings, much darned, one good fur hat, and one felt ditto. Said fellow plays well on the fiddle. Any person securing said negro in any gaol, so that his master may have him again, shall receive four dollars reward, and reasonable charges.

NATHANIEL VANSANT.

57. April 20, 1796

RAN away from the subscriber, in Hopewell township, county of Cumberland, and state of Pennsylvania, on the 9th instant, an indented servant boy, named *William Watson*, about fifteen years of age, of a fair complexion, and short hair; had on, and took with him, two coats, the one long, the other short, jacket and overalls, all of thick cloth filled with grey wool, two shirts, one new, the other old, good shoes, and two pair of stockings, a new pocket bible, and an ink-stand. The same boy got hurt in his left elbow when at school, and can hardly comb his own head with said hands. Whoever takes up said boy, and lodges him in any gaol out of this state, shall receive Twenty Dollars, and if in the state, Eight Dollars, with reasonable charges, paid by

March 11th, 1796. ARCHIBALD MUSTARD.

58. May 18, 1796

WAS committed to my custody, on the 11th instant, a Negro man, on suspicion of being a run-away, who calls himself JACK WILSON, and says his master's name is John Hopkins, and lives in Mountholly. Said Negro is about 5 feet 8 or 9 inches high, wears his hair tied, and of a yellow complexion. His master, if any he has, is requested to come, prove property, pay charges, and take him away, or he will be sold out for the expences, as the law directs, in two weeks from the date of this advertisement, by

CLEMENT ACTON, Sheriff of Salem county, New-Jersey.
May 11, 1796.

59. May 18, 1796

Six Dollars Reward.

RAN-away from the subscriber, on the 8th of this instant, May, living within two and a half miles of West-Chester, an apprentice lad, named FRANCIS COX, between sixteen and seventeen years of age; had on, and took with him, three shirts, two pair trowsers, one pair pieced at the bottom, two sleeveless jackets, one of striped linen, the other linsey, his outside garment a blue coatee, the body a deep blue, and the sleaves a pale blue twilled cloth, an half worn wool hat, and good shoes with strings. He has a remarkable scar over his eyebrow, has a down look, speaks thick, lisps in his speech, and has dark brown hair. Whoever secures him in any gaol in this state, or delivers him to his master, shall have the above reward, and reasonable charges if brought home, paid by DANIEL FITZPATRICK.

60. May 25, 1796

Twenty Dollars Reward.

RAN-away, on the 9th instant, an indented servant lad, named CHARLES ROBESON, about 18 years of age, 5 feet 7 inches high, brown hair tied sometimes, is much pitted with the small pox, speaks generally English; had on and took with him, one green linsey coat, a striped pattern jacket, a good felt hat, four home spun shirts, two pair linsey trowsers, one pair yellow and white striped linen ditto, and one pair tow ditto. Whoever takes up said servant, and secures him in any gaol of this or the adjacent states, and will give information thereof to Mr. DANIEL VANDER-SLICE, No. 89, Callowhill-street, Philadelphia, or to the subscriber, in New Providence township, Montgomery county, shall receive the above reward.

May 20, 1796.   PETER CUSTER.

61. May 25, 1796
Twenty Dollars Reward.

RAN-AWAY last evening, from the subscriber, an indented German servant, aged about 32 years, named JOHANNES GUNEN, about 5 feet 6 or 7 inches high, has grey eyes, a fresh coloured face, short dark brown hair, he speaks little English, though talkative, if indulged, he says he can speak French, and understands it well, low Dutch is his native tongue; he took with him a variety of clothes, is a farmer brought up, says he was in the French army some time, and then set sail to America from Amsterdam; it is supposed he wears a short white homespun coat, a cocked hat flopped down before, corduroy ribbed breeches, and white jacket. Whoever secures said servant in any gaol, so that his master may get him again, shall have the above reward, paid by the subscriber, in the township of Tredryffrin, county of Chester, and state of Pennsylvania.

May 23d, 1796.   WATER LEEVE.

62. May 25, 1796
Twenty Dollars Reward.

RAN-away last evening, from the subscriber, an indented servant German man, aged about 23 years, 5 feet 6 inches high, named CONRAD FREYBERGER, has grey eyes, a light sallow complexion, his hair, which he wears short, is light coloured and straight, he speaks but little English, though talkative, if indulged, in his own language, or in low Dutch, which he speaks very well; he took with him a variety of clothes, is a baker by trade, and says he came from the Duke of Wertemberg's dominions. Whoever secures said servant in any gaol, so that his master may get him again, shall have the above reward, paid by the subscriber, in the township of Upper-Merion, county of Montgomery, State of Pennsylvania.

May 23, 1796.   ISAAC MOORE.

63. June 15, 1796

RAN away, on the 24th instant, from the subscriber, living in Frankford, 5 miles from Philadelphia, an apprentice boy, named CLEMENT SMITH,

by trade a mason; about 18 years of age, 5 feet 7 or 8 inches high, of a fair complexion, short bushy hair, and is pitted with the small-pox; had on, when he went away, a pair of striped homespun trowsers and a homespun shirt, a striped under jacket, and an old drab coloured coattee much worn, and took with him two pair of new shoes, and a pair of yellow Nankeen trowsers; he talks both English and German, but is no scholar in either. Whoever takes up and secures the said apprentice, so that his master may get him again, shall have TEN DOLLARS reward, and reasonable charges, if brought home, paid by DANIEL THOMAS, in Frankford.
    Frankford, May 31, 1796.

64. June 15, 1796
Twenty Dollars Reward.
RAN away, on the evening of Sunday, the 12th of June, instant, a Dutch servant man, named HENRICUS BECKER, but calls himself HENRY, about 24 or 25 years of age, 5 feet 4 or 6 inches high, has a down look, black curly hair, his upper lip very black, and not much beard; he speaks low, and I think does not hear well; had on, and took with him, one pair of pumps, one pair of soaled shoes, one pair of brown cotton stockings, nankeen coloured jacket and breeches much faded, a muslin handker-chief, which he generally wears tied behind, a blue cloth coat lined with dark blue shaloon,[32] with large brass or metal buttons with small knobs on them, a new shirt, and a rorum hat; he also took with him a Dutch Roman prayer book, and an English and Dutch grammar. He calls him-self a butcher, but can do very little at the business. Whoever secures said runaway within 150 miles shall have the above reward, if 200 miles Thirty Dollars, and reasonable charges if brought home, paid by
    Philadelphia, June 14, 1796.   GEORGE G. WOELPPER.

65. June 15, 1796
WAS committed to the gaol of Chester county on the 8th of June, a Negro man, who calls himself Aaron Anderson, and acknowledges he is a slave to Mr. Sidney George, in Middle Neck, in Cecil county, in the state of Maryland. His master is hereby requested to come, pay charges, and take him away, in eight weeks from the date hereof, otherwise he will be discharged at that time, by paying his fees.
    West-Chester, June 6, 1796.   BENJAMIN MILLER, Gaoler.

32. Shaloon or Shalloons: a woolen fabric made in Chalons, France.

66. June 15, 1796

WAS committed to the gaol of Chester county, on the 28th day of May, a
Negro boy, who calls himself John Aaron, and acknowledges he is a
servant to Mr. John Ross, of Germantown, Philadelphia county. His master is hereby requested to come, pay charges and take him away, in four
weeks from the date hereof, otherwise he will be discharged at that time,
by paying his fees.

  West-Chester, June 6, 1796.   BENJAMIN MILLER, Gaoler.

67. June 22, 1796

Eight Dollars Reward.

RAN away from the subscriber, in Falls township, Bucks county, on the
12th instant, an indented Negro boy, named JEREMIAH PETER JULIS,
17 years of age, about 5 feet 7 or 8 inches high, streight made, and large
fore teeth; had on, and took with him, a good wool hat, two shirts, two pair
of trowsers, one of which striped, a dark overjacket, two coloured under
ditto, a pair of new shoes with double leather strings, and an old pair newly
mended and hob-nailed. Whoever takes up said apprentice, and lodges
him in gaol so that his master gets him again, shall receive the above
reward.

  Sixth month, 14th, 1796.   MOSES COMFORT.

68. July 13, 1796

Fourteen Dollars Reward.

RAN away from the subscriber, on the 25th instant, an apprentice to the
joiners business, a lad 19 years of age, named ASA PIATT, about 5 feet 6
inches high, sandy complexion, thick set, knock-kneed, and squints a
little with one eye, had on and took with him, two coats, one of superfine
mixed cloth, the other a bottle green, four under jackets, of different
kinds, two pair of over-alls; two pair of stockings, and two pair of shoes.
Whoever takes up said lad, and secures him in any gaol or workhouse, so
that his master may get him again shall have the above reward, and
reasonable charges, if brought home, paid by JOHN GREEN.

  Easton, Northampton county,
  June 30, 1796.

69. July 13, 1796

Sixteen Dollars Reward.

RAN away from the subscriber, living in Norrington township, Montgomery county, an apprentice boy, named Henry Roosin, about five feet

seven inches high, a little marked with the small pox, and has light coloured hair; nineteen years of age; he took with him a dark blue coat, with large buttons, one yellow striped nankeen coattee, buff cassimer jacket, one pair of thicksett and one pair of tow trowsers, and a pair of coarse shoes, lately soaled. Whoever secures said apprentice, so that his master may get him again, shall have the above reward, and all reasonable charges, paid by LEONARD VANFOSSEN.

June 30th, 1796.

70. July 20, 1796

Three Pounds Reward.

RAN away from the subscriber, living in Chester township, Burlington county, New-Jersey, on Delaware, about 10 miles above Philadelphia, on the 9th instant, an apprentice lad, named *Benjamin Mucklewain*, about 19 years of age, and about 5 feet 10 or 11 inches high, he is slender made, round shouldered, light complexion, somewhat freckled, long thin visage, short strait hair, has a down look, and an impediment in his speech; had on, when he went away, a light brown lindsey coattee, with wooden buttons, olive fustian under jacket and trowsers, all new, a low crowned black felt hat, bound black grained neat's leather shoes, with plain steel buckles, brown homespun shirt, took with him a dirty tow frock, with some things tied up in it, unknown what. Whoever will take up said apprentice, and bring him to his master, or secure him in any gaol within 50 miles of Philadelphia, so that his master may get him again, shall receive the above reward, and reasonable charges paid by CALEB ATKINSON.

N.B. As he has expressed an inclination for the sea, all Masters of vessels are therefore forbid to carry him off, at their peril; but if any person should incline to take him, his indenture may be purchased.

Cinnaminsink, 7th mo. 13th, 1796.

71. July 27, 1796

Five Cents Reward.

RAN away from the subscriber, on the 26th of May last, an apprentice lad, named JACOB CHOOPER; had on, when he went away, an Infantry hat and coat, and took with him other cloathing; he is of dark complexion, and 20 years of age. Whoever takes up said apprentice, shall have the above reward, and no charges, paid by GEORGE SELLERS.

72. July 27, 1796

Eight Dollars Reward.

RAN-AWAY from the subscriber in the township of Mannington, county of Salem, and state of New-Jersey, on seventh day night last, an indented servant man, named PAUL RAIRDON, a native of Ireland, about 5 feet 8 or 9 inches high, some pitted with the smallpox, sandyish hair and fair complexion; had on, and took with him, a swanskin sailor jacket, home-spun shirt and trowsers, and felt hat; a woman went with him, said to be his wife, who has a very mean appearance. Whoever takes up said run-away, and delivers him to the subscriber, or secures him in any gaol, so that he may get him again, shall receive the above reward, and reasonable charges, paid by ZADOCH STREET.

Mannington, July 18th, 1796.

73. August 10, 1796

Twenty Dollars Reward.

RAN-AWAY yesterday morning from the subscriber, living at Haddonfield, in Gloucester county, state of New-Jersey, an indented black lad, named MARK NOER, nearly seventeen years of age, about 5 feet 8 inches high, has a remarkable long head, and large hands and feet; had on, and carried away with him, a roram hat, an old beaver hat, two coattees, one of them olive fustian, the other blue forest cloth, white and black cross-barr'd waistcoat, olive fustian trowsers, black grain neats leather shoes, tied with strings, and other cloathing. Whoever takes up said lad, and secures him in Gloucester gaol, at Woodberry, so that the subscriber may have an opportunity to dispose of him, shall be entitled to the above reward.

8th month 8th, 1796.   JOHN EST. HOPKINS.

74. August 10, 1796

One Cent Reward.

RAN-AWAY from the subscriber, on the 3d of July, an apprentice boy to the blacksmith business, named JOHN ADAMS, about eighteen years old, about 5 feet 7 or 8 inches high, sandy hair; had on, when he went away, a drab coloured coattee, striped muslin jacket, and nankeen trowsers. Whoever takes up said run-away, and will bring him home, so that his master may get him again, shall have the above reward, but no charges, paid by WILLIAM HANSELL.

DARBY, AUG. 6, 1796.

75. August 17, 1796

Five Dollars Reward.

RAN away from the subscriber, living in Abington township, on the 8th of August, instant, a servant boy, named Lewis Evans, between seventeen and eighteen years of age, 5 feet eight inches high, light hair, and tied, smooth face, and a scar under one of his eyes; had on, and took with him, a second hand beaver hat, mixt grey coat, striped cotton jacket, the stripe runs cross ways, dyed homespun tow trowsers, a pair of new calf skin shoes. Whoever takes up said servant, and delivers him to the subscriber, shall receive the above reward, paid by THOMAS LEEDOM,

On the plantation of Robert Fletcher.

76. August 24, 1796

Thirty Dollars Reward.

RAN away from the subscribers, on Staten-Island, on the 13th instant, three NEGRO MEN, one named SAM, belonging to John Journey, thirty-five years old, about five feet ten inches high, middling slim built yellowish complexion, one of his front teeth broke, stoops, and plays on the fiddle.

NEEN, about twenty-one years old, near six feet high, slim and straight, very black, wears his hair tied, big ankles, and clumsey footed.

WILL, belonging to Barnet Parlee, about twenty-two years old, five feet seven inches high, stout built, yellow complexion, a large scar on his forehead and on one of his cheeks, some impediment in his speech, and occasionally wears his hair tied. Their dress would be difficult to describe, as they took changes with them. Whoever takes up said Negroes, and returns them to the subscribers, near the Old Blazing Star, or secures them in any gaol, and gives information that they may be had, shall receive the above reward, and reasonable charges, or ten dollars, with charges, for each of them.

JOHN JOURNEY, ALBERT JOURNEY, BARNET PARLEE.
August 15th, 1796.

77. September 7, 1796

Sixty Dollars Reward.

RAN away yesterday in the forenoon from the subscriber, living in Strasburg township, Lancaster county, in the state of Pennsylvania, the following indented servants, viz.

John Flaugh, born in Saxony, about 27 years of age, of a low stature, stout built, has black hair, and is of a tolerable fair complexion, had on, when he went away, a good hat, a red home made coating jacket, corduroy breeches, white stockings, and a new pair of shoes, tied with thongs, and is a Mason by trade.

Christian Nagle, born in Prussia, about 25 years of age, a little taller then Flaugh; has straight sandy hair, of a fair complexion, and a Taylor by trade, had on, when he went away, a brown home made cloth coat, a pair of bottle green corduroy trowsers and jacket, a good pair of shoes, and a wool hat, almost new, and speaks broken English.

Conrad Dratz, a Hessian, about 24 years of age, is tall and strong built, has black curled hair, which he wears sometimes tied; had on, when he went away, a brown home made cloth coat, almost new, a red home made cloth jacket, a pair of bottle green corduroy trowsers, a good pair of shoes, and a good wool hat, speaks very little English. Whoever takes up the said servants, and secures them in any gaol, so that their master may have them again, shall receive the above reward, or twenty dollars for any or either of them, besides reasonable charges, paid by MICHAEL WITHERS.

September 7th, 1796.

78. September 7, 1796
Twenty Dollars Reward.

RAN away from the subscriber, the 27th of this instant, an indented servant man, named JACOB PHASKEL, about 18 years of age, 5 feet 7 inches high, tolerably well set, long black hair, tied with a black thick set ribbon, dark eyes and eye brows, his forehead bold, his visage long, and his face full of small red pimples. He took with him a square crown castor hat, about half worn, two tow and flax shirts, and four pair of trowsers, one pair of new nankeen trowsers, that tied at the ancles, with a rip in the upper part of the thigh, and vest of the same, a buff colour, one pair of striped lye coloured flag trowsers, a scarlet vest with fustian back, two waistcoats, and a clouded nankeen and a fustian coat, a pair of old shoes newly patched and soaled, and had remarkable long great toes. Whoever secures said servant in any gaol or brings him home to his said master, shall have the above reward, and all reasonable charges, paid by MOSES QUINBY.

Amwell township, Hunterdon county,
New-Jersey, 9 mo. 6th, 1796.

79. September 14, 1796
WAS committed to the gaol of Chester county, on the 29th of August, a negro man, who calls himself ABRAHAM, and acknowledges he is a

slave to Mr. JOHN M'CLEARY, of Cecil county, in the state of Maryland.
His master is hereby requested to come, pay charges, and take him away,
in six weeks from the above date, otherwise he will be discharged at that
time, by paying his fees.

West-Chester, August 31st, 1796.

BENJAMIN MILLER, Gaoler.

80. September 14, 1796

WAS committed to the gaol of Chester county, on the 1st of September, a
negro man, who calls himself DANIEL, and acknowledges he is a slave to
Mr. RICHARD HEATH, in the state of Maryland. His master is hereby
requested to come, pay charges, and take him away, in six weeks from the
above date, otherwise he will be discharged at that time, by paying his fees.

West-Chester, September 3, 1796.

BENJAMIN MILLER, Gaoler.

81. September 21, 1796

Eight Dollars Reward.

RAN-AWAY from the subscriber, living in Waterford township, Gloucester county, state of New-Jersey, a mulatto man, named BOB, about 27
years old, and about 5 feet 6 inches high; had on, when he went away, a
fustian suit, a castor hat, neats leather shoes tied with buckskin strings;
he had a scar on his chin. I forewarn all Captains harbouring him.
Whoever secures him in gaol, shall receive the above reward.

ISAAC FISH.

September 4th, 1796.

82. September 28, 1796

Ten Dollars Reward.

RAN away, on the 22d of the 6th month last, from the subscriber, living
in West-Nottingham, Cecil county, in the state of Maryland, JEREMIAH
FAGAN, better than eighteen years of age, light grey eyes, fair skin, and
freckled, about five feet eight or nine inches high, short curly dark
brown hair, pretty talkative, and apt to swear, when angry; this country
born, had on and took with him, a drab coloured coat, with large metal
buttons, a short coat, ditto with wooden buttons, both lined with blue and
brown lindsey, one fine shirt, two coarse, ditto, fustian jacket and
trowsers, olive colour, one pair of coperas and one pair dyed trowsers,
two wool hats, one new, coarse leather shoes, with large carved buckles,
he is fond of driving a team. Whoever takes up said servant, and secures

him in any gaol, so that his master may have him again, shall be entitled to the above reward, and if brought home, reasonable charges, paid by WILLIAM HAINES.

Sept. 27th, 1796.

83. October 12, 1796

Six Cents Reward.

RAN-AWAY, on the 9th instant, from the subscriber, living in Woolwich township, Gloucester county, state of New-Jersey, an apprentice boy, named WILLIAM RICHARDS, seventeen years of age, five feet eight or nine inches high, very cross-eyed. Whoever takes up said apprentice, and brings him to his master, shall have the above reward, but no charges.

DANIEL MELFORD.

N.B. All persons are forbid harbouring him at their peril.

October 12th, 1796.

84. November 9, 1796

Two Dollars Reward.

RAN-away from the subscriber on Saturday last, an apprentice, named *Thomas Nixon*, he is a fair countenanced lad, about 17 years of age; had on when he went away, a blue cloth coat, fustian trowsers, a round hat, &c. and carried with him several articles of cloathing which cannot well be described. The above reward will be paid for bringing him to his master, or giving information so as he may be had.

JOHN M'CLELLEN.

N.B. All masters of vessels are forwarned not to carry him off, and all persons not to trust him on my account.

Frankfort, November 7th.

85. November 30, 1796

Six Cents Reward.

RAN-AWAY on the 29th ultimo, from the subscriber, living in Goshen township, Chester county, an apprentice lad, named WILLIAM CINSER, about 17 years of age, a short thick set fellow, round visage, short brown hair; had on a hunting shirt, cloth jacket and tow trowsers, when he went away.

Whoever takes up the said apprentice, and brings him home, shall be entitled to the above reward, but no charges.

SAMUEL GARRET, junr.

Nov. 30.

86. December 7, 1796

Six Cents Reward.

RAN away from the subscriber, on the 21st of September, a bound girl, named Sarah Newton, about seven years of age, fair complexion, black hair and dark eyes; had on a striped cotton short gown and brown petticoat, when she went away. Whoever takes up said girl, and brings her to me, at No. 143, North Front-street, shall receive the above reward, but no charges.

PHILADELPHIA, DECEMBER 7, 1796.   JOHN PATTERSON.

87. December 14, 1796

Seven Cents Reward.

RAN-AWAY from the subscriber, on the 20th of November, an apprentice boy, by trade a Miller, named JOHN TANNER, between 19 and 20 years of age, about 5 feet 7 or 8 inches high, light hair; had on, when he went away, a new coat, jacket and trowsers, all of clouded nankeen, and took with him a light colourd broad-cloth coat, a striped jean jacket, and mixed red and blue broad-cloth jacket, two pair of trowsers, one striped purple and yellow, the other fulled lindsey, three shirts, one fine, a fur hat, bound with velvet, two pair of yarn stockings, and a pair of new shoes, and other cloaths. Whoever takes up said apprentice, and will bring him home, so that his master may get him again, shall have the above reward, but no charges paid, by BENJAMIN CHAPMAN.

WRIGHTSTOWN, NOV. 28, 1796.

PART THREE

Daily Life

CHAPTER 5

A Woman of the "Best Sort"

The Diary of Elizabeth Drinker

CATHERINE GOETZ

In April 1795, twelve years before her death at the age of seventy-three, Elizabeth Sandwith Drinker confided to her diary:

> How many vicissitudes do I pass through in the small sphere in which I daily move. Declining health and strength have been my daily lot for a long time past, yet I have abundant cause of thankfulness. If life is a blessing, and it is generally thought so to be, I have been much favored, as I am now near four years older than my dear father was when removed hence, and near 14 more than my beloved mother. May I be thankful for the time past, and

endeavor to be resigned to what may occur in the little that in all probability remains.[1]

This notation on the state of her health and its mild invocation for resignation in the face of future "vicissitudes" is more than an aging woman's melancholy. Drinker's words acknowledge that she had indeed borne witness not only to the daily travails common to most eighteenth-century women but also to a remarkable era of political and social upheaval, changing values, and widespread and recurrent contagion. The entries in her multivolume diary testify to her introspection, her gentle nature, and her spiritual optimism. Begun in earnest by Drinker when in her early twenties, the diary is a record of both public reticence and private candor. It portrays the life of an articulate and wealthy Quaker woman who resided in Philadelphia during the second half of the eighteenth century.

Born in the City of Brotherly Love in 1735 of Irish Quaker parents, Elizabeth Sandwith was the second of three children; her younger brother died in infancy. Elizabeth's father, William Sandwith, enjoyed great material success as a merchant and ship captain. The death of both her parents when she was twenty-one left Elizabeth and her sister, Mary, with strong Quaker beliefs, modest financial resources, and a moderate capacity to earn money in a society where women's employment opportunities were limited. While living temporarily in the home of lawyer and philanthropist Thomas Say, Mary and Elizabeth entered briefly in the feather trade with Dublin merchant Edward Stephans. Like a handful of other privileged and parentless single young women, they engaged in an enterprise that was most likely a vestige of their father's business dealings.

After fourteen months residing with Thomas Say and helping tend the numerous orphans he took into his family, Mary and Elizabeth moved into the household of Ann Warner. Through the Warners and other members of the Society of Friends (Quakers), Elizabeth met an-

---

1. Diary entry on April 11, 1795. Elizabeth Drinker's original diary is in the Historical Society of Pennsylvania, Philadelphia. The excerpts printed below were taken from Henry D. Biddle's edition of the diary because Elizabeth Forman Crane's recent and more accurate edition of the diary was not available when these excerpts were selected. Biddle, Drinker's great-grandson, changed the spelling and the punctuation, so the diary entries were checked against Crane's edition to be sure the meaning was not altered. I also drew heavily on Crane's excellent annotation of the diary. Henry D. Biddle, ed., *Extracts from the Journal of Elizabeth Drinker* (Philadelphia: J. B. Lippincott Company, 1889); Elizabeth Forman Crane, *The Diary of Elizabeth Drinker*, 3 vols. (Boston: Northeastern University Press, 1991).

other Quaker, Henry Drinker, who was to become her life's mate and loving companion until her death in 1807. Elizabeth and Henry married at the Quaker meeting of January 13, 1761, and Mary accompanied her sister when she moved to her new home on Water Street near the docks. Henry prospered as a merchant, and by 1775 the couple belonged to the wealthiest 5 percent of the city's taxpayers (or "the best Sort," in Elizabeth's words), a position they occupied for the rest of the century.[2]

Drinker's diary affords a rare glimpse of the private life of an elite family in eighteenth-century urban America from a female perspective. It sheds light on a variety of daily issues confronting Philadelphians, Quakers, and women in particular. The ways in which one woman felt and expressed her familial duties toward her children, husband, and other kin are evident in scores of diary entries.[3] During her forty-six-year marriage, Elizabeth bore nine children, only five of whom survived the health hazards of childhood (see Chapters 7 and 8).[4] Like most women, Elizabeth spent a great deal of her time raising children, and much of her diary focused on her offspring: Sarah, called "Sally" (1761-1807); Ann, called "Nancy" (1764–1830); William, referred to as "Billy" (1767–1821); Henry, or "HSD" (1770–1824); and Mary, called "Molly" (1774–1866). The diary entries indicate the amount of time Elizabeth devoted to child care. From terse notations in the early years, the entries eventually become longer and more elaborate in the later years, possibly indicating the greater amount of time and energy Elizabeth enjoyed after her children were grown.

As was common among the elite, the Drinker household contained numerous servants, some of whom were considered part of the family. A number were apprenticed during childhood, several were purchased

2. Elizabeth's characterization is from her September 26, 1759, diary entry. Henry Drinker was assessed £116 in taxes in 1772, £10,500 in 1780, £2,170 in 1789, and $300 in 1798, according to the Provincial Tax Lists for those years, located in the Philadelphia City Archives.

3. Like many other eighteenth-century women who left journals or correspondence, Elizabeth Drinker provided few glimpses into her marital relationship. However, her diary does reveal her abiding respect for her husband, Henry, as well as her deep frustration with the demands of his work and the limited time he spent at home with her and their children. On this topic, see Terri L. Premo, *Winter Friends: Women Growing Old in the New Republic, 1785-1835* (Urbana: University of Illinois Press, 1990).

4. Although she gave birth to eight children, Elizabeth referred to nine. Perhaps, as Elaine Crane speculates, she included a miscarriage or stillbirth. See "The World of Elizabeth Drinker," *Pennsylvania Magazine of History and Biography* 107 (1983): 10 n.36.

as indentured servants as they arrived from Europe, others were live-in maids, and a few worked as short-term employees hired for a few weeks or by the day. Elizabeth records her uneasy interaction with several of them, as well as a sense of responsibility to many. The diary also suggests a good deal about the lives workers led outside their masters' homes.

Drinker registers the extraordinary range of medical and health-care practices common in the late eighteenth century. Everything from tooth extractions and gum lancings to regular bleedings and the use of purgatives were employed by household members or by doctors to relieve ordinary and not so ordinary ailments. Further, Drinker provides a vivid firsthand account of the disastrous yellow fever epidemics that afflicted Philadelphia during the 1790s (see Chapter 8).

During an era of political turmoil when many people became radicalized, Elizabeth led a relatively conventional life and generally maintained conservative views. (For a woman with less-orthodox experiences and opinions, see Chapter 6.) Drinker was a British partisan, suspicious of the American Revolutionaries, particularly radicals like Thomas Paine. She also disagreed with much of Mary Wollstonecraft's feminist point of view, especially its emphasis on the need for women to be independent. Even though Elizabeth was well educated and a voracious reader, especially compared with most women or even most men at that time, she believed she had a "dull brain." She was likewise ambivalent about formal education for young girls; she scorned sending them to boarding school and disapproved of their reading certain texts. Yet she sent all her children to a nursery school, although her daughters did not receive an education equal to that of her sons.[5]

The Drinker diary is also useful for its account of the American Revolution and the significance of that war for Quakers and women. Elizabeth chronicles the occupation of Philadelphia by British troops from September 1777 to June 1778. Events often are noted with little personal commentary: "A great number of Soldiers, prisoners, in dif-

5. Quote from diary entry on March 28, 1795. On the education of Elizabeth and her children and grandchildren, see Crane, "World of Elizabeth Drinker," 9–13. For general treatments of women's education and reading habits during the Revolutionary era, see Linda K. Kerber, *Women of the Republic: Intellect and Ideology in Revolutionary America* (Chapel Hill: University of North Carolina Press, 1980); Mary Beth Norton, *Liberty's Daughters: The Revolutionary Experience of American Women, 1750–1800* (Boston: Little, Brown, 1980); and Cathy N. Davidson, *Revolution and the Word: The Rise of the Novel in America* (New York: Oxford University Press, 1986).

ferent Companies, have passed thro' this City, within these few weeks, for New York." But Elizabeth, like many Quakers, was a committed pacifist who did not hesitate to condemn both sides for the evils produced by the conflict: "These are sad times for thieving and plundering; 'tis hardly safe to leave the door open a minute. A number of Friends to Government, about ye country, have lately been plundered and ill-used by the British troops; things wear a very gloomy aspect at this present time."[6] Because of their opposition to the war, Quakers were suspected and often prosecuted by both the Revolutionaries and the Loyalists.

The exigencies of the war encouraged Elizabeth to play a less conventional female role than she may have desired. Her diary recounts her challenge to both American and British officers during the war. And when Henry was jailed for refusing to sign a loyalty oath to the rebel government, Elizabeth made the arduous journey to Lancaster, Pennsylvania, to argue for his release. Drinker thus provides a firsthand account of one woman's wartime experiences and the ways in which her ideas and perceptions were altered by the American Revolution.[7]

More than once Elizabeth Drinker remarked that her journal was meant for the information of her kin and was designed solely to record events for future reference.[8] While she remained faithful to her task, she also revealed a great deal about herself as an individual of keen perception and of felicitous and truthful demeanor. From the vantage of her comfortable home, surrounded by loved ones and within the convocation of Quaker friends, Drinker observed a nation's birth, its bloody and sometimes cruel struggle for political survival. And she experienced the daily difficulties of life common in the eighteenth century, including illness, death, and accidents. Finally, the diary testifies to Elizabeth's "resignation to the Divine will," expressed in her unflinching faith in her God and her dedication to her family.[9]

6. Diary entries on May 11, 1783, and December 11, 1777.

7. On the experiences of women during the American Revolution, see Kerber, *Women of the Republic*; and Norton, *Liberty's Daughters*.

8. See the diary entries for September 16, 1790 and December 31, 1799.

9. Quotation from diary entry on December 31, 1794. As Drinker wrote: "Another year passed over, and our family mercifully kept together. How many calamities have we escaped, and how much to be thankful for. . . . Of the many favors and blessings bestowed on us in this life; the greatest, and from which flows the most comfort and consolation is, resignation to the Divine will. Tho' 'tis hard, very hard in many cases to effect, yet I firmly believe it attainable, and what I think conducive most to this desirable state is, a steady dependence on, and confidence in, the Almighty."

Elizabeth Drinker's Diary

1759

Jan. 15. Stayed at home all day. Began to work a large worsted Bible cover.

Mar. 1. Pulled out a Tooth in ye evening, which ye Tooth drawer had drawn before and replaced.[10]

1760

June 23. Stayed at home all day. Helped quilt Nancy Warner's petticoat in ye afternoon.

July 4. Spent ye greatest part of the Day up stairs looking over accounts.[11] H[enry] D[rinker] came at 10 o'clock, stayed till past 11—unseasonable hours; my judgment don't coincide with my actions, 'tis a pity, but I hope to mend.[12]

Nov. 28. H.D. breakfasted with us. Went to monthly meeting this morning, A[nn] Warner Senior and Sister [Mary] with me; declared my intentions of marriage with my Friend H.D.

1762

Aug. 4. Mon cher [Henry Drinker] went to Town early this morning. Sammy and Betsy Emlen, Hannah and Nelly Moode, spent the day with us; ye day was as agreeably spent as could be in ye absence of my best Friend.

1767

May 3. Billy unwell with Fever. Doct. Redman tends him.

July 8. By Norris's woods we met ye company returning from Ludy's child-burying. A young fellow on a mad colt gallopped against our Mare with such force as occasioned my falling out of the Chair; having the child in my arms asleep, and endeavoring to save it, I fell with all my

10. In early America, the "tooth drawer," or dentist, frequently attempted to implant a false tooth in a patient's mouth. The reimplantation of Drinker's tooth was unsuccessful.

11. The accounts from Elizabeth and Mary's feather trade.

12. Elizabeth understood that, according to the etiquette of the day, a suitor arriving at 10 P.M. was unseemly, but she received her future husband anyway.

weight on my right foot, and it hurt so much that I was unable to set it to ye ground for upwards of 3 weeks. Ye child, through mercy, escaped unhurt. I have lately met with so many frights that I cannot bear to think of riding with any satisfaction.

1773

Dec. 24. An account from Boston of 342 Chests of Tea being thrown into ye sea.[13]

1774

May 3. Governor [Thomas] H[utchinson] carted round ye Town, and burnt in effigy.[14]

1776

Jan. 30. J[ohn] Drinker [Henry Drinker's brother] called before ye Committee [for refusing to take Continental money].

Feb. 15. John Drinker's store shut up by the Committee.

July 16. Friends meeting house at Market street corner broken open by ye American soldiers, where they have taken up their abode.

1777

Jan. 25. We had 5 American soldiers quartered upon us, by order of ye Council of Safety. Ye soldiers were named Adam Wise and Henry Feating—those two stayed 2 or 3 days with us, ye others went off in an hour or two after they came.

Feb. 2. H.D., David Bacon &c. went to Glouchester to visit Mark Miller and Thomas Redman, who are confined in the Jail, for reading a Testimony from the meeting for Sufferings, and for refusing to take the Test proposed to them.[15] [In 1776 the Pennsylvania Assembly required citizens to renounce their allegiance to the British Crown and to declare their loyalty to the new government. But Philadelphia's Quakers resolved: "We are united in judgment that, consistent with our religious principles, we cannot comply with the requisitions of those laws. . . ."

13. The December 24, 1773, edition of the *Pennsylvania Gazette* (Philadelphia) carried the news of the Boston Tea Party, which occurred on December 16.

14. On May 2, Philadelphians pulled a wooden effigy of the unpopular Massachusetts governor through the streets.

15. Mark Miller and Thomas Redman were New Jersey Quakers who refused to take the loyalty oath.

The Quakers also refused to pay taxes levied by the new government. Believing them potentially seditious, Congress declared in 1777 that Quakers were "with much rancor and bitterness disaffected to the American cause" and called for the apprehension and arrest of a number of individuals.]

June 5. An Officer with 2 Constables called upon us for Blankets— went away without any, as others had done, 3 or 4 times before.

July 4. The Town illuminated, and a great number of windows broken, on ye Anniversary of Independence and Freedom.[16]

Sept. 2. H.D. having been, and continuing to be unwell, stayed from [Quaker] meeting this morning. He went towards noon into ye front parlor to copy the Monthly meeting minutes—the book on ye desk, and ye desk unlocked; when William Bradford, one [Bluser], and Ervin entered, offering a Parole for him to sign—which was refused. They then seized on ye book, and took several papers out of ye desk, and carried them off, intimating their design of calling the next morning at 9 o'clock; and desiring H.D. to stay at home at that time, which as he was unwell, was necessary. They accordingly called on ye 4th in ye morning and took my Henry to the Mason's Lodge, in an illegal, unprecedented manner; where are several other Friends, with some of other persuasions, made prisoners.

Sept. 9. Sent Billy to ye Lodge to inquire after his dear Daddy's health; he found him well. Myself, and little Sally went this afternoon to ye Lodge. During my stay there word was brought from ye Council, that their banishment was concluded to be upon ye morrow—ye waggons were preparing to carry them off. I came home in great distress, and after doing ye necessary for ye child, went back near 10 o'clock at night; found ye prisoners finishing a Protest against the tyrannical conduct of ye present wicked rulers.

Sept. 22. Nanny Oat called to day to demand her freedom dues,[17] and was very impertinent and saucy.

Oct. 6. An officer called this afternoon to ask if we could take in a

16. Quakers refused to close their shops to celebrate July 4. Those who did not display candles in their windows to show their support of the Revolutionary cause had their windows broken.

17. Masters commonly gave indentured servants (Europeans who sold themselves into servitude for three or four years in return for food, shelter, clothing, and passage to North America) clothing and cash at the completion of their years of service as part of their "freedom dues."

sick or wounded Captain. I put him off by saying, that as my Husband was from me, I should be pleased if he could provide some other convenient place. He hoped he had given no offence, and departed.

We have had two loads of Hay brought in to day.

Oct. 10. Jenny and Harry went to ye State House with Coffee and whey for ye wounded Americans—Billy went with them.

Oct. 11. Jenny and Harry visited ye wounded again to day with a double portion.

Oct. 25. An officer called to day to know if Genl. Grant could have quarters with us. I told him my husband was from me, and a number of young children around me; I should be glad to be excused. He replied, as I desired it, it should be so.

Nov. 5. A soldier came to demand Blankets, which I did not in anywise agree to—notwithstanding my refusal he went up stairs and took one, and with seeming good nature begged I would excuse his borrowing it, as it was by G. Howe's orders. We have not bought a pound of butter for 3 or 4 weeks past. All we get is from our Cow, about 2 pounds a week, and very few of the citizens have any.

Nov. 18. Nanny Oat came while I was out to ask pardon for her former conduct, which has been vastly impudent.

Dec. 2. Our saucy Ann came while I was at meeting, desiring to know what I would take for her time, and she would bring ye money in a minute.[18] Sister told her she did not know, but that she had heard me talk of putting her in ye Work-House. She replied, "If you talk so, you shall neither have me nor the money." Sister then ordered her to come again at 12 o'clock, but she has not been here since.

Dec. 9. I took a walk after dinner to Bartram's shop in Market street; called at Owen Jones'. Things seem to wear but an unpromising appearance at present, but ye absence of my dear Husband is worse to me than all ye rest put together.

1778

Feb. 23. This forenoon John James brought me a letter from my dear Henry. Our hopes are all crushed for the present; they have again offered ye Test to our Friends.

---

18. Ann Kelly, a troublesome servant, wanted to purchase the remainder of her time as a servant.

Mar. 25. Phebe Pemberton and M. Pleasants came to me to consult about drawing up something to present to those who shall acknowledge our dear Friends as their prisoners. [Elizabeth Drinker and several female friends wrote a plea to General Washington to release the Quakers held for refusing to take the loyalty test oath.]

Apr. 6. [P]roceeded on to ye American Picket guard, who, upon hearing that we were going to headquarters, sent 2 or 3 to guard us further on to another guard, where Col. Smith gave us a Pass for H[ead] Quarters, where we arrived at about 1/2 past one. We requested an audience with the General, and sat with his wife (a sociable, pretty kind of woman), until he came in.[19] A number of officers were there who were very complaisant. It was not long before G. Washington came, and discoursed with us freely, but not so long as we could have wished, as dinner was served, to which he invited us. . . . He told us, he could do nothing in our business further than granting us a Pass to Lancaster, which he did, and gave a letter to Isaac Morris for T. Wharton. After dinner, as we came out of ye dining Room whom should we see but Isaac Penington and Charles Logan, who had been taken up yesterday at Darby, put into ye Provo last night, and now brought to H[ead] Quarters. They were soon acquitted; we have reason to believe that they fared ye better from meeting us there.

Apr. 23. We hear that a number of ye British Light-horse have lately been to Bristol, where they have taken many prisoners.

Where are our dear Husbands to night?

Apr. 25. I can recollect nothing of ye occurrences of this morning. About one o'clock my Henry arrived at J. Webbs, just in time to dine with us. All the rest of our Friends came this day to Lancaster. H.D. is much heartier than I expected; he looks fat and well.

Apr. 30. We set off after 8 o'clock, and travelled on without interruption, and were welcomed by many before, and upon our entrance into ye city, where we arrived about 11 o'clock, and found our dear Families all well; for which favor and Blessing, and the restoration of my dear Husband, may I ever be thankful.

Sept. 10. We are reduced from 5 servants to one, which won't do long, if we can help ourselves. It is the case with many at present. Good servants are hard to be had, such a time was never known here, I believe, in that respect.

19. The American troops commanded by George Washington spent the winter of 1777–78 at Valley Forge, Pennsylvania, which was not far from Philadelphia.

1781

Feb. 1. Charles Mifflin and his Pupils met in our little Front Room; he has lately undertaken to improve a few young girls in writing, teaching them grammar, &c.

Apr. 27. Polly Nugent was this afternoon bound to us by her mother.[20] She has been with us a week, and appears clever—brought ye Itch with her, which I hope we have nearly cured.

May 26. Three men were this morning hanged on the Commons for theft &c.

Dec. 31. [Early in the month the Revolutionaries had mistakenly searched the Drinker house for British goods, which were illegal to purchase. The search was intended for the house of Elizabeth's son, Henry.] 'Tis a bad Government under which we are liable to have our Houses searched, and everything laid open to ignorant fellows, perhaps Thieves. H.D., had he been so disposed, could have make them pay dearly for their mistake.

1782

May 23. Our wicked neighbor Pantlif (in ye alley) beat and bruised Black Tom shamefully (a Negro man we have lately hired); his wife set their Dog at him, who bit his Thigh in two or three places, because he had thrown a Stone at ye Dog, who had run at him some hours before.

May 24. Black Tom lame with ye wound, and under ye doctor's care. He had Pantlif up before William Rush, who bound him over 'till next Court, but by no means humbled him. This man and his wife are two of ye most wicked, spiteful, revengeful persons, I think I ever knew. They are Dutch Folk.

1783

Aug. 11. Molly went first to writing school to Becky Jones.

Sept. 10. Sally, who has been very poorly ever since First day, this day took to her Bed, high fever and sick stomach.

Sept. 12. Billy's fever continued five days without remission—it then intermitted, and he had two regular fits; took ye Bark and recovered, tho' but slowly. During his fever he was lightheaded, and Bled twice at ye nose. Sally was longer recovering than ye others. . . . Ye Doctors called ye disorder the fall Fever,[21] of which many in ye City are ill—some of

20. Polly was bound as an apprentice.
21. "Fevers" were common in the later summer and fall in Philadelphia (see Chapter 8).

nervous, and some of putrid Fevers. Tho' they don't say it is a very sickly season, or not a very mortal one; so much sickness in our Family, and among our acquaintance, made it appear so to me. Great numbers of People up town have been ill.

Dec. 14. H.D. and Children went to ye Funeral of Josey Waln, eldest son of Nicolas Waln—died of ye putrid sore Throat, his Father is in Europe.

Dec. 30. H.D. went to ye Burial of Rebecca Steel.

1784

June 8. One Patrick Dowling, an Irish lad, who H.D. purchased out of an Irish vessel,[22] ye 5th instant: he stayed with us until ye 6th . . . then went in Powel Clayton's Shallop for Maurice's River, where he was to have served his time: we since heard that he was drowned endeavoring to swim, which it appears he did not understand. A very pretty, innocent Lad he appeared to be, between 17 and 18 years of age.

1790

Sept. 16. This book was intended for memorandums of what occurred during my Son's absence, for his information, not a diary of my own proceedings; but as it is the method in which I have been accustomed to write, and know my own movements better than any others—it must serve for an apology.

1791

June 28. Doct. Griffith and a grand man of Colour called this afternoon.

Sept. 29. By deviating from the path of rectitude, eating supper 4 nights successively—which is what I very rarely do—after supper, I drank a small draught of New table beer, and eat some grapes after it. About 3 this morning, I was seized with a severe fit of ye Colic, which lasted for an hour or two. I am much better this morning, thro' mercy, tho' unsettled and weak.

1793

Aug. 23. A Fever prevails in the City, particularly in Water St. between Race and Arch Sts. of ye malignant kind; numbers have died of it. Some say it was occasioned by damaged Coffee and Fish, which were stored at

---

22. Dowling was bought as an indentured servant.

Wm. Smiths; others say it was imported in a Vessel from Cape Francois, which lay at our wharf, or at ye wharf back of our store. Dr. Hutchinson is ordered by ye Governor to enquire into ye report. He found, as 'tis said, upwards of 70 persons sick in that square of different disorders; several of this putrid or bilious fever. 'Tis really an alarming and serious time.

Aug. 28. This afternoon our Carriage, driven by a white man, a stranger, came up with Mattresses, Blankets &c., and Sally Brant behind— poor black Jo[seph] gone away sick to some Negro house, where they have promised to take care of him, and Dr. Foulk is desired to attend him. We have hopes it is not the contagious fever that he has. . . .The inhabitants are leaving the City in great numbers.[23]

Aug. 31. The accounts this day from the City are many and various. Some, 'tis said, die of fear; one or more have died in the street, or on the road; those reports are not ascertained. Some naughty person or persons have broken into our Yard, and stole the grapes and Magnumbonums,[24] and broke ye limbs of that beautiful tree—if they do not get into the House we will forgive them.

Sept. 2. We have heard this day of the death of a poor, intemperate woman of the name of Clarey, who sold oysters last winter in a Cellar in Front Street, a little below Elfrith's alley. She was taken out of her senses, and went out of town; was found dead on the road.

Sept. 4. We were told a sad story indeed, to day, if it be true; it was repeated by different persons, and everything considered, it seems not unlikely, of a young woman who had nursed one or more in Water Street who died of ye disease. She, being unwell, the neighbors advised her to go somewhere else, as none of them chose to take her in. She went out somewhere, I did not hear in what part of the Town it was, and lay down ill at a door. A Magistrate in ye Ward, had her sent in a cart to ye Hospital, where she was refused admittance, and was near that place found dead in the cart, next morning.

Sept. 8. 'Tis remarkable that not one Negro has yet taken the infection—they have offered to act as nurses to the sick.[25]

Oct. 9. Letter this morning from John Drinker. The gloom continues in our City—-the awful disease by no means lessened.

---

23. Between a third and a half of the city's residents fled Philadelphia as the only sure way to escape the disease. Elizabeth and Henry had already retreated to their country estate outside the city, as was their custom during most summers.

24. Magnum bonum: a large yellow plum.

25. It was mistakenly believed that African Americans were not susceptible to yellow fever. A great many blacks volunteered their services.

Oct. 24. By a letter from J. Drinker of this day, we are informed that the malignancy of the disorder is much lessened, tho' many are still ill. We have heard of no death this day—it does not follow that none have died, tho' a proof of amendment. . . . Tremendous times! Wars, Pestilence, Earthquakes, &c.

Oct. 29. The fever appears to be nearly at an end, for which we cannot be too thankful. The newspapers say, that the 11th of this month 2730 odd have died of the Yellow fever; on that day died more than any preceding day, and great numbers since. Very cold.

Nov. 18. There is a report circulated that the Indians have beaten the army that went out against them, and that General Wayne is killed— what a pity peace was not made with them.[26]

1794

Jan. 11. An affecting account in the paper this day of the trial and death of the Queen of France, beyond description cruel. She was beheaded on the 16th Octr. last.

Nov. 20. Polly Chapman, who lived some years ago at service with us, came here yesterday to tell her troubles. She has lost her husband (a poor thing) and left with two young children. Our maid Jenny, who went out of town a little before our family, came here this evening, but talked of returning to ye country again. Good servants at this time are very scarce. Rain or hail this evening. Wind at N.E.

May 5. I was really distressed, and have been at other times when at J. Skyrins' to see the cruelty of the Draymen to their Horses, in forcing them to drag loads too heavy for them up the Hill. They whip them unmercifully, and are frequently, after many vain exertions, obliged to unload. I have long looked on the treatment of Carters and Draymen to their poor dumb servants, as a crying sin that ought to be particularly noticed.

June 19. L. Stoneburner's death was occasioned by an accident, in driving a waggon through a Gateway, he was jammed against the post; his ribs were broken, and otherwise so hurt, that he expired soon after.

July 1. Poor H-y C-p-r put an end to his life this morning, with a pistol, I know not why.

July 13. Finished reading Lavater on Physiognomy. I believe there is a great deal in what he advances, and I am not of the opinion of those who

26. The report of Anthony Wayne's death was erroneous. He subsequently led an American army that defeated Native Americans at the Battle of Fallen Timbers in August 1794 and opened up lands in the old Northwest to settlement by Americans.

say he is a madman, or out of his senses; yet I think he carries some things much too far, and has rather too much conceit of his abilities.

July 29. Heated our oven this morning for the first time; baked bread, pies, rice-pudding and custards.

July 31. Gilbert, Joshua and John making hay. Our little maids Sally Brant and Betsy Dawson helped to turn the hay.

Aug. 23. Read Tom Paine's new piece, entitled The Age of Reason.[27]

Aug. 27. Different persons have different tastes—their likes and dislikes vary; to me the noise of insects is amusing; the Locust, the Criket, the Katydid, as it is called, and even the croaking of Frogs, tho' their notes are inferior, are pleasing.

Aug. 30. A dismal looking object came to the back door this forenoon to ask charity. Our young people were frightened by his appearance; a middle aged man, very lusty, with a staff in his hand—mouth and nose much larger than the common size—long and matted yellow hair; a long beard of the same hue; his clothes very dirty and ragged. I asked him, why we went about the country so frightful a figure? He said, he had just recovered from a fit of sickness (of which no symptoms remained, and I imagine he is more troubled with laziness than sickness). I gave him victuals [food], but no money, and desired him to go quickly off, and shut the gate after him—to alter his appearance—as I thought there was a likelihood he would scare many, and have the dogs set on him. I felt afraid while talking to him, and wished him further off. He said, he intended to change his appearance before he entered the City. . . . I have observed, it is much more common to see those ill looking vagrants about ye Country than in the City; and suppose they are fearful if they enter a town in such a figure, that they will be taken up and confined.

Sept 2. Our girls saw, or conceited that they saw, a man passing more than once by our springhouse, which is opposite the parlor window, where they could easily discern that we have no man with us. We sent for J. Countney, who, with a stick in his hand and Sall with a candle (a fine way to take a thief) went in search of the man, but found him not; but as some of us feel a little cowardly, John has offered to sleep on the carpet in the kitchen, which is agreed to.

Sept. 6. Finished reading Addison's Evidences of the Christian Religion[28] with additional Discourses on eleven different subjects, by the

27. Thomas Paine, *The Age of Reason* (New York: T. & J. Swords, 1794). Paine was one of the most radical leaders of the Revolution and a staunch atheist.

28. Joseph Addison, *The Evidences of the Christian Religion. . . .* (London, 1730).

same excellent author. Those who are capable of much wickedness are, if their minds took a right turn, capable of much good; and we must allow that T[om] P[aine] has the knack of writing, or putting his thoughts or words into method. Was he rightly inclined, he could, I doubt not, say ten times as much in favor of the Christian religion, as he has advanced against it. And if Lewis ye 17th was set up as King of France, and a sufficient party in his favor, and T.P. highly bribed or flattered, he would write more for a monarchical government, than he has ever written on the other side—a time serving fellow.

Oct. 18. Henry has taken a little black boy on trial named Scipio Drake. He has been to several other places, but has run away from them to his mother who lives with M. Fisher. M.F. thought it best to put him in prison, where he was when Henry sent for him. He appears very sulky— is about 11 years old. I can't say I like him.

Oct. 19. Black Scipio, who supped and lodged here, arose early this morning, got his breakfast, and was then ordered to clean the knives. He took them in ye yard, and there left them and set off; in ye afternoon, his father, a good looking negro man brought him back. He is sadly teased with his son; he advised and threatened him, wished us to keep him. He had eaten nothing since morning; we gave him his supper and sent him to bed. M.F. gives him a good character, but if he goes off to-morrow I hope he will not come back to us. . . . A good servant is a valuable acquisition, the want of such is at present a general complaint.

Oct. 28. We discovered a day or two ago, that black Scipio had contracted acquaintance while in Jail, that was really too disgusting to be easy under. We had inquired, and made a search before he left the City, but found none; but since we came up, Sall, after a strict scrutiny found three—which was three too many to be borne with. The difficulty was, he had no change of raiment, linen excepted. I had him stripped and washed from stem to stern in a tub of warm soapsuds; his head well lathered, and when rinsed clean, poured a quantity of spirits over it, then dressed him in girls' clothes 'till his own could be scalded. He appeared rather diverted than displeased. Trifling as are the incidents which I insert, they are occurrences at Clearfield [the Drinker farm], and I trouble not myself with other people's business, but am amused or otherwise with what comes before me, and look out for little else at present, and as 'tis only for my own perusal and recollection, 'tis little matter how 'tis said or done.

Nov. 11. I was walking out with Billy before dinner, when we saw a neighboring Tailor, who I had sent for, going to our house. We turned homewards and had Sip measured for a new Coatee. I have been busy this morning mending his overalls and underments to make him fit to appear when we go to the City, for he looks now like a complete Ragamuffin.

Nov. 22. Little Peter, a negro boy, aged 7 years, came to us today from Virginia. He has not had the small pox, and appears weakly, otherwise well disposed. We are to give, if we keep him, fifteen pounds for his time. Washed him this afternoon in a tub of warm soapsuds, his head with larkspur and rum, and changed his apparel.

Dec. 6. A negro boy of the name of Peter Woodward came this afternoon to us from one of the lower Counties, Kent, I believe it was, and sent here by Warner Mifflin. He was ragged and lousy,[29] having been for upwards of a week on board the vessel, and in poor trim before. Fifteen pounds is said to be the price for him. W.M. writes that he is 11 or 12 years of age; he says his aunt told him he was going on 14; he looks to be between the two. Has not had the small pox. Before he had been here half an hour I had him in a tub of soap and water well washed, afterwards rum in which larkspur was mixed poured on his head; dressed him in Scipio's old clothes. I believe he suffered coming up with cold, for after he had warmed himself and eat something he looked like another creature. His appearance at first was rather formidable, being as I thought, hard favored. One of our Daughters is to have one of the three little blacks that have lately come under our care. I feel much for the poor little fellows—little Peter has no parents here, the other two have.

Dec. 31. Another year passed over, and our family mercifully kept together. How many calamities have we escaped, and how much to be thankful for. . . . Of the many favors and blessings bestowed on us in this life; the greatest, and from which flows the most comfort and consolation is, resignation to the Divine will. Tho' 'tis hard, very hard in many cases to effect, yet I firmly believe it attainable, and what I think conducive most to this desireable state is, a steady dependence on, and confidence in, the Almighty.

1795

Feb. 20. Alice, a yellow woman,[30] who has taken our clothes in to wash for sometime past, came here before dinner in great distress, her child in her arms; her husband, John Wright, a negro man, and a white girl,

---

29. He was infected with lice.
30. Mulatto.

attended by a Constable, who was taking them all to Jail, for keeping, as he said, a disorderly or riotous House. As we knew nothing of the business, and but little of Alice, could say no more in her favor, but that we hoped she was honest. He took them off; I expected we should lose our Linen &c. that was in her custody—a dozen quite new shirts, aprons, and many other things—as they had left their house open and nobody in it. About an hour after she returned in good spirits, informing us that her Husband and self had procured bail, but the white girl was put in Jail. Soon after she brought our Linen home, nothing missing.

May 28. I have been pleased by reading The Morals of Confucius,[31] a Chinese Philosopher, who flourished about five hundred and fifty years before the coming of Christ—said to be one of the choicest pieces of Learning remaining of that nation. A sweet little piece it is. If there were such men in that day, what ought to be expected in this more enlightened Age!

Nov. 14. I have been reading the minutes of the last Yearly [Quaker] meeting, at which a large Committee was nominated to raise subscriptions &c. for the benefit and civilization of the Indians, to build Saw-mills &c., to teach them handicrafts, reading, writing &c. &c. A considerable sum will undoubtedly be realized for their help in many ways.

Dec. 7. Henry has sold Scipio to George Emlen, and we have given him our little Peter Savage. I hope he will be a good boy, 'tho he is but little worth at present.

Dec. 27. I read to day a large Pamphlet entitled A Vindication of Mr. Randolph's Resignation;[32] some say it does not make good the title. . . . I look not on myself as a competent judge.

1796

Jan. 30. While sister was out yesterday, she saw a crowd in Arch street surrounding a woman, who was lying on a cellar door; enquired what was the matter with her, one said she was dead, another said otherwise. She told them, as she passed along, that there were two or three doctors lived near, and advised sending for one. She then went to Jacob Downing's and saw no more of it. Sally's Catty sent us word today that it was poor Molly Hensel, who three hours before was sitting in our kitchen

31. *The Morals of Confucius, a Chinese Philosopher* . . . , trans. and abridged from the Latin translation by the Reverend Fathers Prospero Intorcetta, Philippe Couplet, and others (London: Randal Taylor, 1691).

32. Edmund Randolph, *A Vindication of Mr. Randolph's Resignation* (Philadelphia: Samuel H. Smith, 1795).

eating bread and cheese, and drank a tumbler of table beer. Sister had laid out two dollars of John Jones' legacy for her, and by adding to it, had got for her a flannel petticoat, a shift, an apron, a neckerchief, and a cap. She was rejoiced and thankful for them, and Molly Drinker made them all up for her, and she went away in high good humor, tho' feeble. I had given her a little money, and fear she made a bad use of it, tho' perhaps that was not the case. She lived at service with us many years ago; was an industrious, ignorant, poor woman, lately married to a drunken old man, and was, I fear, addicted to the same failing. I looked upon her with pity and compassion, as I believed her one of the many beings from whom not much was required.

Apr. 22. I have read a large octava volume entitled, The Rights of Women, by Mary Wolstonecraft.[33] In very many of her sentiments, she, as some of our friends say, *speaks my mind*; in some others, I do not altogether coincide with her. I am not for quite so much independence.

Aug. 7. Our queer maid Patience came home near 10 o'clock, with her white petticoat much bedaubed with mud; said she was taken sick in the street coming from an up town Presbyterian meeting, and fell down; was taken into a house where they gave her lavender compound and two men friends were there who knew us; but she did not know them, nor at whose house she was in. She appears perfectly recovered at present. The story may be true, or it may be otherwise.

Aug. 16. I have had a rumpus to day with our ordinary maid Patience, and believe we shall shortly part. No matter how soon, as she is a very bad example to our other servants.

Aug. 17. Clear. Wind N.E. Our girl Patience Clifford left us this morning. Some say a bad one is better than none, but I think that in some cases, none is better than a bad one. We have made out pretty well to day with Peter and Sally.

Dec. 16. Read this afternoon a pamphlet, —A Letter to George Washington, President of the United States of America. On affairs public and private. By Thomas Paine, author of the works entitled, Common Sense, Rights of Man, Age of Reason &c. . . . A better, and more thorough past agent, the *Old one* cannot have, I think, than this same T.P. The wise, the virtuous and informed see through him; but the ignorant, the weak and the vicious readily fall into his snare.

33. Mary Wollstonecraft, *A Vindication of the Rights of Woman, with Strictures on Political and Moral Subjects* (Boston: Peter Edes for Thomas & Andrews, 1792). Wollstonecraft (1759–97) was famous for her writings advocating political and civil rights for women.

1797

May 16. Unsettled. Wind variable. Read a narrative of Elizabeth Wilson, who was executed at Chester, Janry. '86, charged with the murder of her twin infants.[34] A reprieve arrived 20 minutes after her execution, by her brother from Philadelphia. She persisted to the last in her account of the murder being committed by the father of the children, which was generally believed to be the truth.

July 4. Anniversary of Independence. May this day pass without the commission of any enormity, by those who pride themselves on their independence, but know not how to prize or use it.

Aug. 17. There is a man in Water street, opposite us, or nearly so, ill of the fever.[35] Our neighbor Henry Pratt is endeavoring to send him to the Hospital.

Aug. 21. My husband has concluded that W.D. and myself shall go tomorrow to North-bank, as it is thought advisable to leave the city. The Committee of Health have concluded with the Governor's concurrence, that if any person is taken ill, in any house, they shall immediately be removed out of town by their friends, or sent to the Hospital. Several other conclusions are made, and the inhabitants are much alarmed.

Aug. 31. Parker [a servant] had behaved very much amiss—had got in liquor and left the horses in the road near Godfrey Hagger's at some distance from town. A stranger took them back to our stable, with a letter from Godfrey Hagger, informing that the negro man lay dead drunk in the road. Henry gave him a whipping, which he bore with patience and contrition; begged to be forgiven and wept—signs of a very good disposition.

1798

Aug. 15. Dr. Redman called before dinner. He thinks that the disorder is progressing, and will progress.[36] 'Tis according to the nature of things at this season of the year. He talks of going with his wife and daughter into the country. Our black Sarah told me this morning, that she heard a man straining hard to vomit in the mulatto's chamber next door and that she had smelt sugar burning several times yesterday and to

---

34. *A Faithful Narrative of Elizabeth Wilson, Who Was Executed at Chester, January 3d, 1786* . . . (Philadelphia, 1786). On Wilson's conviction, see Sharon Ann Burnston, "Babies in the Well: An Underground Insight into Deviant Behavior in Eighteenth-Century Philadelphia," *Pennsylvania Magazine of History and Biography* 106 (1982): 178.

35. Yellow fever raged through the city in 1797. See Chapter 8.

36. Philadelphians suffered through another yellow fever epidemic in 1798.

day—that a poor sick man boarded there. Upon inquiring of Ben Airs who lives in ye house, we understood it was a man who had a very hard cough, but is no other way disordered. What ye burnt sugar meant, we know not, as they are not very nice or cleanly.

Sept. 16. A comparative table of deaths in Cobbett's paper of the 14th instant.[37] "From the 8th Augt to 31st in '93, there were 264 deaths—from the same to the same in '98, 621. From the 1st to the 14th Septr in '93, there were 375 deaths—from the same to the same in '98, 858 deaths." Our city is at present so deserted that I think it can hardly be possible for so many to be taken, but of this I only conjecture.

1799

Mar. 27. Our black Jacob Turner informed Sister this morning that he was to be married to our Sarah next week. We have had a hint of ye kind before. We may lose a good servant by it, but if it is for her benefit, I shall be satisfied.

Apr. 4. Jacob Turner and Sarah Needham, were, I expect, joined in the bands of matrimony this evening, by Parson Absalom Jones.[38] They talk of coming home next first day.[39] We offered to give them a wedding supper if they would have it here in a sober way. They were much obliged, but had taken a room at his brothers. A wedding without a frolic, would be no wedding, I believe, in their view.

July 22. Black Judy was here today. She is now about 52 or 53 years old. My sister and self sold her when 9 years old into the country. We did not think we were doing wrong, for we did not know what to do with her, as our parents were dead, and we were going to board out. We loved the child, and after a few weeks' consideration took a ride to her mistress's habitation, and offered her 40 pounds for ye child; they [had given] us 25, promising to use her very kindly. She said that she would not part with her for 100 pounds—she thought Providence had directed her to the child, and she meant to treat her with great kindness—we came away disappointed. She was afterwards sold again, but has been many years free, and her children are free when of age.[40] We had formerly some

37. The September 14 issue of the Philadelphia newspaper published by William Cobbett.

38. Jones was the minister of the African Episcopal Church of St. Thomas, the city's first self-regulated black church.

39. Sunday.

40. The Pennsylvania Gradual Abolition Act of March 1, 1780, specified that children of slaves born after March 1 would be free after they had served as bound servants for

uneasy hours on her account, tho' nothing to accuse ourselves of as a crime at the time, except parting with a little child that we loved, to be a slave, as we feared, for life.

Nov. 2. Old Betty Burrage called forenoon. She is, she says, indisposed, and has received a hurt on her side by falling out of a waggon. She wishes my husband would give her a character to recommend her to the overseers of the poor.[41] I gave her victuals and some money—she is to call again—but I don't expect H.D. will give her a good character; he can't, tho' perhaps she may be recommended as a proper object of charity. She called in the afternoon, being very importunate, but H.D. had left nothing for her.

Nov. 6. Betty Burrage came again urging for a character. I gave her one, such as I could give with truth. H.D. wrote it, and I signed it, saying that she was honest as far as I have heard or know, and at present is an object of Charity. The word honest is very extensive, but here it means— not a thief.

Dec. 31. With respect to keeping a Diary—when I began this year I intended this book for memorandums, nor is it anything else. Ye habit of scribbling something every night led me on—as what I write answers no other purpose than to help ye memory. I have seen Diaries of different complections—some were amusing, others instructive, and others replete with what might much better be totally let alone. My simple Diary comes under none of those descriptions. The first I never aimed at, for ye second I am not qualified, ye third may I ever avoid. Tho' I have had opportunities and incitements, sometimes, to say severe things, and perhaps with strict justice, yet I was never prone to speak my mind, much less to write or record anything that might at a future day give pain to any one. The children, or ye children's children of the present day, may be quite innocent of their parents' duplicity; how wrong it is to wound ye feelings of innocent persons, to gratify present resentment. I have seen frequent instances of people, in the course of time, change their opinions of men and things—and sometimes be actuated by pique or prejudice; yet perhaps, tho' convinced that they have been wrong, unwilling to tear or spoil what they have wrote, and leave it to do future mischief. This ought to be avoided by every prudent or sensible person.

---

twenty-one years if they were female, or for twenty-eight years if they were male, after which they would be free.

41. A character reference from respectable citizens like the Drinkers helped impoverished people who applied for aid from the Guardians of the Poor.

1800

Jan. 6. Our black Jane left us today. I believe she wants a holiday, as she appears loath to leave us, and don't choose to have her wages paid, nor will she take her clothes away. If she could go every day to meeting, and take her pipe to bed, she would be very happy. The first I don't like to refuse, the second, I have affronted her about. She is good natured, as far as I have seen, but not worth much in a family.

June 1. Jacob Downing went this morning before 5 o'clock to enter Elizabeth's name for a place at ye boarding school; 14 had been before-hand with him. People are in a great hurry, I think, to get rid of their children; tho' I believe it to be the best thing many can do for them, in some cases; but had I a dozen daughters, and health to attend to them, not one should go there, or anywhere else from me.

1802

Aug. 10. There are no less than eight servants in the kitchen, five of Jacobs' and three of ours, which generally makes confused work—they are seldom what they ought to be. Our Sall is consummately impudent when she takes it in her head, and Peter very fond of idleness and fun. Ye servants of this house are not what they ought to be by any means.

1803

Dec. 14. The old man back of our stable has commenced a suit against Henry Pratt, Henry Drinker, and Isaac Knight. His premises, he said, were injured by the liquid from some of the dungheaps, running on his ground. The matter is to settle from whose dungheap it proceeds.

1806

Sept. 23. Our Peter, a foolish blockhead, was married on first day last to a girl of Hazelhurst's, who is not free, and by all accounts not so good as she ought to be. I am sorry for Peter.

1807

Sept. 24. Last night when I was sitting up with my dear child, I endeavored to feel her pulse, but could find none. She was very ill I think.

Sept. 28. Oh! what a loss to a mother aged nearly 72 years; my first born darling. Oh! my heart—the last 4 or 5 days have been truly trying, tho' I have been supported far beyond my expectations, a poor, feeble, old woman. My son William, daughter Mary and myself were all of our house that accompanied the remains of our dear child to the place of fixedness—to be seen no more in this world.

Oct. 12. Our black Jude, whom we sold 51 years ago when she was a child, was here this afternoon. I thought she was dead, as we have not seen her for many years; she is now not far from sixty years of age. When we sold her, there was nothing said against keeping or selling negroes; but as we were going to board out we knew not what to do with her. Some time after, we were more settled in our minds, and were very sorry we had sold the child to be a slave for life, and knew not what would be her fate. We went to Springfield to repurchase her, but her mistress, a very plausible woman, refused to sell her, tho' we offered her 40 pounds, and had sold her 2 months before for 25. Some time afterward, her mistress sold her to Parson Marshall. It was several years after she had grown up, and when there was much talk of the iniquity of holding them in bondage; my husband called upon her master, and had some talk with him, who did not see the matter in the same light as we did, but at his death, he left her free.

CHAPTER 6

A Working Woman

The Autobiography of Ann Baker Carson

SUSAN E. KLEPP AND SUSAN BRANSON

"All mothers are working mothers." This twentieth-century slogan gains its piquancy from a play on the word "work," which means both to labor and to contribute to the economy. Most women in the past, as in the present, have toiled mightily in a private, domestic capacity, performing tasks that traditionally have not been considered "productive" work in the larger arena of the public economy. While there have always been some married women who worked full-time in the public sphere, and many women who worked before marriage and while they were widows, only in the second half of the twentieth century have a majority of married women in the United States participated in the labor market as employees or employers. Still, the full extent of women's domestic labor and paid work in the past has not been fully studied by historians because of a paucity of sources.

Ann Baker Carson (1785–1824) was one of a handful of women in the early republic to leave a written account of her life and labor in both domestic and public capacities. To a greater degree than Elizabeth Drinker, the focus of the previous chapter, Carson worked in both the domestic and the commercial spheres. While the Drinkers were among the city's mercantile elite, the Bakers and the Carsons ranked just above the average Philadelphia household.[1] In her memoirs, Ann Carson com-

---

1. Both the residence and the income of the Baker family were slightly above average for the city, while the Drinker family was among the very wealthiest in Philadelphia. Henry Drinker evaluated his total real estate holdings (not his total wealth) at $100,000 in the 1770s, and his investments expanded after the Revolution. Their primary residence was known as "Drinker's Big House, . . . a large three-story brick mansion of full forty feet in front, door in the center, parlors each side of the hall, elevation considerable, surmounted by a high flight of gray-stone steps, wide and easy." They also maintained a country residence for use in the summers. Elizabeth Drinker usually had seven servants assisting her, "four in the parlor, three in the kitchen," but this does not include the coachman and other male servants working outdoors. Quotations from Doerflinger, *A Vigorous Spirit of Enterprise*, 132, 246. See also Cecil K. Drinker, *Not so Long Ago: A Chronicle of Medicine and Doctors in Colonial Philadelphia* (New York: Oxford University Press, 1937), 17–18; and Crane, "The World of Elizabeth Drinker," 3–28.

The Baker family at their peak of prosperity in the late 1790s lived in a house one-third the size of the Drinkers'. It contained three stories, each measuring 15 by 26 feet, and a small outbuilding that was probably a separate kitchen. The Bakers' wealth was measured primarily by the income of Ann's father, Thomas Baker, who for most of his adult life was a ship's officer. Thomas was promoted to captain during the crisis with France in 1798, but his $900 annual salary was below the average Philadelphia captain's salary of $1,000, and he held that position for only three years before his alcoholism and mental instability made him permanently unemployable. The family's house was their only other valuable asset. In 1798 it was worth $1,225. This ranked at the 61st percentile of all Philadelphia's house assessments, while its 1,330 square feet of living space ranked at the 72nd percentile. The slight disparity in rank between the assessed value and size was because the Bakers lived in an unfashionable neighborhood on the outskirts of town where housing was cheaper. The house Ann Baker Carson rented for a china shop after 1807 was similar in size to the house of her youth, at three stories and 16 by 26 feet. But the entire first floor was given over to the shop, and ten people lived in the upper two stories. The kitchen was on the second floor, not separate from the house as was preferable at the time. The Bakers and Carsons usually had one or two servants, as did two-thirds of Philadelphia households. This information is from the U.S. Direct Tax, 1798, South Mulberry Ward, Microfilm, Mid-Atlantic Branch of the National Archives, Philadelphia; Stuart M. Blumin, *Emergence of the Middle Class: Social Experience in the American City, 1760–1790* (New York: Cambridge University Press, 1989), table 2.1, p. 44, and table 2.4, p. 51; Smith, *The "Lower Sort,"* table 6, p. 114, and table F.2, p. 233; J.C. [sic], *The Trials of Richard Smith . . . and Ann Carson . . . for the Murder of Captain John Carson* (Philadelphia: Desilver, 1816), frontispiece for floor plan of Carson's shop and house; and Tom W. Smith, "The Dawn of the Urban-Industrial Age:

ments on a host of issues—work, family, marriage, equality, aspirations, values—relevant to understanding women's place in the early nineteenth-century urban economy. Carson provides a wealth of information on the economic activities of one woman and her female relatives, friends, and neighbors as they struggled to maintain a precarious hold on respectability as defined by the emerging middle class.

Born two years after the end of the American Revolution, and growing up amid news of the French Revolution, Carson ardently supported the revolutionary promises of (in her words) "liberty, equality, independence and the rights of man." During her youth, she assumed that women as well as men would enjoy these new rights. Romance and emotional fulfillment were integral to Carson's definition of independence for women, and liberty included contempt for conventional morality when it interfered with her personal desires. But when she wrote her autobiography near the end of her life, she had come to regret her self-reliance and "almost masculine" ideals. This tension between her goals of self-assertion and society's insistence on traditional female obedience, dependency, and docility propelled much of the story of her life.

The daughter of an alcoholic mariner father and a hardworking but timid mother, Carson attended one of the first coeducational academies in America, where she learned to read, write, and sew—basic skills that served her well in later years. While school loomed large in her childhood memories, her formal education was quite limited by twentieth-century standards. Three months of education after having achieved basic literacy was considered sufficient to earn a diploma for a girl. Few girls stayed in an academy as long as three years.[2]

Her childhood came to an abrupt end at age fifteen when her unemployed, sick, and often violently drunk father pressured her to marry a forty-year-old ship captain. It was not a happy union, and her husband left her without financial support for years at a time as his own alcoholism worsened. To earn a living for herself and her four children, Carson toiled as a seamstress and sometimes hired other women to assist her. She also opened a retail china shop in 1807 and used the proceeds to

The Social Structure of Philadelphia, 1790–1830" (Ph.D. diss., University of Chicago, 1980), 64–66.

2. Ann D. Gordon, "The Young Ladies' Academy of Philadelphia," in *Women of America: A History*, ed. Carol Ruth Berkin and Mary Beth Norton (Boston: Houghton Mifflin, 1979), 80.

support her parents, brother, and sisters in addition to her own children. In these enterprises, Carson differed little from numerous other women heads-of-household in the new republic whose manufacturing and retail ventures contributed to the early stages of the industrial revolution.

A composite portrait of women's public economic activities drawn from city directories and censuses helps place Carson in the larger context of early nineteenth-century Philadelphia. Married women whose husbands were present at home generally did not work outside the household or conduct independent economic ventures, at least as indicated in official documents. But not all women were married or lived with spouses who could or would support them; many were single, widowed, or, like Carson, abandoned by their husbands. Women headed 13 percent of the city's households in the 1811 city directory, when Carson kept a shop. More than a third of these women listed no occupation, usually describing themselves as widows or gentlewomen, implying that they did not need to labor for a living. The majority of the white women recorded in official or public documents were independent retailers, providers of services, or producers of wearing apparel who operated on a small scale and clustered in four occupational groups: 31 percent were shopkeepers and hucksters, 21 percent were teachers and nurses, 19 percent were seamstresses and milliners, and 16 percent were boardinghouse keepers. Another 13 percent kept inns or worked as servants or in factories. Not listed in the official records were the thousands of women who worked as domestic servants, wet nurses, laundresses, spinsters, seamstresses, nurses, market women, barmaids, prostitutes, and in other occupations. Those not recorded were usually poorer, less independent in both their economic and familial relations, and sometimes less reputable than the women whose occupations appeared in print. Contemporary ideas of propriety meant that only a few occupations were considered appropriate for respectable, genteel women.[3]

Carson and the female members of her family typified these more independent, more reputable working women. With the assistance of her mother and sisters, Ann Baker Carson ran a china shop, while her sister, Sarah Baker, operated a small school. Their mother took in boarders. In addition, all the women in the family sewed to earn money. Carson's account affords a rare glimpse of the variety of women's money-making activities, about which little is known because it so infrequently surfaces in

3. Claudia Goldin, "The Economic Status of Women in the Early Republic: Quantitative Evidence," *Journal of Interdisciplinary History* 16 (1986): 375–404, esp. table 4, p. 396.

official documents. City directories, for example, listed Sarah Baker's school between 1807 and 1811, but not afterward, and Carson's china shop was listed for only about half the years of its existence between 1807 and 1816. Both the boarding and the sewing work would be entirely unknown to us except for Carson's memoirs. So not only was women's domestic work not viewed as productive labor by contemporaries, but a great many of women's public economic contributions remain invisible to historians due to the silence of the existing records.[4] The public record also reflects the assumption that women had a single occupation, but the autobiography reveals the multifaceted employment of women as well as the importance of supportive friends and kin.

Like her contemporaries, Carson emphasized her contributions to the formal economy as symbols of her success, independence, and middle-class status, but she devalued the domestic labor performed by her and by most other women. Routine housework—cleaning, washing, shopping, and cooking—received scant attention, in part because one or two full-time servants, often African American women, did many of these tasks for the Bakers and the Carsons, and in part because these humdrum chores were too commonplace to mention. It is only by chance observations that we know the Baker women cared for boarders and sewed to earn money. Carson and her mother, like many other women, organized domestic "manufactories." They were labor contractors who sometimes hired live-in seamstresses to help make shirts and other clothing, or who cut the cloth at home and distributed garment pieces to out-workers.[5]

The economic strategies employed by families teetering between comfort and poverty are clearly evident in the memoirs. Carson's family

4. Recent innovative studies have greatly expanded our knowledge of women's lives in the early republic. See Christine Stansell, *City of Women: Sex and Class in New York, 1789–1860* (Chicago: University of Illinois Press, 1987); Laurel Thatcher Ulrich, *A Midwife's Tale: The Life of Martha Ballard, Based on Her Diary, 1785–1812* (New York: Knopf, 1990); Jeanne Boydston, *Home and Work: Housework, Wages, and the Ideology of Labor in the Early Republic* (New York: Oxford University Press, 1990); and Jean R. Soderlund, "Women in Eighteenth-Century Pennsylvania: Toward a Model of Diversity," *Pennsylvania Magazine of History and Biography* 115 (1991): 163–84. The authors of this chapter currently are engaged in a study of the life of Ann Baker Carson.

5. Joan M. Jensen, "Needlework as Art, Craft, and Livelihood Before 1900," in *A Needle, a Bobbin, a Strike: Women Needleworkers in America*, ed. Joan M. Jensen and Sue Davidson (Philadelphia: Temple University Press, 1984), 1–19; Ava Baron and Susan E. Klepp, " 'If I Didn't Have My Sewing Machine . . . ': Women and Sewing Machine Technology," in *A Needle*, 20–59.

repeatedly moved from house to house in and around Philadelphia, constantly adjusting their residence to fit their immediate economic circumstances. The size and the composition of the household also changed as boarders, servants, and employees (usually seamstresses) moved in and out of the home. Even kin were maneuverable. Family members were incorporated into the household during good times and forced out during bad times.

Marriage likewise was occasionally a partial solution for economic problems, despite both the cultural ideal that free choice and romance should govern courtship and the emphasis during the Revolutionary era on individual rights. By 1800, most young adults made their own marriage choices based on mutual attraction and love; parents had, at most, a right to veto a potential match. Still, fathers occasionally arranged the marriages of their offspring, especially in times of economic crisis when the rights of individuals might be sacrificed to benefit the entire family. Ann's father, Thomas Baker, seems generally to have been an authoritarian rather than a permissive and affectionate parent. The marriage of his two elder daughters would lessen his household expenses, and he insisted that they marry at the unusually tender ages of fifteen and seventeen. By contrast, the average Philadelphia woman married at age twenty-one. Only 3 percent of the city's women married before their sixteenth birthday, while just 10 percent were married by the age of seventeen. In general, the custom of later marriages afforded parents less control over the decisions of their more mature and more independent children.[6]

Carson's views about the economy, especially the benefits of industry, commerce, and private enterprise, were in accord with her advocacy of freedom and liberty in social and political relations. The belief that unlimited material expansion promised prosperity for all was shared by many Americans at a time when the most devastating features of an industrializing economy were still in the future. Like many other small producers (see Chapter 10), Carson took pride in the fact that "My business continued prosperous; I daily increased my little capital, and added to my stock in trade." Indeed, this venture brought her the independence and the status that marriage had failed to provide. As an unhappily married wife, Carson posed a question in 1803: "If not to a

6. Klepp, *Philadelphia in Transition*, 74. Another coerced marriage that was as unhappy as Ann Carson's was that of Ann Shippen, described in *Nancy Shippen: Her Journal Book,* ed. Ethel Armes (Philadelphia: J. B. Lippincott, 1935).

husband, where can a woman look for happiness?" She answered it four years later from the perspective of a shopkeeper: "whence did this happiness arise? —from industry. I was now a useful and active member of society."[7]

Carson continually strove to harmonize her economic independence and her precarious middle-class status, on the one hand, with her desire for romantic love, on the other, a quest that would precipitate the later unhappy events in her life. At several points in her narrative she compared the lot of women in marriage with the position of African Americans in slavery. These comments generally occurred after she and her husband quarreled. For Carson, love made a married woman's condition bearable; without shared emotional ties, marriage was merely a form of enslavement for women. Her ultimate failure to combine domestic tranquillity with material independence, and her subsequent regrets about her spirited, autonomous behavior, reflect the contradictions many "respectable" women encountered. It further highlights the disjunction between the revolutionary promise of the universal right to life, liberty, and the pursuit of happiness and the social realities for women in the early republic.

Carson and her family prospered for many years by combining income from her shop, her sewing, and her father's Navy pension. But the economic depression following the War of 1812 and her involvement in a sensational murder case in 1816 destroyed her business and her personal reputation, and created a financial crisis for Carson. She then entered into a lower-class world inhabited by petty thieves, fences, prostitutes, "kept women," abortionists, and counterfeiters. In a desperate attempt to earn money, Carson wrote and published her autobiography, *The History of the Celebrated Mrs. Ann Carson,* in 1822. She died two years later in prison while serving a sentence for passing counterfeit bills. Mary Clarke, the editor and friend to whom Carson addressed her autobiography, published a second edition of her memoirs, "revised, enlarged and continued to her death," in 1838. Excerpts that cover the years between the late 1790s and 1812 are reprinted below from the 406-page second edition of the autobiography, but in a much abridged and edited form.[8]

7. Tom Paine similarly combined a belief in the promise of laissez-faire economics and the ideals of limited government and civil rights for citizens; Eric Foner, *Tom Paine and Revolutionary America* (New York: Oxford University Press, 1976), esp. 145–82. On the ideology of small producers, see Schultz, *Republic of Labor.*

8. Ann Carson, *The History of the Celebrated Mrs. Ann Carson, Widow of the Late Unfortunate Lieutenant Richard Smith . . .* (Philadelphia, 1822). The second edition was published as *The*

The Memoirs of Mrs. Ann Carson

My maiden name you know, my dear Mary, was Baker. My grandfather, on my father's side, was a native of Leicestershire in Great Britain; he was by trade a house-carpenter. Fortune smiled on his industry, and he enjoyed in age the blessings of health, ease and independence. The first alloy to human happiness his family ever experienced was occasioned by the death of my grandmother, for which her children were inconsolable: this event took place when my father was but ten years of age. My grandfather soon after married his housekeeper. This marriage so incensed his children, that my uncle Edward, his eldest son, who had been raised to the same trade as his father, bid adieu to his native place, and embarked for America, which was then a colony, dependent on Great Britain, and at that period looked on by the high-spirited and enterprising Englishmen as the land of *Promise*. On his emigration he brought my father with him, then twelve years of age. At this time the disputes between Great Britain and the colonies (which terminated in the *Independence* of the latter) had commenced; remonstrances and replies were passing, thus, party spirit began to disturb this once happy region. My uncle Edward in a short time became disgusted with the new country and returned to England. My father, having during this short period imbibed a strong portion of the then prevailing mania for liberty, equality, independence and the rights of man, soon evinced his enthusiasm by concealing himself from his natural protector, till he quitted the country; and remained in Philadelphia. After my uncle's departure, my father articled himself to captain Gustavus Cunningham, as an apprentice to the sea. With this man he continued several years, enduring all the severity a harsh and cruel master could inflict; but he was in a land that holds liberty and equality for its motto, and had the prospect of becoming a citizen when his apprenticeship expired: this idea supported him through all his trials and enabled him honourably to fulfill his contract.

Memoirs of the Celebrated and Beautiful Mrs. Ann Carson, Daughter of an Officer of the U.S. Navy, and Wife of Another, Whose Life Terminated in the Philadelphia Prison, ed. Mrs. Mary Clarke, 2nd ed., 2 vols. (Philadelphia and New York, 1838). The excerpts reprinted here include portions from the 2nd edition, 1: 1–77.

My mother's father was a native of Ireland, as was her mother (his name James M'Cutchen), and on their emigration to America they settled near Brandywine-creek, in the state of Delaware; his occupation was that of a farmer. He then removed to Philadelphia, wherein it my grandfather commenced grazing.[9] He was so successful that his family lived in ease and plenty. But in an ill-fated hour, he endorsed notes [for Mr. Garrett] to the amount of all his worldly wealth. The failure of his friend reduced him to penury, while Mr. Garrett, for whose debts my grandfather suffered, having secured his property, continued in affluence. Such are the deficiencies of our laws, that while an honest man sinks into poverty, the villain that effected his ruin continues rolling in wealth.[10] This was the death of my maternal grandfather. My grandmother endeavoured for some time to keep her family together. My father then received the old lady into his house, where she remained for several years.

[Carson's parents married around 1782, when her father was twenty-three years old and her mother was only fifteen. Her father served in the American navy during the Revolutionary War, then hired out as a ship's officer or sea captain, employed by merchants trading with the Caribbean islands. Their first child was a daughter.]

Shortly after this, my unfortunate self made my *entree* into this vale of tears, for such indeed it proved to me. I was their second child [born in 1785]; my father continued in the mercantile trade with considerable success; his family increased rapidly; and I can truly say that my days of childhood and youth were uninterrupted scenes of perfect happiness. I received my education at the best seminaries Philadelphia then afforded; no expense was spared. Oh! could we think of the anxiety of our parents, the expense they incur in our education, and the blessing that it may prove to us, how few would waste, as I did, those precious hours, days and years in idleness, frivolity and carelessness; and would teachers be more attentive to the solid and genuine improvement of their pupils, by

9. Graziers fattened cattle for the market by grazing them in suburban fields. They served as the middlemen between the farmers who raised the cattle and the butchers and tanners who bought them.

10. Carson felt so strongly on this issue that she spent time in debtor's prison (c. 1813) rather than renounce her husband's debts or declare bankruptcy. She ultimately paid all his debts by sewing and by selling her furniture and china. Her husband was frequently unemployed and often in an alcoholic stupor by this time. See J.C., *Trials of Richard Smith*, 19.

enforcing the performance of their duties on their minds, not as they do, in a light trifling manner, but with a proper understanding, more real utility would rise from our seminaries than they at present afford; for notwithstanding my carelessness in studying, and repeating my lessons, and the wild volatility of my disposition, I was ever a favourite pupil of my preceptors, who suffered all to pass with impunity. Thus encouraged by those who ought to have restrained me, I grew up a proud, careless, self-willed girl, in defiance of all my fond mother's care, who, having a number of children to share her attention, could not govern me with that despotic authority so essentially requisite for a mind as firm and decided as mine naturally was.

At school I formed an acquaintance with two young ladies and with them passed those hours in diversion that ought to have been devoted to study. I must here also remark on the gross impropriety of associating boys and girls in the same seminaries, as at school I imbibed those seeds of coquetry, which have essentially injured me in the estimation of the world, and acquired many of those opinions that have tinctured my mind with ideas almost masculine. I was ever an admirer of personal beauty, and my young mind even then aimed at conquest; we all had our favorite beaux, and ever ambitious of excelling my companions to attract and hold the attention of the handsomest boys in the school, was an object to my young heart of pleasure and triumph.

My mother's anxiety to make me a proficient in needlework was more conspicuous than the cultivation of my mind (she being a matron of the old school). In this I forwarded her views by an unremitting attention to my work; I therefore became complete mistress of my needle, and ex-celled in plain sewing and fancy work. This gratified my fond parent, who overlooked many of my failings in consideration of my attention to, and excellence in, this her favourite branch of my education; this, and writing, were the only arts I ever excelled in while at school.

My father's profession keeping him so much from home, the care of the family devolved solely upon my mother, and as there were seven of us, all small at one time, viz., five girls and two boys, she could not be expected to have time to eradicate from my mind those weeds. Thus I grew up fair to the eye, and of a pleasing exterior; my heart was warm, rather than tender, generous, humane, and susceptible; affectionate to those that were kind to me; but haughty, cold, and vindictive to those that attempted to controul my will, or restrain my pleasure. Fond of dress, and amply provided with the means of gratifying this my favourite propensity, vanity formed a conspicuous trait in my character. My figure increased rapidly; I was ever uncommonly tall of my age; before I had attained my fourteenth year, I was of the middle stature. This rapid growth gave me the appearance of womanhood, before age justified the idea, or my understanding was sufficiently cultivated to render me a suitable companion for gentlemen of my father's standing in society and profession.

My father's affairs continued prosperous. The luxuries of the West Indies were in our family added to the delicacies of our plentiful city. I knew not a care but to amuse myself or perform my part of the plain work of the family.

[The decline of American commerce at the end of the 1790s limited employment opportunities for Mr. Baker, Ann Carson's father. He started drinking heavily and was overdosed with mercury for an unidentified disease (perhaps syphilis) acquired in the tropics. His increasing debility eventually made him unable to work, and he was in and out of the Pennsylvania Hospital with bouts of "derangement" caused primarily by excessive drinking.]

His keeping my mother in total ignorance of the actual state of his affairs, at length introduced pecuniary embarrassment, that awoke me in common with the rest of my family from our dream of pleasurable tranquility. [My mother] communicated to my elder sister and myself, with many tears, the situation of my father's affairs; and this, I can truly say, was the first sorrow I had ever known. We then agreed to retrench our family expenses, hoping by frugality and economy to continue our independence. This was a precarious support for a family consisting of seven children, five of them girls educated in ease and plenty and taught to look forward to brilliant prospects. Now were their views obscured, if not annihilated, and themselves reduced to comparative poverty. This we bore with patience, and some degree of fortitude; every retrenchment was made in our household establishment consistent with comfort. My grandmother returned to the house of my uncle.

My mother, from habit and her early marriage, was considered by my father incapable of conducting any business, and we knew not what method to adopt to add to our scanty income, my father's pride forbidding the idea of his daughters' learning any trade. Had he permitted my mother to keep a *shoe*, *grocery*, or *grog shop*, now at this time our family might have been opulent, and some of its members probably lawyers, doctors, and even clergymen.

[Ann Carson did begin to learn something about business. Her father, "having confidential letters to write, would trust no one but myself to be his amanuensis." But her parents decided further to minimize household expenses by marrying off the two oldest daughters and sending the eldest son to sea. Nearly halving the number of dependent children would significantly ease the financial straits of the family. Ann's parents consequently encouraged a parade of suitors for their daughters.]

This was my debut in the society of gentlemen; hitherto I had in some measure been secluded from the company of our male visitors. My father, though he had been in the custom of receiving all the young men hospitably, and affording them his support and protection in their naval careers; he being a man of the most humane, generous and liberal sentiments; yet he never suffered his daughters to join the company who, he was aware, were generally dissipated young men. His idea of the delicacy and dignity of the female character was high and almost peculiar to himself; a pupil of the old school, he wished us to be educated as retiring, than as forward girls. Judge then what were my feelings to find myself, as soon as I did, an object of general attention; and to some of admiration. I was released from my leading strings;[11] the watchful eye of my tender parent no longer restrained my youthful and exuberant fancy.

[She was engaged to Captain John Carson, a colleague of her father's and an officer in the U.S. Navy.]

William Carson, grandfather to Capt. C. was a barber, whose ambition induced him to educate his sons to the learned professions. He therefore made the one a doctor; this was Capt. C.'s father. Dr. Carson was sent over to Scotland, to finish his studies at the college of Edinburgh, where he married a Miss Agnus Hunter. This the Carson family considered an improper marriage, and it cruelly disappointed the hopes of his ambitious father, who had formed expectations of uniting his son to some of the affluent young ladies of Philadelphia. They had nine children, all of

11. Toddlers, both male and female, wore dresses with two cords or "leading strings" attached at the shoulders. Parents used the cords to help steady their children's movements. A major milestone in childhood occurred at about age three, when children could walk independently and the leading strings were removed. See Philippe Aries, *Centuries of Childhood: A Social History of Family Life* (New York: Vintage, 1962), 52–54.

whom attained to maturity. John, his eldest son, was apprenticed to William Crammond, then a respectable merchant in this city. . . .

On the termination of the yellow fever in the city, my mother determined to receive a few gentlemen boarders, properly recommended, and for this purpose, a house in Dock-street had been prepared for our reception, to which we removed, and to increase our income eight gentlemen were taken. My father, not aware he had a right to receive the half-pay allowed to officers who had lost their health in the public service, did not immediately solicit for it; and being wholly incapacitated from engaging in any employment by his late deplorable illness, sold his real estate, paid his debt and appropriated the residue to the use of his family.

Precluded by my father's engagements with Captain Carson for me, of amusing myself with our male visitors, a total change took place in my habits and disposition. I became serious, studious and retired; reading was my favourite source of amusement and I pursued it with avidity. I forsook all company, confining myself to a chamber appropriated to the children's use, called the nursery; here with my younger sister Sarah, I constantly passed my time. My eldest sister, Eliza, assisted my mother in the care and management of the family, and being fond of company, my retirement did not interfere with my duty to my parents.

And here I must digress to give you, my dear Mary, my opinion on the danger of suffering a young, ardent, and docile mind, to inhale the sentiments of authors, who, however celebrated they may be for their talents, ease of style, and elegance of language, ought to be condemned for the impurity of their ideas, and the grossness of the scenes they present to the eye of innocent and unsuspecting youth. I do sincerely declare, that half the inconsistencies of my life originated from the perusal of Rosseau, Gesner, Ovid,[12] and various other authors of the same description. . . .

In June [1801] Captain Carson and myself were married by the command of my father, who was lying very ill. I then wanted two months of being sixteen years of age. Oh Mary, how cruel, how weak in parents thus to almost force, or compel a girl, scarce past the days of happy childhood, to enter into a state that forever afterwards stamps her future fate with happiness or miseries extreme. I did not love Captain Carson, to

---

12. Jean Jacques Rousseau (1712–78) was a French writer and philosopher who espoused reason, liberty, and emotion and who was often critical of conventional morality. Salomon Gessner (1730–88) was a Swiss writer of prose idylls, and Ovid (43 b.c.–a.d. 17?) was a Roman poet whose works include some erotic poems.

that passion I was a perfect stranger. It is true, my girlish vanity was flattered by his dashing appearance, elegant figure, and handsome face; nay my pride was gratified by being the bride of a United State's officer, and my sense of right satisfied by my obedience to my parents in becoming his wife.

[Within a few weeks of their marriage, John Carson left the U.S. Navy, "as there was no war," and he sailed for India, having obtained "a lucrative situation" on board a commercial vessel.]

I must proceed rationally and methodically. On the sailing of Captain Carson, I returned to my family. Here I found a great change had taken place during my absence; my father had been again removed to the hospital, as the return of his malady rendered it dangerous to suffer him to be at large. My sister Eliza, after our return, went to reside with her mother-in-law, Mrs. Hutton.

During Captain Carson's absence, the yellow fever broke out in Philadelphia; all the family were immediately sent to the country, except my parents and myself.[13] I remained with them, as they refused to quit the scene of danger, and I knowing no duty superior to that I owed to them, determined to remain also, even at the risk of life. Mrs. Harriot Moore was my particular friend, became my companion. She very soon caught the prevailing epidemic, and I became her only attendant and nurse, as a nurse was not to be procured for love or money. From her my mother caught the infection. We had then three or four boarders, and only one servant, the other having quitted us as soon as Harriot took sick. During this day of peculiar distress, Nathaniel Hutton [brother of Ann's sister's husband] evinced the sincerity of his attachment to me; forgetting all apprehensions for his own safety, he participated in my fatigues, setting up with my patients part of the night that I might enjoy that repose so requisite to enable me to support the fatigues of the day; the morning he generally passed in shooting birds for them, as all kinds of poultry were scarce and dear. Thus were his days and nights devoted to my assistance, nor could a father's commands remove him from the city, or my abode. My mother soon recovered her health, but my poor Harriot languished, drooped and died. The next day beheld me a victim to the same cruel disease that then was making its ravages through the family.

13. On the seasonal yellow fever epidemics in Philadelphia during these years, see Chapters 7 and 8.

[Captain Carson returned from India at this point and became furiously jealous of Nathaniel Hutton's presence. Nat certainly was infatuated with Ann, and she, in turn, considered him a close friend.]

Captain Carson now determined on having an establishment of his own; he therefore rented a house in Lombard-street, which he furnished in a genteel manner, and thither I removed. This was my first departure from my family, and to me the house appeared as a tomb, no fond parents to cheer me with their approving smiles, no kind sister to converse with; in sad and gloomy state I sat, my mind sunk and depressed by the death of Harriot, and the loss of Nat's society, which habit had rendered pleasing. I was really miserable; to this I may add Captain Carson's paroxysms of ill-temper, which was a continual source of grief to me. I learned to scorn and despise him, only regarding him as a slave does an austere master whom he is compelled to obey, and to whose authority he must submit. I began to recriminate and became in my turn his tyrant. I was no longer the mild, tender, gentle girl I had thitherto been, yet something I must be, nature did not create me for a *non entity*, so I became a heroine, and bravely bid defiance to Captain Carson's authority.

The unfortunate Mary Wolstonecroft, when forsaken by the ingrate Imly, sought consolation in the theory of religion for a time, and the practice of philosophy; she justly observes in her letters from Norway,[14] none but the Creator can fill the heart he has formed with confidence of not being forsaken. Would to heaven I had followed her plan, and sought the happiness from above, man had robbed me of, but of religion I knew only its external formalities.[15] I was young, the world called me handsome; I had been admired, and, the gossip Fame said, beloved tenderly, ardently; by a man, young, sensible, accomplished and attractive. My tyrant was madly jealous, my heart was untouched with love for any man.

[John Carson sailed for the West Indies after two months in Philadelphia.]

14. Mary Wollstonecraft (1759–97) was most famous for her writings advocating political and civil rights for women, especially *A Vindication of the Rights of Woman, with Strictures on Political and Moral Subjects* (Boston: Peter Edes for Thomas & Andrews, 1792). Her *Letters Written During a Short Residence in Sweden, Norway, and Denmark* (1796) were addressed to Gilbert Imlay (1754?–1828?), her lover and the father of their child, who had taken advantage of her absence to establish himself with another woman. A modern edition of the *Letters* has been edited by Carol H. Poston (Lincoln: University of Nebraska Press, 1976).

15. No advocate of religious formalities, Wollstonecraft sought happiness primarily in personal, emotional terms.

Soon after his leaving Philadelphia I discovered I was in the way to become a mother; this gratified me as I hoped the little stranger would henceforth be a bond of unity between us, and that I might yet see some domestic happiness with him. I once more commenced a career of pleasure; card parties, plays, and dress, succeeding each other, occupied my time, and banished the remembrance of the last two months I had passed with my capricious *cara sposa*.[16]

A few months disgusted me with house-keeping; I gave up the establishment and returned to my mother. Here I was not long suffered to remain idle, being engaged in preparing for my expected stranger, whose birth I hourly anticipated, when the (by me dreaded) yellow fever made its appearance in the house next door to our's, and I was soon compelled to remove to the small town of Darby, a distance of seven miles from Philadelphia, where my mother had taken a house. A few hours after my arrival at this little village I gave birth to my first son, John.[17]

Here we resided six weeks, and I was treated with all the politeness and hospitality we could desire or expect. My health daily improved, and in nursing the little urchin, and tracing in his baby face the likeness of his father, I found a new source of pleasure. —Nat Hutton, my books, and all were forgotten as I pressed this my first darling boy to my bosom. Oh! what language can portray the rapture of a fond mother as she hangs delighted over the first pledge of matrimonial love: all Captain Carson's caprices, jealousies, and petulancy were forgotten and forgiven as I kissed the baby lips of his infant boy, and felt I was a mother.

My son John was near five months old when his father arrived. I resigned all my former pursuits, devoting my time wholly to the care of my infant, who was seldom or ever from my sight, and whose growth was rapid as his beauty fascinating; his grandfather almost doted on him, as did the whole family. I was now to feel a portion of that pride and pleasure I then enjoyed, when smiling I presented to Captain Carson his infant cherub and he enraptured received from my arms the darling babe, and pressed him to his parental bosom. This fondness for his son I gladly hailed as the harbinger of peace, and future domestic happiness; and for a time I enjoyed a degree of peaceful pleasure I had never expected.

16. Italian for "beloved bridegroom."
17. John Carson was born September 13, 1803, and baptized on June 18, 1805, at the Third Presbyterian Church of Philadelphia.

On Captain Carson's return I was again established in a house of my own in Front-street, and he soon after took the command of the Pennsylvania packet, then in the East India trade. I shut up my house and fixed my residence with my mother; thus endeavouring, by seclusion from society to preserve that unblemished reputation which ought to be every woman's care.

[Ann Carson moved from her mother's house in rural Montgomery County to Philadelphia and then to the home of the Hutton family outside the city, where "Nat was almost a constant visitor" for six weeks. She afterwards returned to her mother's house.]

My principal employment was nursing my boy, but all my leisure hours were devoted to reading. My sister Sarah had attained to the age that rendered her an agreeable companion. Together we pursued our studies nor ever found the day too long. This rational scheme of life I pursued, and lived happily in the bosom of my family, till the return of Captain Carson again recalled me to the busy, bustling haunts of men. My dearest boy could, at his father's return, walk, and lisp papa.

[The domestic quarrels soon began again.]

I had married Captain Carson without loving him. The flame his kindness kindled in my heart one day, his stormy temper extinguished the next; accustomed to the kindest treatment in his absence, from all my family and friends, and experiencing only the extreme of misery when with him, at my own house, both became alike hateful to me; for can human nature love a being that tantalizes, teazes, and even domineers over her—impossible. The slave toiling beneath the burning sun, and shrinking from the lash of a cruel overseer, can still anticipate a respite from his labour when the sun shall have sunk down beneath the western waves, or be secure if he fulfills his duty by performing the task marked out for him. But alas! I could never find a mitigation of my sufferings, night or day; a word, a look, might raise a storm in his mind. Thus was my naturally haughty temper rendered fierce and intractable from self-defence. To tell the truth, I was a spoiled child, and never could from my infancy endure the slightest contradiction. If Captain Carson ever presumed to command me, I recoiled with abhorrence from this assumption of power; and, when after our differences, his harshness melted away, and he would sue for forgiveness, I would repay him back with scorn and contempt.

I was very young when married to him, my heart unbiased by any attachment; he had received my unreluctant hand and vows of fidelity. Had he then endeavoured to gain it, my heart would soon have accompanied them; but his haughty soul disdained to try to gain the affection of a girl he fancied bound to love him, and like the Turkish bashaw, who, when his female slaves are endeavouring to attract his attention by their blandishments, haughtily throws a handkerchief to the happy she with whom he condescends to pass an hour. So did Captain Carson fancy that I was compelled to meet and return his love, when he condescended to be in a good humour. To this kind of conduct, I never could or would bend. I was an American; a land of liberty had given me birth; my father had been his commanding officer; I felt myself his equal, and pride interdicted my submitting to his caprices. Therefore the ill treatment I received from him (but which many a simple wife might consider good) I resented. Thus we lived: can any thing on earth equal the misery of matrimonial infelicity? —to find a tyrant where we expected a soothing companion, and to know that dire suspicion is corroding the bosom on which we depend for protection, sympathy, consolation and confidence. If not to a husband, where can a woman look for happiness?

[John Carson sailed for India.]

After his departure, I returned to my mother's abode, and resumed my former habits of reading, which I pursued with avidity, until interrupted by the illness of my son. I wrote to Dr. Proudfit in Philadelphia, who advised my immediate return to this city. With his advice I complied, and for many months every other care subsided in maternal anxiety for this my darling boy. It pleased God to restore my son to perfect health, as the skill of those two medical gentlemen, Drs. Proudfit and Wistar, both eminent in their profession, made a perfect cure, and my bosom once more became tranquil. After his recovery, finding myself lonesome, I took boarding with Mrs. R. in Third-street, opposite the Mansion-house hotel, where I resided for some time, until my family's return to the city.

By the active exertions of my mother, my father had been placed on the half pay establishment; their circumstances were therefore easy, although not so affluent as my mother desired. With her I again went to reside, until Captain Carson's return. She had taken a house in Front-street below Catherine: to this house I removed from Mrs. R's. I knew no care, no discording domestic jars destroyed my peace, my health was good, I grew tall and of a full firm figure.

[Years passed with only an intensification of marital conflict. Two more children were born, and John Carson was again absent. The year was 1807.]

I had now been one year without receiving any means of support for myself and children from him. The money he left me on his going to Baltimore, was rapidly wasting away, and I found that I could not depend on Capt. C. for a renewal of my funds, when they would be exhausted. I had never been accustomed to any employment, except needle-work for myself and family. How then could I seek for it?—from the rich and great?—that seemed impossible—my soul shrunk from the idea. Of business I knew nothing; yet something I must do, else become the victim of penury, or a dependent on my parents, who had a large family and very slender income, my father's half pay being then their sole dependence. After devising and revising a variety of plans, all of which my mother opposed, saying, as none of the family had ever been in business, I could not expect encouragement, and would quickly exhaust my finances in stock, which would lay dead on my hands. My mind ever active and enterprising, was not to be intimidated by her imbecile doubts and false pride. Independence was my idol, and I resolved, flattered by hope, and impelled by my guardian angel, to endeavour to realize my plans. I therefore sold all my superfluous furniture, and as Capt. C. had brought me a considerable quantity of china in the early stages of our marriage, which, at this time, was getting scarce, as the India trade was very much embarrassed by the national disputes between Great Britain and these States which terminated in the late war [the War of 1812]. Those articles were therefore to me a valuable acquisition, as I had determined to enter into the sale of china and queens-ware.[18] I therefore rented a house in Second-street [for $500 per annum], a part of the city well calculated for business, where I commenced with a slender capital; and being, as I thought, too young to live entirely alone in so public and exposed a situation, I prevailed on my parents to remove to the same house, and reside. Thus protected by parental care, I entered into business, with hope, confidence, and activity. Heaven smiled on my endeavours, and prosperity crowned my exertions; peace and plenty were the inmates of my humble dwelling; industry is the parent of both, as indolence is that of vice, want, and misery. I now had no leisure for painful reflections, or dis-

18. That is, porcelain and stoneware.

agreeable retrospections; time flew on downy pinions; the day was never too long, for I was usefully, pleasantly, and profitably employed. My children engrossed my affections, and promised to amply reward my paternal cares of them. My sisters were my companions, my parents my friends, the public patronage was equal to my most sanguine expectations, and I was happy. Yet whence did this happiness arise?—from industry. I was now a useful and active member of society; I lay down with ease and arose but to be content and happy.

> I envied not the rich and great,
> Contented with my humble state.

PART FOUR

Marriage, Mortality, Migration

CHAPTER 7

Marriage and Death

The Records of Gloria Dei Church

SUSAN E. KLEPP AND BILLY G. SMITH

The Reverend Nicholas Collin was rector of Gloria Dei, a Swedish Lutheran Church in the Philadelphia suburb of Southwark, from 1786 to 1831 (see Figure 9). During his tenure, Collin recorded in five volumes the marriages, births, and deaths that occurred among the predominantly working-class people Gloria Dei (also called Old Swedes' Church) served. These documents not only contain genealogical information and records of significant events in the lives of laboring Philadelphians, but also provide valuable insights into the daily existence of the city's poorer citizens. Brief descriptions of their housing, health, attire, recreation, behavior, material conditions, familial relationships, and attitudes are included.[1]

1. For information about Collin, see Amandus Johnson, *The Journal and Biography of Nicholas Collin* (Philadelphia: New Jersey Society of Pennsylvania, 1936). Collin's records

Figure 9. "Preparation for War to Defend Commerce. The Swedish Church Southward with the building of the FRIGATE PHILADELPHIA," 1800. Gloria Dei (the Swedish Lutheran Church), identified with an "A," is in the background. From W. Birch and Son, *The City of Philadelphia . . . As It Appeared in 1800.* Courtesy of the Historical Society of Pennsylvania.

Besides recording the ages, previous marital status, parents' names, and place of residence of brides and grooms, Collin commented on many of the unsuccessful applicants for marriage. His observations reveal a great deal about the attitudes of poorer Philadelphians concerning marriage, personal relationships, and individual independence. As early as November 30, 1789, Collin began making notes in the marriage register of his church. Starting in January 1794, he set aside a section of the

are at the Pennsylvania Genealogical Society, Historical Society of Pennsylvania, Philadelphia. For a more extensive discussion of them, see Klepp, *Philadelphia in Transition.*

register that he entitled "Remarkable Occurrences Concerning Marriage." "The continuance of licentious manners and defective laws," Collin subsequently explained, "renders necessary the recording of such incidents as may prove the prudence of my conduct against blame for cases against which no caution can secure, and also to instruct my successor on the rules of proceeding, so necessary in the lamentable disorders of the society." Entries in the "Remarkable Occurrences" appear through November 17, 1818, although Collin continued thereafter to include other comments in the marriage register itself. Collin's attention to his commentary was sporadic. There were notations every week or month in some years, but hardly any at all in other years. The record is particularly valuable because Gloria Dei was the city's most popular church for weddings in Collin's tenure, during which he officiated at the marriages of more than 3,000 couples from Philadelphia and the surrounding countryside. One reason for the large number of ceremonies was the widespread belief that it was especially lucky to be married in Old Swedes' Church.[2]

Collin denied many applicants for marriage for a host of reasons. By Pennsylvania law, written parental approval was required for all marriage applicants younger than twenty-one years old. To protect himself from both legal action and irate citizens who had not approved the betrothal of their dependents, Collin demanded evidence that minors had obtained the consent of their parents, guardian, or master. He consistently refused to perform the ceremony for young men and women without both the permission of their parents and freedom papers proving that they had completed their apprenticeship, indenture, or, in the case of blacks, that they were not slaves. Because property might be at stake, Collin also declined to marry some older couples without their parents' approval if their family name was the same as a nearby inhabitant of "respectable station." Other applicants of the age of majority had to prove their single status or the death of their previous spouse. More than half of all couples Collin refused failed to show proper evidence (see Table 3). Some were subsequently married in Gloria Dei, but most did not reapply. Collin also would not join blacks and whites, although he believed that "these frequent mixtures will soon force matrimonial sanction."[3]

2. Quotation from entry dated January 1799. On Gloria Dei Church, see Lillian Ione Rhodes, *The Story of Philadelphia* (New York: American Book Company, 1900), 82.
3. July 2, 1800.

Table 3.   Irregularities of Marriage Applications,
Gloria Dei Church, 1793–1818

Reason for Refusal	Percent of Refusals
No Evidence	
Of independence, both parties	24.1
Of independence, woman	16.8
Of independence, man	11.3
Improper Behavior	
Drunk, levity	6.6
Late hour	8.4
Request for clandestine marriage	14.2
Detected in a lie or fraud	4.4
Coerced marriage	4.0
Bigamous marriage	3.3
Interracial marriage requested	1.7
Remarriage, certificate lost	1.1
Disparity of ages	1.1
Request for divorce	.6
Miscellaneous other	2.4
Total	100.0%
Sample number	274

SOURCE: Calculated from data in Susan E. Klepp, *Philadelphia
in Transition: A Demographic History of the City and Its Occupational Groups, 1720–1830* (New York: Garland, 1989), 97.

Fraud, the independent attitude of young people, bigamy, and premarital sex contributed to the "extreme want of order" that Collin found in
America. A great many applicants resented the existing laws, feeling that
they unjustly infringed on their natural rights—perhaps a legacy of the
rhetoric of the American Revolution. After being refused marriage because he did not possess his freedom papers, one shoemaker left with a
"miff, saying he was free and independent," reported Collin. The man
"behaved otherwise civilly," Collin observed further, "but has no idea of
civil order. If one or two other clergymen refuse he will probably either
quit the woman, or live with her without wedlock." Many others evinced a
similar contempt for law and custom, often tinged with class consciousness.
Thus, when Collin turned one man away for not having his freedom papers, the intended "bride's sister abused me for this hardship to the poor,
tho' I told her similar precaution is taken with people of all conditions."[4]

4. Quotations from May 11, 1801, November 8, 1806, and April 3, 1795.

Political and religious regulations were not the only ones that chafed against the libertarian ideals of many applicants. A couple refused for not having the permission of the woman's father "thought it very odd, as many others, having no idea of parental authority." Minors often scandalized Collin with demands to be married without the consent of their parents, instead "insisting on their capacity and right of choosing for themselves." These attitudes suggest the continuing struggle between generations during this period over who would make important life decisions for young people. That so few middle- and lower-class parents even attended the wedding ceremony of their children further indicates that many couples selected their own mates.[5]

The lack of serious purpose displayed by many of those who came to be married exasperated Collin. One woman whom he refused to marry because neither she nor her partner had brought evidence responded (according to Collin's notes), "If I do not now marry him, I never shall, for I may marry his rival," to which Collin replied in writing: "Liberty! Liberty, in a shape often seen by me! Wretched manners!" Liberty it was, but in the sense of impulsiveness as well as freedom. The ultimate in impulsiveness can be found in one man's retort to a refusal, as reported by Collin: "The bridegroom gave as a strong reason for his importunity, that his love was so violent that he might suffer if he refrained from bedding with her that night."[6]

Marriage was occasionally contracted for appearance's sake, to legitimize temporary affairs, or merely to provide access to a respectable inn. After a short time, one or another of the partners would either desert or return to the minister and inform him of some fraud, usually bigamy, and the marriage would be annulled. The frequency with which mariners were betrothed on the night before their departure suggests a similar ploy. One man was bold enough to admit to such a purpose, requesting "a certificate of marriage to be filled up, but without performance of the rites, that he might have opportunity of bedding with the woman any place, as she was to be his fellow traveller for a year." At times the complexities of the fraud imitated the intricacies of eighteenth-century art, as in the case of *The Vicar of Wakefield*. In Collin's words, "Martin Murray's wife

5. Quotations from July 15, 1805, and July 1797. On the struggle between parents and children about the marriage decision, see Daniel Scott Smith, "Parental Power and Marriage Patterns: An Analysis of Historical Trends in Hingham, Massachusetts," in *The American Family in Social-Historical Perspective*, ed. Michael Gordon, 2nd ed. (New York: St. Martin's Press, 1983), 87–100.

6. Quotations from May 29, 1797, and May 1805.

came to know if her husband was lately married. Three years ago she was married to him by a fellow who assumed the clerical character, Joseph Cassel, as she afterwards learnt, and who signed the certificate John Smith, this her husband took from her three weeks after."[7]

Some instances of fraud concerned bigamous relationships, of which apparently a large number existed. Some "New England men, as well as other Americans," Collin observed, "not seldom have 2 or more wives by getting married in diverse places."[8] One case involved the collusion of a husband and wife to marry her to a third party so that the husband would be clear of her debts.[9] In other instances, various women, described as "strumpets," "hussies," and "town drabs," brought drunken men to wed. This may have been a method for women of easy virtue to marry, or a form of extortion that their vows would later be "forgotten" for the right price. So common was this type of swindle that Collin eventually tired of recording every such occurrence. Pregnant women and their prospective husbands often applied for nuptials, imploring Gloria Dei's pastor to antedate their marriage certificate.[10] A number of couples, like their modern counterparts, chose to beget children and live together without the benefit of ceremony. Many of those who decided after several years to legitimize their union also requested antedated certificates.[11] Collin steadfastly refused to participate in these deceptions.

The machinations of the couples who applied for marriage should be read with caution. They were recorded precisely because they were exceptions. Moreover, Nicholas Collin was biased; he disliked Philadelphians, believing that they behaved like heathens. He was an elitist who mistrusted the liberty of the lower classes, the young, and women. Collin blamed much of their freedom on "false ideas of liberty," assuming that

7. Quotations from August 1817, and June 17, 1797. Mr. Thornhill used a false priest in order to marry a number of wives; Oliver Goldsmith, *The Vicar of Wakefield* (1803; reprint, Worcester, Mass.: American Antiquarian Society, 1965), 403.

8. July 2, 1800.

9. June 1, 1796, Gloria Dei Marriage Register.

10. April 1800. In the Early National Period, one in five Philadelphia brides was pregnant or had previously given birth; see Klepp, *Philadelphia in Transition*, 87. Daniel Scott Smith, "The Dating of the American Sexual Revolution: Evidence and Interpretation," in *American Family*, 426–38, presents evidence on the extent of premarital pregnancies in early America.

11. October 19, 1806. For a discussion of the willingness of some ministers to antedate certificates, see Stephanie Grauman Wolf, *Urban Village: Population, Community, and Family Structure in Germantown, Pennsylvania, 1683–1800* (Princeton: Princeton University Press, 1976), 259–61.

society had been more orderly in an earlier day.[12] Yet, as Gottlieb Mittelberger remarked in the 1750s, "Liberty in Pennsylvania does more harm than good to many people, both in soul and in body. They have a saying there: Pennsylvania is heaven for farmers, paradise for artisans, and hell for officials and preachers."[13]

The most significant change may have been that during the Revolution laboring people embraced an ideology that enabled them to articulate their own views of morality without the cloak of deference. And in terms of marriage, many Philadelphians obviously felt free to act as they pleased regardless of their parents' wishes, to select their mates on the basis of attraction, and to disregard laws and customs that interfered with their immediate desires. The late eighteenth-century city did not resemble a "traditional" society as much as a conglomeration of individuals each going his or her own way.

The first section below contains the bulk of the Reverend Nicholas Collin's notes about the "Remarkable Occurrences" concerning applications for marriages from 1794 through 1802. Information about the brides, grooms, and witnesses in the weddings Collin performed during the first three months of 1795 is included in the second section. Collin recorded information about the marriages he performed, in the same format for each ceremony. Thus, on January 1, 1795 (the first entry of the second section), Collin married Mathias Weaver, who was past thirty-five years old ("p. 35"), and Hannah Cabellaw, who was at least twenty-nine years old ("p. 29"). Mathias did not know whether his parents, Mathias and Susannah, who lived in Germany, were alive or dead. Hannah's father was deceased, and her mother, Elizabeth, resided in Germany. Both Mathias and Hannah were residents of Philadelphia. The entry for January 2, 1795, specifies that Arthur Davison and Rebecca Mela presented evidence ("Ev. p.") for and witnessed the wedding of George Adams and Sina Boice. All of them were black, and all lived in Philadelphia.

The burial records for Gloria Dei's cemetery contain commentary by Collin on a variety of issues, as well as indications of causes of death, as Philadelphians understood them at that time. Fatalities among young children often were attributed to worms, vomiting, purging, teething, weaning, measles, and smallpox, and adults commonly expired from fevers, diarrhea, consumption, and on occasion from walking barefoot,

12. January 1812.
13. Gottlieb Mittelberger, *Journey to Pennsylvania*, ed. and trans. Oscar Handlin and John Clive (Cambridge: Harvard University Press, 1960), 12–13.

cooling off too fast, and being driven insane by Methodist preachers. Collin was an educated man with a keen interest in medicine, and despite his use of now obsolete terms and his misconceptions about disease, his diagnoses were as adept as those of the best physicians. His registers reflect the precariousness of life itself and the physical hardships so many Philadelphians suffered.[14]

Southwark, where Collin's church was located, was the city's rapidly growing southern suburb. Its population of 5,663 in 1790 increased to 9,621 in 1800 and 13,707 in 1810. During those years the suburbs were the least desirable residential districts because they were distant from the markets, shops, services, and jobs of the central city. Houses were more ramshackle, streets were less often paved, public water pumps were scarcer, and garbage collection was less common, while doctors, pharmacists, churches, and charities were all rarer than in the city proper. Southwark also contained a higher proportion of poorer artisans and unskilled workers than Philadelphia. Laborers, mantuamakers (dress and cloak makers), seamstresses, and weavers were among those who congregated in the suburb because of the cheaper rents. Southwark was also the center of local ship-building. Mariners and ship carpenters lived there, as did artisans who outfitted ships, including coopers, ropemakers, and blacksmiths. The area likewise accommodated a transient population of mariners and their families who moved frequently from port to port throughout the Atlantic world. And the suburb served as the first stop for many newly arrived European migrants, for young artisans just getting established, and for country folk searching for new opportunities in the city.

Gloria Dei Church was among the few public institutions in Southwark, and the Reverend Nicholas Collin was one of the few university-educated professionals there. He was in charge of a congregation comprised primarily of Lutherans of Swedish descent and served the entire neighborhood as a medical adviser, dispenser of charity, social worker, teacher, and interpreter. He baptized, married, and buried almost every-

14. Mortality in Philadelphia is analyzed by Susan E. Klepp, "Demography in Early Philadelphia, 1690–1860," *Proceedings of the American Philosophical Society* 133 (1989): 85–111; Billy G. Smith, "Death and Life in a Colonial Immigrant City: A Demographic Analysis of Philadelphia," *Journal of Economic History* 37 (1977): 863–89; and Tom W. Smith, "The Dawn of the Urban-Industrial Age: The Social Structure of Philadelphia, 1790–1830" (Ph.D. diss., University of Chicago, 1980). On medicine and sickness in early America, see John Duffy, *Epidemics in Colonial America* (Baton Rouge: Louisiana State University Press, 1953); and Richard Harrison Shryock, *Medicine and Society in America, 1660–1860* (New York: New York University Press, 1960). Also see Chapter 8 in this volume.

one who applied, whether they belonged to the church or not. But members did have privileges, one of which was the important right to a free burial. While people could apply for church membership, it was often granted by hereditary right.

The records of interments in church grounds from 1800 and 1801 are reproduced in the third section below. The January 16, 1800, entry for burials can be understood as follows: Seventy-year-old Hester Guest died of "Palsey" (an uncontrollable tremoring of the body), which had afflicted her for eleven years. She was the widow of William Guest, who had formerly lived in Raccoon, a Swedish Lutheran parish in southern New Jersey. Hester was considered a member of the church and therefore entitled to a free burial because her husband's mother's family had been members. Collin's brief genealogical sketch proved her right and justified the absence of a fee to the church coffers. Among the categories of burials were "Strangers," as Collin labeled nonmembers. Their relatives paid ten dollars for an adult's burial and five dollars for a child, although Collin accepted a lower fee in cases of special hardship, which he usually described. Deceased adults who would occupy a full burial plot were separated in the records from children who required only a half plot. In explaining his reasons for allocating the deceased into these groups, Collin inadvertently provided an unusual window on the details of life and death in the Philadelphia suburb.

Part I
Remarkable Occurrences
Relative to Marriages

January 1794

2. Widow Fletcher came to inquire whether her daughter Jane had been married to a young Frenchman, Francis, as they had lately eloped; on hearing that they were not, she forbid the bans,[15] the girl being only 16 years of age, and he a very young tradesman.

---

15. The "banns" refers to the notice of a proposed marriage published in advance to allow people to object to the ceremony if they so desired.

8. A young man of 24 requested me to join him, secretly, to a lady of 18, as he was going on a journey for 3 months and would, til his return, avoid the eclat;[16] alledging that her father was willing, both as to the match and mode. I refused, without personal appearance of the father. Putting the question to him which I had on similar occasions put to an hundred others, "Suppose you come to have a young amiable daughter, would you approbate a clergyman who should not ask your consent?" to which he returned the answer which many others have, "No, I must confess that I would not."

8. Came Margret Power, who was married to John Martin, on the 22d of December last, for a new certificate,[17] as he had taken the first from her, and had left her on the very evening of the marriage. She was a widow, 27 years old, and he 26; natives of Ireland.

8. A negro came with a white woman, who called herself Eleonore King, widow of a sea captain. They were refused.

10. Came a man to ask whether a certain Mary White had been married. She was on the 10th of December last, as per record. He declared her to have been his wife, though she pretended widowhood. He had been from her in New York for 3 years. Note well—Hajams and his wife declared, at the time of marriage, that this woman was pregnant by the party Philip Land.

12. Sunday. At night came a party, and with strong entreaties called me out of bed. On my refusing to marry the couple, they went off in a vicious manner throwing a large stone against the entry door.

21. A man about 35 years of age, entreated me to come as far as Campentown to marry him. On my referring him to Mr. Pilmore, who liveth in that neighbourhood, he said that he was out of town. Next morning I went, enquiring from the tavernkeeper at the Green Tree, I found cause for doubt. I waited on Mr. Pilmore (hearing of his being at home), and was informed that this man had made application, but had been refused until he could produce satisfactory certificates of his being disengaged.

February

1. Rudolph Bartholomew and Alsey Levering, who had a child together, were married.

16. He would avoid publicizing the marriage.
17. A new marriage certificate.

March

2. A Spanish mariner was to be married to a young girl, but did not come. I had requested a certificate from her father, though her mother was to be present, this he could not obtain because the father, who came that day to enquire, had refused his consent until his intended son-in-law had returned from the voyage on which he was going the next day. Same evening, late, came a couple; were refused chiefly because the hour was unpardonable, and no previous notice had been given.

5. McLeroy and Mary Couglin were joined. They had cohabited for six years.

31. Adam Cleland and Lydia Frances, married without fee, being very poor.

April

24. At 11 at night came a party to be joined. I refused in a manner complaisant.

From the 1st of June till 11 of July I was on a tour through New England. Just before a French captain of a privateer came with a young lady, from Baltimore. Begged very hard but were refused.

July

12. Came a man of mature age, to bespeak his marriage for the next day, his bride was an orphan. These came accordingly but she confessed that her father was living; were refused.

September

6. Came a young man, sincerely confessed that his father was not willing—refused, with advice to procure his consent.

7. A young Frenchman would be married without the bride's parents consenting—refused.

Note well—Here are omitted many who came late in the evening, also such as endeavored to procure an antedating of certificates.

12. A drunken man, from Burlington, came with a dirty town-drab; refused, and the man warned of his danger. The company also reproved.

23. The Wiljam Britton upon record for this day, proved to be the son of a person living in Philadelphia, thus the marriage is false.

24. Came a Frenchman with a young woman, brought good evidence but were refused for the present. Next day I went to their lodgings, above the market; in the afternoon they were joined, after previous testimony of an elderly woman, the bride's relation, that her mother, living in New Jersey, would be satisfied, and that she was past 22.

October

28. Came a couple twice, were refused because he was not quite sober; were married next morning.

28. Came a couple from Wilmington, he a middle aged man, she a girl between 20 and 23, to appearance. A female cousin testified that her father had not, for 12 years, spoken to her. Refused till further certificate.

In November three companies, most of these persons drunk, applied in vain.

December

Parents came with their son and a girl, by him pregnant, as they said. He was not free,[18] and therefore refused until his master should certify his consent, the declaration of said parents to the purpose being insufficient.

The licentious manners which in this part of America, and especially in Philadelphia, are evidently striking, and which in matrimonial affairs are so pernicious, render a continuation of these memoirs necessary.

January 1795

6. A non-commissioned officer came with a young woman about 19 years old, whose parents live in the country, about 18 miles from Philadelphia. He strongly entreated me to dispense with certificate of the father's consent. She also appeared very uneasy, but less anxious about the marriage. They were refused.

13. A seaman, belonging to the Danish Ship *Unge Victoria*, came to request me to marry him to a widow. I, in the first instance, sent inquiry to the Captain, who answered personally that he had no further objection than prudential care for the young man's well-being. I enforced this motive on him, but he was determined to get married; I then promised, if she proved clear of impediment. On examination of herself and others, I found reason to believe that she had a second husband living, and refused. They were, however, married by some other clergyman.

In the course of two months several were refused.

18. The prospective groom was still an apprentice or indentured servant.

March

15. Came a young man to bespeak the marriage ceremony for to-morrow, promising to bring certificates.

16. Said person did not come.

April

3. A young couple was refused because he did not produce sufficient proof of his being out of his apprenticeship.

3. A young couple refused because the man could not produce certificates of his being out of his apprenticeship. The bride's sister abused me for this hardship to the poor, tho' I told her similar precaution is taken with people of all conditions.

6. A swedish mariner came to engage my service in his intended nuptials; refused until he produced testimony of the woman's character; warned not [to] forget his national character in this foreign alliance.

5. (Easter Sunday) A young couple came in a chair.[19] Refused on suspicion of being runaways.

20. Two men urged me to marry a woman pregnant by a man who had taken care of her since the desertion of her husband, who had (as they say) cruelly abused her by stabbing, etc., and thereby killing the fetus in her womb. These also remonstrated the impossibilities of procuring legal divorce because of her poverty. Refused with prolix demonstration. Bad manners, crooked laws! Oh when shall I be cleared from this detestable place.

24. Came a young sailor, with an uncle and other company, to be joined to a small young girl. They asserted that her father and mother were dead. Refused.

25. Came 2 men, from the country up Lancaster road, with a young girl who confessed that her mother is living and had given consent. Refused til better evidence [presented].

28. A woman who had been published,[20] came to declare that she had broken off the match on discovering the bad character of the man.

May

7. A young decent couple came without company, seemed to act sincerely, but were refused til certificates should be obtained.

---

19. They arrived in a horse-drawn carriage.
20. The banns for her marriage had been proclaimed.

13. A man about 50 years old came to bespeak marriage with a girl of 18. I advised him to consider better of it. He did not return.

14. A couple after 10 o'clock. Refused as irregular.

23. A decent man used many persuasives to be married without consent from the bride's father. I refused, but offered to confer with [the father] as I knew his whimsical temper.

June

3. A young couple refused. She said that her father does live 200 miles from here, that she left him 18 months ago because her stepmother was unkind. I offered to enquire about her from the family in which she resides, but she refused this piece of service.

18. A young pair, just, as they said, come from Ireland, were refused until a certificate on their circumstances could be obtained from the Captain.

July

15. A young man late from Ireland came to be joined to a young woman, with whom he had a child, and in consequence thereof was threatened with imprisonment by her father. I refused until this man could be heard, but this he, the bridegroom, positively rejected, expressing bitter ill will against his intended father-in-law.

28. A couple of elderly persons came, alledging as a great motive of the intended union, that he had something, and she also which by joining might be worth something. Nevertheless they begged the marriage for one dollar. Refused with the same reasons as frequently are used to such people—that I baptize gratis, visit the sick gratis, aid many poor, bury the indigent without fee, but that marriage is not charity, that if they would swallow less rum they could pay.

September

Some couples refused; one, very decent and both of age,[21] because she was a Friend[22] and could not produce an open certificate thereof from her mother, it being against the statutes of that denomination.

October

8. A young man refused because he did not bring certificate from the girl's father.

21. Both the man and the woman had reached their age of majority.
22. She was a Quaker.

November

2. A couple refused for the want of better evidence. She seemed to be of age, but asserted that her parents live in New York, which wants confirmation.

8. A young couple refused as the bride, about 18, had no certificate from her mother.

30. A couple came to request my parting them. He gets drunk and beats the wife. She seems to have a cutting tongue. Dismissed with proper advice.

December

9. A drunken man came at 9 in the night, urging me to marry him; ill pleased by the refusal.

Runaways advertised in the Gazettes,[23] here registered to prevent my being imposed to marry any of them. Ann Kelly, 20 years old, short, thick. Time of deserting last of April, 1795. James Dunbar, 18 years, 5 foot 7 inch high. Ditto time. Samuel Carty, Salder, 19 years. Samuel Miller, Taylor. George Darman, Irish servant, 20. Susanna Ware, Irish servant, 26 years old. Benjamin Hannis, about 18, pale complexion. Nicholas West, Irish, 20 years. William Gormly, Irish, 19 years old. Elizabeth Henry, about 18, advertised Feb. 8, 1796, servant. Martin G. Parsons, about 70, Johannes Sell, about 25, Dutch servants, advertised March. Thomas King, Country born,[24] about 18, advertised Mar. 18. John Cook, apprentice of James Mathews, Sept. 27, 1796.

Forbidden

Dennis McFardin, about 20. Nicholas Miller. Mary Kinnard. Clement Plumstead. Mary Keen.

February 1796

3. A young couple coming alone, refused until proper evidences were brought. They returned with such the 8th and were married.

March

13. A young girl refused because she had not brought certificate of her freedom; the witnesses appeared creditable.

23. The *Pennsylvania Gazette* was one of the newspapers published in Philadelphia. Advertisements for runaway servants, slaves, and apprentices from that newspaper are reprinted in Chapter 4.

24. "Country born" meant that he was born in America.

May

13. A young man, as he said, merchant's clerk, young though possibly of age, denied because a nephew of a respectable person in town whom I would first consult. The young man said that his uncle never had any regard for him because a poor lad.

13. Two men and four women came. The bride looked very young and seemed much alarmed; she and some of the company said that her parents, formerly of Burlington, were dead. The chief woman, who would give the bride away, pretended to be a sea captain's wife and to live in a street not very distant, said that the girl had been two years her maid. Refused. Note well—They came in chairs, no doubt from the country.

June

18. A young man refused because he would not bring certificate from the girl's father.

July

3. A young couple (though of decent appearance) refused for want of certificate.

5. A young man late from Ireland, who had brought a girl from that country with intent of marriage, refused til he could produce certificates. He pleaded in vain his coming from New York and having no acquaintances in this place.

Two more refused this month.

August

19. A young couple of decent appearance, with several attendants, among them a middle-aged couple who were intimately acquainted with the girl, applied and offered bonds to any amount. Her father, as they said, had given consent, but was out in the country. The young man was going to sea in 2 days. Positive refusal without certificate from her father.

September

25. A young couple refused though they brought as evidence a man whom I had married 1 1/2 year ago. The reason was the girl being young and having no certificate of being free. She has come from England 3 years ago, as they said.

October

29. A young couple of decent appearance and attended by many persons, refused for want of proper certificates. She was but 16 years; her mother lives near Wilmington.

November

15. A Boston mariner was refused though attended by a person who said he was cousin of the bride, and affected that her father (belonging to Burlington) had been abroad on a voyage for 2 years.

The same licentious disorders in public manners render it necessary to continue the notes in the former way.

January 1797

17. A couple came after previous notice; the bride being young, I required peculiar information, and in the course of inquiries found prevarication. A fellow who pretended to be her brother, and asserted that their parents lived in New Jersey, proved to be of Irish origin in this manner: a female of the company, to quiet any suspicion from his dialect, said, without my previous remark thereon, that he was born in Ireland, but his sister here. They were dismissed with advice to the intended bride not to deceive her parents or near friends.

February

12. A couple came alone, of decent appearance and mature age; he about 30, she about 24. The bridegroom hesitated on pretence that her parents had not consented. She reproached him passionately for his infidelity, having so long baffled her. She told me that they had had a child together which is dead. On this he would have consented by a small additional persuasion from me, but I withheld this, yet put the matter to his conscience, with advice to marry her if he thought there was a prospect of happiness.

May

24. A woman desired me to search the records for the marriage of a couple, premising the request with an offer of two dollars if it could be found. I answered that half a dollar only is the charge for the renewal of a certificate. She made me look throu 2 or 3 years, and then said she was surprised that the lady should pretend to being married when she was not. A fresh proof of the artful and still absurd tricks of these hussies.

29. A young couple came, without previous notice, at 10 in the evening. I refused until they brought evidence. The girl behaved with levity, yet earnest desire of the rite. She said, if I do not now marry him, I never shall, for I may marry his rival. Liberty! Liberty, in a shape often seen by me! Wretched manners!

June

Some refused. A man refused because the bride had no certificate from her father.

17. Martin Murray's wife came to know if her husband was lately married. Three years ago she was married to him by a fellow who assumed the clerical character, Joseph Cassel, as she afterwards learnt, and who signed the certificate John Smith, this her husband took from her three weeks after. She had no evidence.

July

29. A couple from Virginia, just come in the stage, sent word about 4 or 5 o'clock that they would be married in the evening. Came, but had no evidence but a Virginian residing here for a short time. The man was middle age; the woman about 20, having no parents, as they said. Refused. Probably runaways.

On the succeeding time may be observed that similar cases happen not seldom: young girls, some 15, coming with improper men, as strangers, etc., insisting on their capacity and right of choosing for themselves; young persons being, or appearing to be, apprentices or servants; persons demanding secrecy. Occasionally, but not often, persons of too near relation applied, as a woman and her first husband's brother's son. (Note well—Some people regard this as proper.) Black and white seem to approach, I having been solicited by several, and well-looking girls.

The continuance of licentious manners and defective laws renders necessary the recording of such incidents as may prove the prudence of my conduct against blame for cases against which no caution can secure, and also to instruct my successor on the rules of proceeding, so necessary in the lamentable disorders of the society.

January 1800

25. Thomas Snowden proved to be a son of ——— Snowden, in Philadelphia. He asserted that he had come from England to the West Indies, when a boy, and from there to Philadelphia; that he was a comedian, belonging to the theater here; that he was not in the least related to any of that name in the city. His bride had assumed a false name, proving to be a daughter of ———.

The deception was more plausible from his having notified his intention of being married by a written message, at 3 o'clock P. M. of same day, in which he mentions himself as a stranger and being unable to pay more than a low fee.

The witness, Thomas Bisset, had heretofore been present at a wedding, and I recognized him. The father of this Francis took him from the partner and sent him off to ———. I declared to him that the marriage was undoubtedly false.

February

2. A very young couple were refused, although they brought several witnesses. The bridegroom said that he was midshipman of a vessel of war, lying at New Castle. Suspicion arose from his very thin dress, and his total want of resemblance with a pretended brother who came as evidence, and was, by his own assertion a mariner, being several years older.

In same month another couple were refused.

March

Beginning of March a couple came at midnight, rapping hard at the door, requesting to be married, as he (being a captain by assertion) was going to sea next morning. Were refused, and did not return.

April

12. An Irishman, about 30 years, came with a young girl, in appearance 17, but as he said 20. They alleged that they had just came from Baltimore, but not in the same stage; that he had left her, but she had followed him, being pregnant by him and near her time. The appearance did not show so much, and how far it went her dress concealed. The fellow was ragged and smelt much of the stable. Her name was that of a sadler and harness maker in this city, but she denied any relation to him. He went away after vain sollicitation, saying that he must try and get married this night to save the girl's reputation.

13. A young couple, both being hired to the Swedish Consul; his father, an Englishman, being hired to a gentleman in the city, had not given his consent, as I required, because this son was a minor; therefore they were refused.

About this time a young man in trade, of good connections, applied three times with earnest sollicitations and offers of reward for being married with ante-dating the certificate, in order to conceal his premature connection with the bride, for whose reputation he expressed great anxiety. I refused with ample demonstration of the necessity for official veracity, and the pernicious consequence of falsifying records. He was under great perplexity how to act. I strongly advised him by no means to delay the performance of the nuptial rites, though his misstep might not be concealable. He did not repeat the request. He offered a generous fee for my trouble, but I declined acceptance of it, being always happy to give salutary advice.

In second week of April, a young officer in the American Army, by birth a Russian, requested being married to a young woman from Reading, alledging that her father had given consent; I refused until he should produce certificate.

24. A young negroe, not free, refused.

27. A young German servant, refused until his master's certificate of consent may be produced.

May

24. A good looking pair came; she was 19, and had, as she said, the consent of her father; I refused until that should be produced. The bridegroom was ill pleased but not indecent in his quick departure.

July

2. A negro came with a white woman, said that he had had a child with her which was dead, and was uneasy in his conscience for living in such a state. I referred him to the negro minister, not willing to have blame from public opinion, having never yet joined black and white. Nevertheless these frequent mixtures will soon force matrimonial sanction. What a parti-coloured race will soon make a great portion of the population in Philadelphia.

2. A captain of a small vessel, Bostonian, came after previous notice, with a genteel girl, 20 years old, and brought her sister and her husband Simeon Dillingham, innkeeper in North Water Street. Though no particular cause of suspicion existed against the assertion of them all that her parents were both dead, that her step-father was living and took no care of her, that she kept house for a gentleman, etc., yet I ventured not to marry her for fear that her father might be one of the Gibs in the city, though all denied any relationship. Such is the standard of honesty in this American metropolis! It is possible that the very evidence had taken false names; besides these New England men, as well as other Americans, not seldom have 2 or more wives by getting married in diverse places.

August

9. A party of Irish came. The bride had been a bound servant to Penrose, in this vicinity, probably she was free, but refused to wait until one of the company should bring a certificate from him.

10. About midnight a fellow, by dialect Irish, waked me by rapping at the door, and insisted on my getting up to marry two couples, promising a liberal reward. I refused because of the improper time.

September

22. A negro wanted to be married to a white woman; he had commissioned a black woman to speak for him. The intended bride warmly pleaded her cause in person. She is a European, her father Irish and her mother English. I refused with complaisance on the ground of public opinion disapproving such wedlocks.

October

A young couple earnestly requested of me to ante-date the marriage certificate by some months, on account of premature intimacy, the man offering money, etc. They acquiesced finally in being married regularly, but could not be made to comprehend my reasoning on the impropriety and many bad consequences of such fraud.

13. A young couple, he 16 years, and she 1 or 2 years less, made earnest sollicitation to be joined. They were attended by a pair not much older. The female being sister of the intended bridegroom, and also, as himself, second cousin of the bride. These two female friends reside in a village 5 miles from Philadelphia, and keep house together. They pleaded the independence of both parties, her parents being dead, his father also, and his mother in the West Indies. The male witness had moreover privately, a few moments before, apprized me of a premature connection. I endeavored to convince them of the necessity I was under to seek information from their next friends or kindred, particularly from the bridegroom's brother, a public officer of respectable character, but in vain. They were dismissed with suitable admonition and gratuitous offer of my future advice, if it should be required. The bride appeared much distressed.

December

26. Two women brought a sailor. He is a native of England, but came a boy to America; is 32 years old, sails from here. Being a little in liquor he was refused, although he and the bride's attendant pleaded his going to sea to-morrow.

February 1801

21. Half-past 10 at night, two couples came, two of them as evidences. The intended bridegroom was said to be a sailor, who must go to sea next morning. Being refused on account of the late hour, they knocked at the door and kept entreating for 15 or 18 minutes.

March and April some cases happened, and I omit particulars because of the similarity, and of my being engaged in other important affairs.

May

11. Being the second day of Vestry,[25] a woman came in the afternoon, during the Vestry dinner, to prohibit the marriage of her daughter with a seaman. She said that said daughter had, at the age of 15, been married by Mr. Turner, to one Starke, a kind of Doctor, without her knowledge. That said person, being now at New York, had sent for her in vain; that she was going to be married to a sailor, therefore forbid the marriage. She also appeared extremely agitated. In the evening a young couple came to get married, after previous notice given in the afternoon. On examination I found the woman's name to be Starke, and that she, on close examination, hung her head and would not give sufficient information; that the destined bridegroom had not been here more than 6 weeks from Hamburg. His Captain was with him. I represented the extreme want of order in America, and the great danger of strangers engaging in such contracts without previous knowledge. I told them how many men, without reason, leave their wives, etc., etc., but that the danger of marrying such women, before a legal divorce, is very great in case of the party injured suing, and advised postponing at any rate. Some of the company did say it might be some other person of the same name. I advised postponing at any rate, and so dismissed them. Spoke also to the captain and bridegroom in German. They departed. Some pleased, some not.

In the summer several refused.

---

25. Collin is referring to the meeting of the people responsible for administering the temporal affairs of the parish of Gloria Dei.

October

29. Two men came, P.M., to bespeak a wedding. The bridegroom was represented as a very genteel, well educated young gentleman who had been appointed Chaplain for one of the Frigates, but on being out of service (the number reduced) had turned shopkeeper. The lady was under age and had not the consent of parents, but the said gentleman would give his bond for my indemnification in case of suit. They were dismissed.

November

5. Two couples of blacks refused for want of certificates. The next day one of the couples returned, the girl had her indentures as free, but the man was a slave, and showed a certificate of consent from his master which appeared suspicious by the badness of composition and hand.

10. A couple from Woodberry, in West Jersey, were refused because the girl, not quite 18, had no certificate from her parents, and the man was also of very disproportionate age, probably 60. Several persons attended them, one a housekeeper in this neighborhood. The girl was very desirous. The old bridegroom boasted of being one of the first men in the said place.

January 1802

12. A young Englishman, settled since a year in Philadelphia, came with a girl of 17, had a decent appearance. After a little demur he told me honestly that her father knew of his addresses to her, but would not consent. I adviced them to sollicit his consent and in [the] mean time postpone the marriage, declaring that I would by no means join them according to law.

In the course of the winter and spring, several persons made earnest sollicitations for ante-dating the certificates, and were told how impossible such grants are, how necessary true statements are in official records.

Some drunken men, brought or came by their own consent, to get married and were refused.

June

14. A company of 4 or 5 brought a man so drunk that he could not stand. He nevertheless expressed great unwillingness to be married. The company endeavored to persuade me that he had given full consent and was not much in liquor, etc. The intended bride was also very desirous, giving for one important reason that putting off the nuptials was an unlucky omen, as she had experienced in her first marriage (she being or pretending to be a widow). I gave to all proper reproaches and dismissed them. Two of the men were so angry at the bridegroom as to give him several thumps.

Part II
Marriages in Gloria Dei Church

January 1795

1. Mathias Weaver, son of Mathias and Susannah Weaver, now or late in Germany, p. 35, and Hannah Cabellaw, d. of dec. Henry and Elizabeth Cabellaw, of Germany, p. 29, both of Philad.

2. George Adams, son of the dec. George and Nelly Adams, late of the island of Curasoe, p. 38, and Sina Boice, d. of the dec. Cuffey and Diana Boice, heretofore of Delaware State, p. 32, both Africans. Ev. p. Arthur Davison, Rebecca Mela, of same race. All of Philad.

3. John Schnider, son of Casper and Elizab. Schnider, in Philad., p. 24, and Mary Earl, d. of dec. Asa Beck and his relict[26] Hannah, in W. N. Jersey, p. 26, widow, both of Philad. Ev. p. John Ward Easby, in Philad., Asa Beck, in W. N. Jersey.

7. Wiljam Burke, son of Paul Burke, in Maryland, and his dec. wife Judith, p. 24, and Susannah Sergeant, d. of dec. Joseph and Sarah Sergeant, heretofore of New Jersey, p. 40. Ev. p. James Gildea. All of Philad.

10. Samuel Hosier, son of dec. John Hosier and his relict Ann, in New York, p. 22, and Letitia Warren, d. of dec. John and Elizab. Warren, heretofore of Ireland, p. 23. Ev. p. Bryon McCraith, Francis McArdell. All of Kensington, near Philad.

10. John Michael Burckhart, son of dec. Philip and Margret Burkhart, heretofore of Philad., p. 41, and Ann Mary Musgrove, d. of Charles and Margret McKean, now or late of Ireland, p. 34, widow. Ev. p. David Clemons, Mary his wife. All of Philad.

11. Thomas McCoughley, son of John and Jane McCoughley, in Ireland, p. 21, and Rebecca Hughs, d. of Duncan and Christina McDonel, in Philad., p. 28, widow. Ev. p. Joseph Wilson, his wife Jane, sister of the bride. All of Philad.

---

26. A "relict" is a widow.

18. John Peter Wright, son of dec. Jacob Wright and his relict Dorothy, in Philad., p. 21, and Ann Jane Durand, d. of John and Cathrine Durant, in Ireland, p. 18. Ev. p. Ann Lea, Levinus Skellinger. All of Philad.

20. John Fisher, son of the dec. John Fisher and his relict Elizabeth, in Bucks City, of Pensilv., p. 25, widower, and Ann Brown, d. of James Alexander, dec., and his relict Lydia, in Philad., p. 25, widow. Ev. p. Lydia Alexander, Joseph Burden. All of Philad.

21. John McMullen, son of James and Sarah McMullen, in Ireland, p. 28, and Elizabeth Campbell, d. of John Dixon, in Ireland, and his dec. wife Mary, past 36, widow. Ev. p. Arthur McConnel, Elizab. McMullen. All of Philad.

21. Charles McCalla, son of Michael and Nancy McCalla, in Ireland, p. 20, and Sarah McGloghlin, d. of James McGloghlin, dec., and his relict Sarah, in Ireland, p. 20. Ev. p. John McFeale, Ann, wife of Thomas Cannon. All of Philad.

22. Laurence Deurbreec, son of the dec. Jacques and Clara Deubreece, heretofore in France, p. 26, and Sarah Hugh, d. of dec. Robert Hugh and his relict Elizabeth, in Philad., p. 19. Ev. p. the said Elizabeth Hugh mother of the bride, John George Cresson. All of Philad.

22. Isaac Mason, son of dec. Abraham Mason and his relict Cathrine, of Pensilv., p. 25, and Mary Hababacker, d. of Peter and Mary Dick, in Philad., p. 30, widow. Ev. p. Richard Folwell, Rachel Mason. All of Philad.

24. Archibald Murray, son of Archibald and Florinda Murray, in Ireland, p. 24, and Mary Carr, d. of dec. James and Rebecca Carr, heretofore of Philad., p. 19. Ev. p. Wm. Forsyth, Sarah McClelland, widow. All of Philad.

25. Thomas Hoy, son of John Hoy, in Philad., and his dec. wife Sarah, p. 22, and Eva Cress, d. of the dec. Casper and Cathrine Cress, heretofore of Philad., p. 20. Ev. p. Wiljam Hoy, Samuel Hoy. All of Philad.

29. Wiljam Trump, son of Daniel and Mary Trump, in Philad., p. 22, and Mary Tilford, d. of dec. Robert and Jane Tilford, heretofore of Philad., p. 16. Ev. p. John Brown, uncle of the bride, Nelly Stone. All of Philad.

30. Matheu Moran, son of dec. Dominick and Margret Moran, heretofore in Ireland, p. 46, and Sarah Page, d. of dec. George and Deborah Page, formerly of Philad. City, p. 25. Ev. p. Edward Riley, Elizab. Rutter. All of Philad.

February

4. John McGonnigel, son of Philip and Marget McGonnigel, in Ireland, p. 25, and Biddy Brislin, d. of dec. James and Hannah Brislin, in Ireland, p. 20. Ev. p. John O'Donnel and his wife, the bride's sister, [and] John McCannan. All of Philad.

6. Wiljam Whetherly, son of dec. Wiljam Whetherly and his relict Mary, in England, p. 33, and Ann McKean, d. of dec. James and Marget Martin, in Ireland, p. 32, widow. Ev. p. Hugh McConnel, John B. Pothamus. All of Philad.

7. John Boggs, son of John and Isabella Boggs, of Ireland, p. 23, and Biddy Devine, d. of dec. Michael Devine and his relict Biddy, in Ireland, p. 20. Ev. p. James Mitchell, Margret wife of Emanuel Svain. All of Philad.

8. Samuel Carson, son of John and Jane, in Africa, p. 32, and Sophia Hand, d. of James Hand, in Trenton, N. Jersey, and Tinna his wife, in Philad., p. 24, both Africans. Ev. p. Tinna her mother, Cesar Pickering, Africans. All of Philad. He [is] a servant of Paul Cox, she [a servant] of Joseph Warner; from both certificates of consent were presented.

8. Fredric Quigley, son of dec. John and Eleonore Quigley, heretofore of Ireland, p. 18, and Mary Anderson, d. of dec. Andrew and Mercy Anderson, in East N. Jersey, p. 22. Ev. p. Abigail Anderson sister of the bride, Hugh Gallaher, John McDevet. All of Philad.

16. Wiljam Crotty, son of Morris and Cathrine Crotty, now or late of Ireland, p. 24, and Cathrine Furey, d. of Thomas & Eleonore Gibbons, now or late in Ireland, p. 29, widow. Both of Philad.

17. James Alexander Bartram, resident of Bucks City in Pensilv., son of Alexander Bartram, in England, and his wife Jane in said county, p. 22, and Ann Nicholson, resident of Philad., d. of dec. John and Ann Nicholson, heretofore of Philad., p. 22. Ev. p. Philip Dick, Phebe Palmer, widow, both of Philad.

18. Peter Pierce, son of Henry and Deborah Pierce, in Gloucester City, W. N. Jersey, p. 20, and Mary Smith, d. of dec. Abraham Smith and his relict Mary, in said City and State, p. 21. Ev. p. Thomas Runyan, Joseph Smith. All of Philad.

21. Samuel Moser, son of the dec. Philip Moser and his relict Sophia, in Philad., p. 21, and Marget Grison, d. of dec. John Grison and his relict Jane, in said city, p. 19. Ev. p. Peter Adams, Jane Grison sister of the bride. All of Philad.

22. Wiljam Barry, son of Wiljam and Mary Barry, in Ireland, p. 30, resident near Philad., and Ann Barry, d. of Henry and Mary Carrig, in

Ireland, p. 45, widow, resident of ditto. Ev. p. Peter Dubrej, Marget Carnes, widow, both of Philad.

22. Agnew Campbell, son of John and Jane Campbell, in Ireland, p. 25, and Ann Alexander, d. of dec. Joseph and Mary Alexander, heretofore in Pensilv., p. 20. Ev. p. Tim O'Brien, John Henry. All of Pensilv.

22. Charles Dobbin, son of the dec. John and Marget Dobbin, heretofore of Ireland, p. 18, and Christiana Montgomery, d. of dec. Hugh and Christiana Montgomery, of Ireland, p. 24.

22. Thomas Britt, son of Marcus and Cathrine Britt, in Ireland, p. 30, and Mary Price, d. of Wiljam and Sarah Carell of Ireland, p. 26, widow. These two couples all of Philad., and evidences to each other.

26. Laurence Cashin, son of dec. James and Sarah Cashin, of Ireland, p. 30, and Ester Abenetty, d. of dec. Wiljam and Margret Abenetty, of Ireland, p. 30. Ev. p. Michael Walsh. All of Philad.

26. Jacob Smith, son of Conrad and Hester Smith, in Mifflin City, Pensilv., p. 22, and Cathrine Houston, d. of James Houston, in Philad., and his dec. wife Cathrine, p. 18. Ev. p. John Baxter, widow Margret Stuvdeune, the bride's aunt. All of Philad. Her father is at sea.

26. Cornelius Scanlin, son of Thomas and Elenore Scanlin, in Ireland, p. 30, and Mary Wiljams, d. of the dec. Thomas and Elizab. Wiljams, in Pensilv., p. 26. Ev. p. Edward Scanlan, George Nunemaker. All of Philad.

March
1. Andrew Maclean, son of dec. Andrew and Elizab. Maclean, of Ireland, p. 22, and Margret Giles, d. of dec. Thomas and Margret Giles, of Maryland, p. 18. Ev. p. Samuel Clark, James Smith, all of Philad.

1. Mathew Gold, son of Mathew and Margret Gold, in Lancaster, of Pensilv., p. 21, and Marget Muhlenberg, d. of Michael Mulenberg, in Germantown, near Philad., and his dec. wife Mary, p. 21. Ev. p. Wiljam Crotty. All of Philad.

5. James Shaw, son of the dec. Ezechiel Shaw and his relict Jemima, in Bucks City, p. 21, and Rebecca Smith, d. of the dec. Robert Smith and his relict Seiah, in said City, p. 18. Ev. p. said Seiah her mother, Joseph Wills. All of Bucks City, in Pensilv.

6. Philip Vance, son of the dec. Philip Vance, and of his relict Mary in W. N. Jersey, p. 27, and Mary Midleton, d. of Jacob Midleton, in W. N. Jersey, and his dec. wife Sarah, p. 19. Ev. p. Aaron Midleton, Elizab., his wife. All of Philad.

7. Daniel Bannerman, son of dec. John and Elizab. Banneman, in

Scotland, p. 34, mariner, and Margret Swain, d. of dec. Joseph and Alice Swain, in Philad., p. 37. Ev. p. Thomas White, James Scott. All of Philad.

12. Peter Fox, son of the dec. Ephraim Fox, and his relict Elizabeth, in W. N. Jersey, p. 32, and Elizabeth Hutson, d. of John and Mary Hutson, in Maryland, now or late, p. 25. Ev. p. Robert Levick John Plamer, all of Kent C'ty in Delaware St. N.B.[27] They brought a child named Jonathan, near a year old, whom they declared to be their common child.

12. Thomas Cummans, son of George and Elizab. Cummans, in Ireland, p. 23, res. of Philad. City, and Hannah Berry, d. of dec. Redman Berry, and his relict Eleonore, now wife of George Alms, in Montgomery City, Pensilv., p. 18, resident of said City. Ev. p. Martha Berry her sister, Hugh Hart, of said Montgomery C'ty. N.B. His name may perhaps be Cummins or Cummings, but his own mode of spelling is as above.

15. Wiljam Durvis, son of James and Jane Durvis, in Ireland, p. 20, and Mary Durvis, d. of Oliver and Ann Durvis, in Ireland, p. 20, Ev. p. Thomas Hamilton, Mary his wife. All of Philad.

15. George Griffith, son of Griffith and Sarah Griffith, in Philad., p. 24, and Mary Truck, d. of dec. Thomas Truck, and his relict Mary (now wife of Francis Deport), in Philad., p. 21. Ev. p. Wiljam Gilbert, Susannah Griffith, sister of the above George, all of Philad.

17. James Jockum, son of the dec. Andrew Jockum, and his relict Hannah, in Montgomery City, p. 24, and Deborah Eagens, d. of George and Jane Eagens, in said City, p. 20. Ev. p. Isaac Eagens her brother, all of Montgomery City, Pensilv.

18. Esaiah Hunt, son of dec. Edward and Christina Hunt, last of East Jersey, p. 49, widower, and Eleonore Bee, d. of the dec. Samuel Packer, and his relict Eleonore, in Gloucester City, Jersey, p. 40, widow. Both from Gloucester City, in W. New Jersey. Ev. p. John Moffet, Sarah his wife, of Philad.

19. Moses Lincorn, son of dec. Jacob Lincorn, and his relict Ann, in Kingsess, p. 33, and Barbara Kinch, d. of Caspar Kinch, and his relict Margret, in Kingsess, p. 26. Ev. p. Jacob Yocom, Ann Rambau. All of Philad. City.

19. Jeremiah Mathews, mariner, son of dec. Edward and Abella Mathews, heretofore of New Jersey, p. 20, and Sarah Cox, d. of John Huddel, in Philad., and his dec. wife Ann, p. 27, widow. Ev. p. John Huddel, Sarah Huddel wife of Samuel Huddel, all of Philad.

---

27. "N.B." is an abbreviation for a Latin phrase meaning "note well."

21. St. John Harvey, son of dec. St. John and Ann Harvey, heretofore of Ireland, p. 42, widower, and Margret Cheina, d. of dec. Guy and Marget Charleton, heretofore of Ireland, p. 30, widow, both of Gloucester City, in W. N. Jersey. Ev. p. Joseph Harvey, of Philad.

23. Stephen Conyers, son of the dec. Clement and Marget Conyers, of the Island Bermuda, p. 28, and Susanna Parram, d. of the dec. Wiljam and Hester Parram, heretofore of Philad., p. 19. Ev. p. Jeremiah Mathews, Wiljam Huddle. All of Philad.

24. Joseph Bolton, son of dec. Joseph and Susanna Bolton, heretofore of Pensilv., p. 23, and Hester James, d. of dec. Gabriel and Sarah Cottman, late of Pensilv., p. 24, widow. Ev. p. Charles Dominick, Maria his wife, all of Philad.

26. Moses Levi, son of dec. Henry Levi and his relict Elizabeth, in London, p. 29, and Ruth Crowel d. of dec. Esaiah and Temperance Crowel, heretofore of Cape May, in N. Jersey, p. 18. Ev. p. Joseph Greenway, Hannah Greenway, his wife, sister of the bride's father, all of Philad.

29. Henry Spence, son of Henry and Elizab. Spense, in Ireland, p. 22, and Mary Charlesworth, d. of James and Ann Charlesworth, in Ireland, p. 21. Ev. p. James Dobbins, Cathrine his wife, all of Philad.

29. John Washington Green, son of dec. Solomon Green and his relict Jane, of Philad., p. 20, and Sarah Lone, d. of dec. Henry and Cathrine Lone, heretofore of Philad., p. 19. Ev. p. said Jane Green, George Dyer, all of Philad.

Part III
Burials in Gloria Dei Cemetery,
1800–1801

1800

Members, Grown

January 16. Hester Guest, widow of William Guest, heretofore near Raccoon; about 70. Sick 11 years with Palsey; generally bed-ridden. Note: The mother of said Guest was of the Halton family.

April 29. George, son of William & Mary Cursain, in Front Street Alley, near the new Cemetery. This lad was apprentice to Thomas Mason, Windsor-chair maker in Callowhill Street. He came last Sunday to visit his parents; Walking, after service, with his father, they were accosted by William Henderson an unruly and drunken man; he having been robbed by his wife, who broke open his chest, had taken great ill-will against the said Cursain & his wife, being next neighbours, for not having observed and to him notified his wife's crimes. Meeting him and the son he renewed former abusive language and threatened to murder this man and his wife. The lad, being much frightened, could not on his return home get clear of his terror, in consequence of which he was taken with chills in the night and fits which never left him til he died this morning at 2 o'clock. He had not spoken since yesterday 10 o'clock. He had been a healthy lad; his age was 16 years within a month. His father's membership is from his mother who was a daughter, only one, of Peter Rambo, in Upper Merion.

June 22. Samuel Davis, aged 71 and 1/2. Had been bed-ridden since last week in August of last year. Then he was taken with rheumatism; this after two months fell upon his intestines and caused a very troublesome diarrhea. During the two last months he literally ate almost nothing but drank weak mixtures of wine with water. He also smoked.

July 23. Debora, widow of George May & wife of Patrick Haye, aged 50 and 5 months.

Member's Children

April 19. Ann, daughter of Charles & Elizabeth Grant. Sick only 3 days with hives, or as the name also is, *croup*.[28] She had next before got a very great cold; a co-operating circumstance might be that an issue on her neck below the ear, which she had since 1798, had stopt.

July 12. A still born male of Jacob & Elizabeth Rusk, son-in-law of deceased Nicholas Forsberg.

August 1. John, son of deceased Andrew Armstrong (the Swede) and his relict Brita, born Svanson, 24th January, 1799; disease, vomiting, purging, teething, worms.

August 4. Christiana, near 20 months, daughter of William & Elizabeth Shillingsford, born 12th December 1798. Disease, Worms, vomiting, purging.

August 22. Anne, 22 months old. Sick for 8 weeks with vomiting and purging. Also worms, having voided 4 of the white kind, one of them 1/4

28. "Hives," a corruption of the word "heaves," signified the childhood disease characterized by extremely difficult breathing and a hoarse, rasping cough. At this time in medical history, it was being replaced by the term "croup." Samuel Powel Griffiths, *Domestic Medicine . . . by William Buchan, Revised and Adopted to the Diseases and Climate of the United States of America* (Philadelphia: Dobson, 1795), 558–59.

of a yard long. Daughter of the deceased Francis Pap and his relict Mary, now wife of Peter Andrews, and daughter of William Foy with his first wife.

November 22. Dead born daughter of William & Julip Dairs; his right by the Smith family.[29]

Members, Grown

September 23. Thomas Tallman, 25 years old; son of deceased Augustine Tallman & his relict Margaret; residing in Pottsgrove, of Pennsylvania, daughter of deceased Andrew Bancson. He had been sick for three weeks with a kind of decay. By imprudence he had got into jail and there fell sick.

Strangers, Grown

February 3. Emelia Fultz, 21 years old. Sick 5 days; daughter of Fredric and Patience, both deceased. She had been ailing from her childhood. Last sumer she had a severe intermittent 4 weeks.[30] Now she had been exposed to cold previous to sickness. The disease was malignant, attended with much green-dark pewking, pain and great weakness in the knees, etc, also a mixture of Pleuresy. Being buried at expense of relatives, 8 dollars were accepted.

February 12. Oliver Ross, 60 years, died suddenly yesterday, having gone to work in the morning; had no previous sickness.

Strangers Children

January 8. Female child of Thomas Donnel, 4 months old.

January 17. Female child of James Cogel, 5 weeks old; had fits for 10 days.

January 27. William, 5 weeks and 3 days old. Parent John Coppinger.

January 29. Maria Matilda, 7 weeks old. Disease, hives. Parents Benjamin and Sarah Svane. Note: He is a Swede, sailing under the Swedish flag, in the Bartholomew trade, but not yet become a proper member by election, according to charter, by neglect of petitioning. In consideration of all this and of her poverty, late sickness, etc., I took only half price.

March 1. Captain Peter Foster's male child. Still-born.

March 17. David, son of James Simpson, 1 year old. Note: Another child, a little older, being left alone with it burnt it in playing with fire, which occasioned the death.

March 19. A female child of John Morrison, near 2 years old.

---

29. The daughter of William Dairs could be buried for free in Gloria Dei's grounds because of Dairs's relationship with the Smith family, who were church members.

30. Intermittent: recurring attacks of a fever.

Stranger's, Grown

March 23. Latitia, wife of Thomas Dilworth, about 33. Sick since last August.

March 24. Robert Gage, about 28 years. Sick 4 weeks. Pleuresy. He left a wife and 2 small children.

April 18. Patience, wife of Henry Louderback, 48 or 9 years old. Sick since beginning of winter. This disease owing to the change of the female constitution, usual at her age. In the course of it her bowels seemed reduced within a small space. She was also out of her senses. Being very low spirited she had refused food.

July 29. James Jackson, in Love Lane; about 30.

August 27. James Frazer, past 50. Sick since the 23d in morning, being last Thursday; then was affected as with an intermittent, but by persuation of two men he went down the river, below Wilmington, in an open boat and got worse. Was brought home on Monday evening (day before yesterday) very ill. As he had no property, and had also buried three children here, one dollar was abated; thus 9 paid. He had been a healthy man. The origine of the disease probably getting wet on a raft, his business being in that line, it naturally increased by exposure to the sun and to night air in an open boat, to such a degree as to render him delirious etc., before he got ashore.

August 31. Caleb Combs, 24 years 9 months. Sick nervous fever, joined with previous diarrhea. Mariner. 2 dollars abated on account of the family's want.

September 5. William Johnston, about 40; sick for six weeks. Pleuresy. Chestnut Street near Eight.

November 8. Debora, wife of Peter Flootwell, about 51. Taken sick last Sunday night; died this morning (Saturday). Inflamatory fever of the head, vulgo *head pleuresie*. Had been middling healthy.

November 29. Francis Lovat, past 50. Taken yesterday morning with convulsive fits and died last night between 12 and 1 o'clock.

December 27. John Caldwell, between 30 and 40. Seaman just came from sea; had been ailing a good while, decay. His family from Ireland only 3 months.

Stranger's Children

April 1. Sarah, daughter of William & Sarah Galfrey, 5 months & 2 weeks old. Died Small-pox.

May 16. William, son of deceased William Rook and his relict Sarah. Had fits and eruptions similar to Small-pox.

June 7. Cathrine, daughter of Anne, widow of Christopher White and of John Keen (first husband), near 12 years old. Died of a severe natural Small-pox on the 14th day.[31] Place, Mary Lane, between Cathrine and Christian Streets, near the rope-walk.

July 11. Henry, son of Thomas & Cathrine Babington (in Mead Alley, resident 5 years), born 21st August 1799. Ailing since 3 weeks; the first a diarrhea, afterwards pewking with it.

July 13. Joseph Shaffer, son of Alexander & Sarah Dunbar; one year & 7 months (vomiting & purging).

July 13. Sarah, daughter of Joseph & Martha Smith, 15 months. Vomiting, purging.

July 16. Hannah, daughter of Andrew & Elizabeth Robeson, 11 months. Vomiting, purging.

July 19. Phebe, daughter of John & Elizabeth Saring; six months. Vomiting and purging.

July 20. David, son of Joseph & Sarah Manning, 2 weeks and 3 days old.

July 25. Male child of Mr. Pane; past 4 months. The disease dropsy[32] of the head for 13 days. Had a bad cold when 3 weeks old; then an eruption, which by ointments had been repelled into the head.

July 25. Susannah, born 10th April this year. Parents Christopher and Susannah Mirtetus. Sick but two days with constant fits; had been healthy.

July 30. James, son of Fredric & Mary Wiliams, born 29th of January 1797. Disease, flux[33] without much vomiting. Sick 13 days. Place of residence in 3d Street by Plum.

August 1. Thomas, son of Thomas and Ann Moore, 16 months old; disease not specified.

August 2. Daughter of John & Mary Lancaster, not quite 2 days old.

August 3. Still born, of James & Cathrine Morrison.

August 7. Ann, daughter of John & Anne Hall; 4 months. Disease, Vomiting and purging.

August 7. Mary Ann, daughter of John & Rachel Davey, 21 months. Vomiting and purging.

---

31. Catherine did not contract smallpox through inoculation, a process whereby individuals were infected with the disease, usually at a young age, in order to build up an immunity to it. For a discussion of this procedure, see Donald R. Hopkins, *Princes and Peasants: Smallpox in History* (Chicago: University of Chicago Press, 1983).

32. Dropsy or edema: an abnormal accumulation of serous fluid in connective tissue causing puffy swelling.

33. Diarrhea.

August 10. William, son of Charles & Margret Brommel, 11 months. Disease, Vomiting and purging.

August 25. Robert, son of Robert and Martha Allen, 6 months. Sick 6 or 7 weeks. Vomiting and purging.

August 30. A still-born of John Boyd.

September 2. Elizabeth, daughter of Peter & Ann Green, 5 months old. Disease lax of bowels.[34] He is a Swedish seaman now at sea. The woman indigent.

September 2. Cathrine, daughter of Jacob & Eleonore Waters, 1 year & 17 days. Disease, purging.

September 3. A new born, 7 months, male child of John & Nancy Drake. He has been at sea for 4 months, the funeral is at the expense of friends. Paid 3 1/2 dollars.

September 18. Son of Alexander & Elizabeth Ramsey, a year old. Purging & vomiting. 9 weeks sick at intervals with it. Paid 3 dollars as he [was] buried in the same grave with a former young child.

September 19. Elizabeth, daughter of Alexander & Sarah Adams, 4 years old. Disease, worms.

September 23. George, past 12 months; son of George & Jane Alkorn, in Shippen Street, Number 46. He was inoculated last March, and sickly ever since. Died Vomiting and purging.

September 30. James, son of John & Elizabeth Saring, 2 years, 4 months & 2 weeks. Disease, diarrhea, little vomiting. Had been sick 3 weeks. 2 worms had come from him, one down, in part decaid, the other up, about 4 days ago, with a pointed head, whitish 7 inches long. In Christian Street.

October 27. Elizabeth, daughter of Richard & Judith Woolfall; born 4th of April this year. Disease hooping cough. The father at sea.

November 8. Female, still-born of John & Elizabeth Mansell.

November 19. Son of John Williams, 2 weeks.

November 26. William, son of Samuel & Mathilda McCutchen, 5 weeks.

November 30. Son of Nehemiah & Eunice Eires, ten months old. Disease, hives for three days. Healthy before. In Parram's alley.

December 1. Son of Alexander & Sarah Ray, 10 weeks old or 12. Hives.

December 14. Edmund, son of Edmund & Jane Potter, three years old. Taken sick last Wednesday; died yesterday, 4 P.M. (Sunday).

34. Diarrhea.

December 19. A daughter of Richard Dulap, one year. Hives.

December 25. Daughter of John McConnachy, 4 weeks old.

December 31. William, son of Robert McDorvel, 5 years old. Had the stone and underwent an operation; got a fall on the edge of the gutterstones which caused a swelling that required cutting. The stone taken from him was large as a pea.

1801

Members, Grown

January: None, except the wife of Basset and her child, recorded under the list of Strangers.

February 18. Captain Samson Harvey.

Children

May 15. Rosannah, daughter of George & Hester May, 13 months; disease, hives; it had, some weeks ago, been inoculated. Note: The right of the mother by her father Moses Lang. Her first husband was George Cook.

Members, Grown

May 5. Sarah, widow of Captain George Blewr, daughter of Lindmeyer, sister of Mrs. Nordenlind & Mrs. Ord, in her 64th year.

September 13. Mary, wife of John Taylor, on Tinnicum Island; near 75 years old. Sick for a week with vomiting and purging. Her parents were Conrad and Christina Neithermark. She was born 21st November, 1726.

Children of Members

June 28. Elizabeth, daughter of William & Judith Davis, three years and six months; disease, flux for 2 weeks. His right by the Smith family.

July 21. Leanard, son of Charles & Rebecca Jutkis; 22 months old; died of the so-called blood hives. Born 23d September, 1799.

July 26. A still-born daughter of Mary Featherbridge. His right by the wife who is a daughter of Peter Matson.

July 27. William, son of Garret & Elizabeth Boon, born 20th September last year.

July 30. Cathrine, daughter of Jacob Smith Junior & his wife Cathrine, born 11th January, this year.

Grown Members

October 16. Jonathan Brady, aged about 60. He had been ailing many years with rheumatic pains and consequential infirmities, particularly in the back, but was seldom bed-sick, and had til within six months been able to saw wood some times. The 27th of July last he entered the

Bettering house;[35] grew weaker so as hardly able to walk, and died without confinement or sensible sickness. He and his wife are of Irish race and akin to Swedes. But as they had been educated by Swedes in Ridley and came to Swedes service frequently, this favour was granted.

October 30. Mary, wife of Peter Halton, aged about 33. Sick with intermittent fever for 10 weeks, beginning with vomiting and purging. She had recovered but relapsed by exposure barefoot to damp ground, etc. Note: Said man is 2 years ago from Racoon, where his mother, now Cathrine Davenport, lives. She speaks well Swedish. Her husband, Peter, did also.

November 5. Lydia, wife of William Causey (in Cathrine Street between Front & 2d). She has been in a weak state since her child-bed, six weeks ago, but bed-sick only 5 or 6 days. Dropsy in chief was a leading symptom. Her parents were Zebulon & Drusilla Lock in Rapapo; Members of the Swedish Racoon Church.

November 29. Edward Murray, about 20 years; has been sick with dropsy and consumption. He was buried from the Bettering house where he had been. He was married to a daughter of the widow Louder, whose maiden-name is Helms.

Children of Members

August 5. James, son of Solomon & Rebecca Supplie (now living near Lebanon in 11th Street), 3 years old. Disease, Hives with racking pains in the bowels for a day.

August 9. A still-born male child, not come to full age, of same parents.

October 28. Elizabeth, daughter of Thomas & Mary Loudon, born 22d of September 1796. First she had pewking for 4 days. On 5th day became speechless and was in a high fever, her face very red and flushed. A doctor gave medicine to expell the disorder, supposed the measles. She continued speechless for 2 weeks, until death; only once asking for a bit of potatoe; appeared in no pain, and in perfect senses. Doctor Pasc, who was called, attempted to bring out the measles, but only small watery pimples came out on her neck and breast. Dissection showed the intestines mortified and the heart corroded with many spotted holes.

Strangers, Grown

January 14. Hannah, wife of Zebedia Basset, 23 years, had been in decay, and died in child-bed.

---

35. The bettering house generally served as the last refuge of paupers, either physically capable of working or physically incapable. See excerpts from the Daily Occurrence Docket in Chapter 2.

Children

January 5. A female child of John Connor, 2 weeks.

February 6. John & Cathrine Thompson's son John, above 2 years old. Had a fall 5 weeks ago down the cellar steps, but the hurt was not visible. In the course of a week got sick; disease chiefly in the head. The Doctor said that mortification had taken place.

March 12. Robert, son of Thomas & Mary Ann Crawford, 9 months old. Supposed hives or teeth. Note: They have had two, both dead; the first a female still-born, 2nd 2 months old, died in 1799 during the fever.[36]

Strangers, Grown

February 8. Hannah, widow of John Payton (dead 19 years ago) aged 61. Had been ailing for 3 months and had failed much for 4 or 5 weeks, but was bed-sick not quite 3 days. Was first attacked by a pain in her breast.

February 19. Angus McCloud, aged 51. Had been ailing for some years and subject to fits. In the morning he was taken in or near the market and fell down, was taken home and died.

March 28. Mary, daughter of Andrew & Elizabeth Robeson, born 11th September 1800. Sick 5 weeks with the Scarlet fever. Note: He is from Norway, son of a Swede who married his mother, a native of that country. He came to America [as a] Seaman, but settled here for life.

April 14. Female child, still-born, of Captain Peter Foster.

April 23. Mary, wife of Peter Widdy, seaman, about 26 years. She was brought to bed 5 weeks ago. Her breast had gathered and broke; but she was recovering and yesterday sitting up, died suddenly against all expectation. Paid 9 dollars. The husband being at sea, 4 children left in great poverty and the funeral expenses falling on a brother-in-law.

April 24. Elizabeth Low, or Loe. Had been unwell since last sumer and spit blood at times. She has had four children buried here, as appertaining to one Scarlet, who died in the fever. As her friends must bear the funeral expenses and also for the present take care of her surviving children, they paid only 8 Dollars. Note: As her mother was anxious to bury her in the old cemetery along with her children, I consented, strictly charging the sexton to find out the vacant spot in order to make the grave sufficient deep.

Children

April 24. A male, still-born, of John Hendricks.

April 27. A female child of William Saunders, Seaman, 4 days old.

---

36. The yellow fever epidemic of 1799 was one of several outbreaks of the disease which plagued Philadelphia during the late eighteenth and early nineteenth century.

Strangers, Grown

May 12. Simon Atsong, a German from Frankfort on the river main; had been in America since 1794. Kept shop for a while and got broke; was 32 years old, had a decay for 2 years or more. Buried from the house of Fredric Oeler in Second Street.

May 23. Joseph Wayne, about 40. Ship Carpenter. He went to St. Mary, on the frontier of Georgia, 17 months ago in good health. About 9 months ago he got hurt by carrying a heavy weight. He came back by water having a stormy and wet passage of 20 days, laying also among wet sails at times. He has now been at home six weeks; died in a deep decay. In consequence of the said accident something had broke within him. To the last much blood issued from his ears. He was buried at the expense of his friends.

Stranger's Children

May 6. William, son of George & Cassandra Hews; inoculation of Small-pox. [The eruptions] came out, but flattened.

May 15. John, son of John & Sarah Cole, 11 months, 2 weeks. Sickly from his birth. Had a gathering inward; was inoculated; the pock had come out and turned yellow. The gathering broke and he voided much blood from his ears.

Strangers, Grown

June 16. Peter Frazer, aged 28 years, 7 months 11 days. Disease consumption.

June 16. Mathew Robeson, a person about 30 or less, lately come from Ireland.

June 21. John Howard, native of England, seaman of the American Vessel Surprize, about 30 years. He fell from a horse yesterday near the market in South Street, and broke his scull. As the Landlord, John Green, Spruce Street, Number 94, pleaded the hardship of entering him at his own expence, he paid only 8 dollars.

June 24. Richard Bateman, native of South Carolina; had come from Charleston a week ago for his health, being far gone in dropsy. He had walked about yesterday evening. Craved several light articles of food and drink. Age about 40. Buried from the house of Mrs. Vare, corner of Spruce and Water Street, where he lodged.

July 10. Daniel Conover, aged 21 or more. 6 weeks ago a horse trod on the top of his foot and caused a sore. This had not healed up but was skinned over, when it was renewed by the same accident three weeks ago. Still it had produced no extraordinary consequences in all probability, but for the following accident: On the 4th of this he joined with other young people in the frolies of the days; and being heated by dancing in the evening, laid down upon the grass. The consequence of which was a very great cold. Tuesday his jaw was locked; and could not be loosened by abundance of mercury taken inwardly, and rubbed externally. Samuel Heyms, blacksmith, paid 9 dollars, one was abated on his pleading the great expense of the sickness and funeral of the deceased.

Stranger's Children

May 29. Esther, daughter of deceased William & Mary Williams, 3 years old, disease, Small-pox, natural, very-full, rose and lurrid black. Buried at expense of Thomas Fitzgerald, whose wife is a relation.

June 12. Anne, daughter of Patrick & Grizle Cathall, one year. Was sick with vomiting and purging a good while. 16 weeks ago she got a sore mouth which continued til said malady came.

June 16. Eleanor Jeffrys, aged 13 years. Had her scull broke by a window shutter falling upon her.

June 21. A female child of George Cline, aged 3 months.

July 9. Lambers, son of John & Jane Wharf, 10 months & 8 days.

July 9. Sarah, daughter of Christopher & Susannah Myrtetus, born 1st of this month. Place, Christian Street between 1st and 2d. Paid only two and a half dollars, as the babe was put into the grave of its sister, that was buried last August, four months old.

July 10. Still born of Doile Sweeny.

July 16. John, above 6 months, son of John & Elizabeth Balbier, died with the flux; sick one and 1/2 weeks.

July 20. A son of William Dunwick, 2 weeks.

July 25. John, son of Patrick & Mary McClasky; 13 months. Disorder, Vomiting, purging.

July 26. Sarah Ann, daughter of Daniel & Anne Brown, 14 months, purging, vomiting, also by being weaned and cutting teeth.

Strangers, Grown

July 19. Wife of Doyle Sveney (or Sweeny), mother of the above mentioned child; died in child-bed.

August 4. Martha, wife of Adam Lamb, in Parram's Alley; near 60. Disease, Nervous fever.

September 6. John Hendrick. Died after a few days illness; but his constitution was impaired by excessive drinking.

September 23. John Kean, aged 39; had been long in a Consumptive decay and often bed-sick for the last 20 months. Daniel Kean, Grocer, in Queen Street declared that he is at the expense of his burial, wherefore he paid but 9 dollars.

October 1. Mathias Miller, past 70. Sick 7 days; disease, stranguary.[37] Resides in Front Street near Christian.

October 28. Phipps Brenn, a mariner from New Haven, Connecticut; about 23. Died of a complex intermittent.

November 11. Sarah, wife of Joshua Barns, between Almond & Cathrine Street. Died in child-bed.

November 21. Edward Kirby, son of deceased Timothy & Mary Kirby, 14 years of age. Had been ailing all his life, owing probably to his having been dropt and got his back broke, when a child, 9 or 10 months old. He had been supported by his two sisters, the widow of Doyle & her sister a young woman, and they are indigent; the former having two small children, therefore I took but 8 dollars.

Stranger's Children

July 28. Hannah, daughter of John & Rachel Loyd, 2 years next month. From birth unwell; sick since 2 months; first vomiting and purging, the first not continuing long.

July 30. Henry, son of Henry & Elizabeth Jennings, 8 months old. His father is a ship carpenter, come from Boston to settle here. The passage was 21 days owing to North west winds. They had only coarse bread and salt provisions during a considerable part of the time which in some degree, at least, effected the child.

July 30. Mary, daughter of William Elder, 11 months old. Disease, flux. In South street near 5th.

July 30. Thomas, son of David & Elizabeth Rush, 6 weeks. George street, between South & Shippen. The husband is at sea & the mother poor.

July 31. Mary, daughter of John & Rebecca Robeson, born 23d September 1800. Disease, Natural Small-pox. In Front near Cathrine.

August 1. Elizabeth, daughter of Samuel Fleming, 18 months. Disease Vomiting, purging. Resides in Cathrine Street between 2d & 3d.

August 2. Margret, daughter of Hugh McBrag, 3 weeks old. Resides in George Street.

August 8. Hannah, daughter of Thomas & Martha Smith, in German Street. Disease, Measles, finally mortification in the bowels.

August 10. John, 6 months. Son of Mary Wood; disease, fever, diarrhea, fits. Had been hearty til last friday. Resides Robert Carr's, in Cathrine Street, above 5th.

---

37. Stranguary: a slow, painful discharge of urine produced by spasmodic muscular contractions of the urethra and bladder.

September 1. Mary Ann, daughter of William & Sarah Grimshaw, 18 months, disease, Vomiting and purging, the first which stopt but the other continued.

September 16. John, son of John & Elizabeth McLochlin, 2 weeks.

Strangers, Grown

December 5. James Norris, Mariner, from New England, about 25 years old. Had been sick near a twelfth-month, confined 3 or 4 weeks and died with a diarrhea, etc. Being very poor, the parties concerned paid 9 dollars.

Stranger's Children

September 18. Samuel, son of Samuel & Ann Shepard (corner of Plum & Second Street). Disease, by a fall. His step-sister-mother's daughter by a former husband, had let him fall divers times, and last 2 weeks ago, by which his head had been hurt. Age 7 months & 11 days.

September 29. William, son of William & Elizabeth Williamson, 14 months old. Disease, Dropsy in the head. Resides Penn Street below South.

September 29. Male child of William Wiseman, 2 weeks old, nursed by wife of John Macks, his mother being dead.

October 7. William, son of William & Jane Brooks, 18 months old. Disease, flux. Resides 2d between Christian & Queen. The parents being very poor, having come from Ireland 10 weeks ago.

October 14. Alexander, son of Morgane & Elizabeth Alberris, 2 months.

October 23. Thomas, son of deceased Barney Clayton & his relict Margret, aged 2 years; died in Measles. Paid 3 Dollars. So much was abated on account [of] her poverty, having 3 children now sick of the Measles. Besides, her husband was buried here in December 1799. He laid long in consumption and they had lost all their property in the Moravian Alley that fall.

October 25. Samuel, son of deceased Francis Haines & his relict Elizabeth. Died of Measles. Aged 3 years.

October 31. George, son of William & Ann Elkins, in the vicinity, five weeks old.

November 6. Sarah, daughter of John & Eleanor Steel, in Queen Street, between 1st and 2d.

November 7. Thomas, son of John & Lydia Sylvin, 6 weeks old. Two and 1/2 dollars. The woman assuring me that her husband is a Swedish seaman, and she being very poor in his absence at sea, an half was abated of the usual price.

November 9. John, son of Walter & Jane Foster (corner of Mead Alley in Water Street), 9 months. Disease Small-pox. He had buried a child before and is indigent.

December 8. Rosannah, daughter of John & Mary Veymer; 2 years old. Died of Measles after 2 weeks illness.

December 22. A male babe of Manuel & Abigail Peterson, 5 days old. Paid 2 dollars. He is indigent, supporting himself by carrying fish for sale; he pleaded with tears his desire to enter the babe in consecrated ground, and his being a member of the Lutheran Church, having been brought up in Hesse-Darmstadt, from whence he came two years ago. By his earnest request I also attended the funeral, and he insisted on giving me a string of perch for my trouble.

December 24. William, son of Isaac & Elizabeth Rickards, 4 years last 23d of August. Was sick with Measles and could walk about, but took cold, and fell into an intermittent or bilious fever of which he was sick 16 or 17 days. He is an indigent journey-man taylor, working at very low wages, like many others at this time.

December 26. A still-born, son of James Farley.

December 31. Robert, son of Braycroft, 2 years old; died of Measles.

December 31. A still-born male child of Alexander Taylor. As he had buried a child before & has part of a pew in the church, I was content with 3 dollars.

CHAPTER 8

Zachariah Poulson's Bills of Mortality

1788–1801

SUSAN E. KLEPP

The practice of publishing tables of "vital events" (births, marriages, deaths) was not common in British North America before the middle of the nineteenth century. Vital events, particularly births and deaths, are useful for judging the health of a community, past and future rates of growth, and rates of migration. Since the sixteenth century, most churches had tried to keep records of their members, some congregations more successfully than others, but these notations were rarely analyzed for statistical information. Starting in the seventeenth century, many European cities began to publish the annual numbers of deaths and baptisms on printed broadsides called "Bills of Mortality," and before the disruptions caused by the American Revolution a few colonial towns, notably Boston and Philadelphia, kept similar records. The statistics of births and deaths in Philadelphia published annually by Zachariah Poulson in the first thirteen issues of his *Town and Country Almanac* (1789–1802) are among the first to be collected systematically after the American Revolution. They provide an unusually detailed record of public health during a decade of dramatic contrasts.[1]

Poulson's almanacs provide demographic data about Philadelphia that are superior to any available for late eighteenth-century America. They record the total number of baptisms and burials from Philadelphia's churches and meetinghouses, and the births and deaths of "Strangers"—a category that includes both immigrants and poorer residents who had no church affiliation and who were buried at public expense in the "Stranger's Ground." Each category is subdivided by sex, and the race of each Stranger is noted. For one year at the turn of the century, age distributions are calculated for many of the deceased. These Bills of Mortality preserve the vital events of the entire community—men and women, blacks and whites, churched and unchurched. They also provide information about ethnicity, religious affiliation, and immigration.[2]

The last decade of the eighteenth century was significant. It began with the lowest recorded death rates in the city's history, as disruptions in trade to the West Indies cut off a major source of disease and as some greater attention was paid to sanitation and nuisance abatement by city authorities. Then major epidemics of yellow fever between 1793 and 1805 caused the death rates to soar, as they had previously in the colonial period—a devastating reminder of the fragility of health in a society where there was little understanding of the causes of disease. The period also began with very high birth rates, but within fourteen years births started a sustained decline that would continue, with only a few major exceptions in the 1820s and 1950s, to the present.

The demographic data that Poulson collected and published appear to

1. Poulson's *Almanacs* for 1789 through 1800 are at the Presbyterian Historical Society, Philadelphia. The *Almanacs* for 1801 through 1807 are at the Historical Society of Pennsylvania, Philadelphia. These and all other surviving bills of mortality have been reprinted in Susan E. Klepp, ed., *"The Swift Progress of Population": A Documentary and Bibliographic Study of Philadelphia's Growth, 1642–1859* (Philadelphia: American Philosophical Society, 1991).

2. For example, these bills indicate a higher rate of religious affiliation than does the analysis by Robert Gough, "Towards a Theory of Class and Social Conflict: A Social History of Wealthy Philadelphians, 1775 and 1800" (Ph.D. diss., University of Pennsylvania, 1977), 138. According to Gough, Quakers accounted for 5.4 percent, the Swedish Lutherans for 1.6 percent, and Catholics for 9.8 percent of the population in 1800, but data in Poulson's *Almanacs* indicate that those groups were much larger (see Table 11 below).

be complete. The numerical totals are similar to those found in the surviving, less-detailed Christ Church Bills of Mortality for some of the same years.[3] But how reliable are these statistics? One potential deficiency in Poulson's Bills of Mortality may have been an undercount of births. Like other compilers of Bills of Mortality, Poulson had to rely on the number of baptisms from churches practicing infant baptism. Baptisms do not include those infants who died in the weeks or months that customarily elapsed before christening. Under normal conditions in the United States, an average of 105.5 males are born for every 100 females, but Poulson's data show an equal ratio of newborn boys and girls. Because the initial days and months of life are more fatal to boys than to girls, the equal sex ratio of the baptisms in Poulson's record probably indicates an undercount of the number of children born in the city. Evidence from the Strangers category tends to confirm this argument. Here the basis is births, not baptisms, and the sex ratio is 103.5 males born for every 100 females.

Still, the number of infants that Poulson's records missed was undoubtedly small, because there was another factor that influenced the sex ratio at birth. This was the epidemiological crisis of the 1790s. During medical and nutritional crises, fewer boys than girls are born because males, physically more fragile than females, face a higher risk of spontaneous abortion, just as they are more likely to die as newborns. Philadelphia's population suffered from major epidemics of yellow fever in 1793 and 1798, and during nearly every year between 1793 and 1801 many died of the disease. The sheer number of burials suggests only part of the devastation, because for every person who died one or two others were desperately ill. Other people, especially laborers and the poor, might have escaped yellow fever, but they faced malnutrition as the economy collapsed during the epidemics. Consequently, the lowest recorded sex ratios among the newborn are found during the major epidemics (93 and 96 males for every 100 females in 1793 and 1798, respectively). The congregations closest to the riverfront, where the infected mosquitoes swarmed, were especially hard hit as pregnant women were bitten by the

3. One reason for the slight differences in the baptisms and burials recorded by the two sets of records is that the Christ Church Bills of Mortality covered the calendar year while Poulson's data generally included the period from September to September, or August to August. Scattered bills for the final years of the century are available on microcard, listed as "An Account of the Births and Burials in the United Churches of Christ-Church and St. Peter's," in Charles Evans, *American Bibliography: A Chronological Dictionary of all Books, Pamphlets and Periodical Publications Printed in the United States of America from . . . 1639 down to . . . 1820* (Chicago and Worcester, Mass.: American Antiquarian Society, 1903–59).

diseased mosquitoes, became exhausted from nursing the sick, or failed to get enough food during the crisis. The low sex ratios can be attributed both to an underregistration of births and to the unhealthfulness of Philadelphia after 1793.[4]

Poulson's almanacs do not give a source for the counts of births among Strangers. Because the city did not officially register births until 1820, Poulson, as manager of the Pennsylvania Hospital for the Sick Poor, might have gathered data on births from the hospital and from the Philadelphia Dispensary and the Almshouse. These institutions provided free medical care to the needy. While it cannot be checked for accuracy against any other source, the record on Stranger's births is internally consistent.

White "Strangers" had fewer births than deaths. These more transient Philadelphians gave birth to only 58 children for every 100 burials, while there were 122 births for every 100 deaths in the city's total population. Destitute whites—Strangers in the language of the day—were often infirm, handicapped, widowed, orphaned, elderly, and/or alone. A majority were too young, too old, or too sick to have children, while even the young and healthy adults were sometimes too poor to marry. They were therefore less likely than other city residents to have children, and more likely to die. The impoverished population of immigrants, laborers, and sailors living around Gloria Dei Church in Southwark (see Chapter 7) also experienced a surplus of deaths over births.[5]

4. On the city's yellow fever epidemics, see J. H. Powell, *Bring Out Your Dead: The Great Plague of Yellow Fever in Philadelphia in 1793* (1949; reprint, Philadelphia: University of Pennsylvania Press, 1993), 67, 178; M. A. F. Mansfield, "Yellow Fever Epidemics of Philadelphia, 1699–1805" (M.A. thesis, University of Pittsburgh, 1947); and Smith, *The "Lower Sort,"* chap. 2. The sex ratios of newborns is discussed in William Peterson, *Population* (New York: Macmillan, 1975), 67.

5. On Poulson, see M. Atherton Leach, "Zachariah Poulson: A Study of Danish-American Achievement in Philadelphia in the Eighteenth and Early Nineteenth Centuries," *American Scandinavian Review* 8 (1920): 516–17. Fertility was reduced for the lower classes even within marriage. Chronic illness, malnutrition, poor housing, and the absence of husbands who worked as mariners, soldiers, and laborers all contributed to lower birth rates among laboring people; see Klepp, *Philadelphia in Transition,* 206–218. One final point on the birth data for Strangers is that some of their children may also have been baptized. The cost of a church burial far exceeded that of a baptism, so that poorer families who were forced to inter their members in the Stranger's Ground still may have been able to afford to baptize their children. William Barton estimated that one-third of the births among blacks recorded in Poulson's *Almanacs* had been christened and should be subtracted from the total number of births. While the effect of such duplication would have minimal importance for demographic analysis, it is interesting that Barton made no such adjustment for white Strangers. White families with even a tenuous claim to church affilia-

The circumstances of African American Strangers and white Strangers in the late 1780s and the 1790s were different. At the beginning of this period, all African Americans—whether unchurched and poor, or church members and successful—counted as Strangers. Few white-dominated churches permitted blacks to be buried in their cemeteries, so nearly all African Americans were interred in a segregated corner of the "Stranger's Ground," as the local potter's field was called. By 1797, both the African Episcopal Church and the African Methodist Church had their own cemeteries, to provide the black community with more dignified burials than the hasty, unceremonious interments in the Stranger's Ground. However, the poverty of many Philadelphia blacks, who were no longer slaves but often indentured servants, meant that a majority continued to be buried in the Stranger's Ground.

Still, Pennsylvania's abolition of slavery in 1780 made Philadelphia an attractive destination for the new nation's African Americans, even if few occupations were open to them. Most African Americans were recent arrivals in the city. The black population nearly doubled between 1783 and 1790, and almost tripled during the 1790s as blacks migrated to the city from rural Pennsylvania, Delaware, Virginia, or as far away as the Caribbean. Immigrants tend to be young adults who marry and start families when they reach their destination. The age structure and marital status of the African American population were responsible for the relatively high ratio of births to deaths among black Strangers (133 births for every 100 burials). However, when the data on African Americans are compared with the records on Roman Catholics—another predominantly immigrant group—the effects of the greater poverty of African Americans is clear. Catholics, many of whom arrived from Ireland in the 1790s, christened 188 infants for every 100 deaths, while among the churched and unchurched African American population the ratio was 142 : 100. Both immigrant status and poverty affected the vital rates of African Americans. Compared with other immigrant groups, African Americans had lower fertility and higher death rates, but compared with the poor, white Strangers, African Americans were more successful in forming families.[6]

---

tion apparently might have their members buried or baptized by the church as a charitable act. For Barton's claims, see "Duration of Human Life," *Transactions of the American Philosophical Society* 3 (1793): 37.

6. African Americans in Philadelphia are considered in Nash, *Forging Freedom*. The city's population of Catholics doubled between 1787 and 1801 when as many as 7,000 Irish

Philadelphia burial statistics are more reliable than the baptismal and birth statistics. By the end of the eighteenth century, recording burials was a well-established practice in large cities. Poulson's figures on burials are, however, least likely to be accurate during the yellow fever epidemics of 1793 and 1798. Normal record-keeping broke down when many residents fled the infected city, and when clergymen and sextons fell ill, died, or closed their churches and cemeteries out of fear of contagion. It is therefore not surprising that different sources give different figures for the epidemics. For the twelve-month periods following August 1, 1793, and August 1, 1798, Poulson lists 4,992 and 4,463 deaths, respectively. The Christ Church Bills of Mortality record 5,105 and 4,120 for the calendar years in 1793 and 1798. Historian Tom W. Smith estimates that annual interments may have been as high as 6,085 and 5,348 for those two calendar years. These enumerations of deaths should be considered as low estimates for the epidemics.[7]

To return to the question of the accuracy of these statistics, the conclusion is that Poulson's Bills of Mortality are quite accurate by eighteenth-century standards. Even though a count of baptisms will underenumerate births, the shortfall is unlikely to have been large. The death rates minimize mortality during the two major yellow fever epidemics. These data are, on the whole, the most complete demographic records that survive for late eighteenth-century America.

Poulson's records provide a basis for insights into the social, demographic, and economic characteristics of the city at the end of the eighteenth century. Combined with population figures from the first federal censuses of 1790 and 1800, the data on births and deaths can be used to compute crude birth and death rates. The crude birth rate (CBR) is a measure of fertility that calculates the births per 1,000 population, while the crude death rate (CDR) measures deaths per 1,000 population. The average (mean) Philadelphia CBR for the fourteen years of Poulson's record was 45—somewhat lower than the colonial average of 49, but an indication that the long-term decline in American

---

disembarked at the docks; see Edward C. Carter II, "A 'Wild Irishman' Under Every Federalist's Bed: Naturalization in Philadelphia, 1789–1806," *Pennsylvania Magazine of History and Biography* 94 (1970): 342.

7. T. W. Smith, "Dawn of the Urban-Industrial Age," 89–92. Poulson's records are seriously deficient in enumerating burials in the black Stranger's Ground in 1793. He records only 159 deaths there, while the Christ Church Bills of Mortality list 305. The higher number probably is more accurate, although in most of the following calculations the lower figure is used for consistency.

fertility rates was just beginning in this period. And despite the presence of yellow fever, the average death rate of 35 was a substantial improvement over the average of 45 during the colonial period, when many more diseases swept through an even dirtier city filled with a higher proportion of immigrants.

Compared with modern industrial societies, these rates are quite high. In 1990 the CBR in the Philadelphia region was 18 and the CDR was 12. Public sanitation, central water supplies, and regular garbage collection—as well as advances in medicine, including knowledge of the germ theory of disease, vaccines, and antibacterial drugs—have been major factors reducing the death rate. Family planning, the availability of birth control devices, and changing attitudes toward children have reduced birth rates in industrialized nations. Eighteenth-century Philadephia had vital rates that are unfavorable even by the standards of war-ravaged and famine-stricken Third World countries today. In 1990, for example, Afghanistan had a CBR of 48 and a CDR of 22, and Ethiopia had a CBR of 44 and a CDR of 24. Philadelphia experienced neither war nor famine during the last decade of the eighteenth century, yet its death rates in nonepidemic years equaled or surpassed these most dismal of modern rates.[8]

Crude birth and death rates must be interpreted with care because they do not take into account the characteristics of the "population at risk"—the inhabitants of Philadelphia, in this case. Crude rates are especially sensitive to the age structure of the population. A population with a high proportion of young married couples naturally tends to have a higher CBR because it contains more people in their prime childbearing years, while a population with a great many young unmarried people or elderly people has a lower CBR. Similarly, because humans are most vulnerable to death in infancy and over the age of sixty, a population with a large number of infants or older people usually has a higher crude death rate than a population comprised mostly of adolescents and adults.

Ideally, age-specific fertility and mortality rates should be computed in order to correct for differences in the age structure of populations, but the necessary information on age and sex is often not available to historical demographers. Because federal census takers did not collect adequate

8. Current Philadelphia rates are from the Bureau of the Census, *Statistical Abstract of the United States, 1990* (Washington, D.C.: Government Printing Office, 1990). The data for Afghanistan and Ethiopia are from Carl Haub, Mary Mederios Kent, and Machiko Yanagishita, *1990 World Population Data Sheet* (Washington, D.C.: Government Printing Office, 1990).

age or sex data until 1830, only crude birth and death rates can be calculated, but a few clues about Philadelphia's age and sex structure can help in interpreting these rates. Like the rest of the nation in the 1790s, Philadelphia had a very young population, especially compared with the late twentieth century. Of the free white males living in Philadelphia County in 1790, some 43 percent were younger than sixteen (in 1990 only 22 percent of the nation's inhabitants were under fifteen). The city's youthful age structure in the 1790s was the result both of a high birth rate, which produced a large number of children, and of a flood of immigrants in the 1780s and 1790s. Many of these immigrants married and started families soon after settling in Philadelphia. In the records reproduced below, some groups—such as African Americans and Roman Catholics—experienced very high immigration rates and high birth rates, while others, notably Episcopalians and Quakers, did not attract migrants and had lower birth rates.

Philadelphia's youthful population also partially explains the city's high death rates. Infants and young children are particularly vulnerable to death resulting from poor sanitation, limited knowledge of disease, and neglect. Among Episcopalians, children under five years old accounted for 36 percent of deaths, compared with only 2 percent of all Philadelphia deaths in 1987. Migration also elevated the city's death rates, because migrants were not only more susceptible to new diseases but also introduced and spread infections through the crowded urban environment.

Yellow fever devastated Philadelphia in the series of major epidemics between 1793 and 1805. The first outbreak, in 1793, was probably caused by mosquitoes transported with refugees from the revolution in Santo Domingo. The city's death rates of 26 per 1,000 between 1788 and 1792 more than tripled as a consequence of yellow fever in the autumn of 1793. Yellow fever is a viral disease common in the tropics and spread from an infected human (or monkey) to a new host by the bite of one species of mosquito, the *Aedes egypti*. This mosquito is a domestic species, preferring small, calm bodies of water for its habitat, such as the water barrels on board ships, the rain barrels Philadelphians left next to their houses, or even an undisturbed wash basin or forgotten glass of water. It is domestic too in that it never flies far from the place where it finds its first meal. The mosquito's limited range meant that outbreaks of the disease were quite localized. In Philadelphia, the disease rarely appeared far from the waterfront and almost never in the countryside. Fortunately for Philadelphia, the *Aedes egypti* cannot tolerate cold weather, so each epidemic ended with the first frost of winter.

The yellow fever virus attacks the liver, producing a yellow pallor in its victims and thus giving the disease its name. It is also quite deadly; between a third and a half of those obviously infected go to an early grave. Survivors acquire complete immunity. People who live in places where yellow fever is common often catch mild cases as infants and consequently have a lifelong immunity to the disease. Because yellow fever rarely appeared in Philadelphia, most inhabitants were at risk of catching the disease, but not all residents faced the same probabilities of death. Invalids and the elderly, who were apt to stay indoors and were therefore less exposed to mosquitoes, were often spared. Babies often suffered only mild cases. Immigrants from the Caribbean, Africa, or the coastal regions of the American South sometimes had immunity through previous exposure. And a handful of older Philadelphians enjoyed immunity because of previous epidemics in the 1740s and perhaps in 1762. If the very old and the very young were at less risk of death, it was otherwise healthy young and middle-aged adults who died. In nonepidemic years, 39 percent of deaths among Episcopalians were adults between twenty and sixty years old, but in epidemic years that figure rose to 55 percent. Orphans, invalids, and the elderly were left without family support as these epidemics seemed perversely to single out the most productive residents, not their dependents. The only sure way to avoid the disease was to flee the city, which middle- and upper-class Philadelphians did by the thousands, especially after 1793. Because the poor could not afford to leave their jobs or to support themselves in the surrounding countryside, they were a disproportionate percentage of the fever's victims.[9]

Yellow fever was a dramatic killer in the 1790s, but other diseases were as deadly. Between 1789 and 1801, yellow fever caused the deaths of 18 percent of Episcopalian decedents, while tuberculosis (consumption) caused 24 percent of deaths. Other infectious diseases, including smallpox, whooping cough, measles, diphtheria, and vaguely defined "fevers," accounted for 22 percent of deaths. Convulsions, diarrhea, and other common causes of infant deaths accounted for 18 percent of the total. Deaths of women in childbirth, which now are only 0.01 percent of all deaths in America, comprised 1.5 percent of the deaths. In the late twentieth century, two out of three deaths are the result of cancer, heart disease, stroke, and accidents, but two centuries ago these degenerative and accidental deaths were only 8 percent of the total. A young, mobile

9. Sir Macfarlane Burnet, *Natural History of Infectious Disease* (Cambridge: Cambridge University Press, 1953), 167–69, 334–37.

population with little understanding of infectious disease and with poor sanitation faced very different life chances than people in the late twentieth century. Contemporaries calculated a Philadelphian's life expectancy at birth to be only thirteen to nineteen years at the end of the eighteenth century, compared with seventy-five years in the United States today.[10]

The decade of the 1790s encompassed enormous contrasts. Philadelphia began the decade healthier than it had ever been, with a crude death rate of 25 per 1,000 in 1788 and two births for every death (see Table 13 below). As William Barton commented, "Must not the mind of every American citizen . . . glow with emotions of a virtuous pride, when he reflects on the blessings his country enjoys?" But pride goeth before a fall, and the appearance of yellow fever in Philadelphia after an absence of thirty-one years brought disaster. High mortality levels and faltering birth rates meant that by 1800 the city's rate of natural increase was a mere 5 percent for the decade rather than the 200 percent that optimistic residents like Barton had forecast earlier.[11]

French refugees and their slaves fleeing from the Santo Domingo revolution probably reintroduced yellow fever into the Quaker City. They joined thousands of Irish, Scots-Irish, and Germans on the ocean voyage to Philadelphia and a large flow of itinerants from the American countryside. If the records of Gloria Dei Church reflect overall migration patterns, then about one-quarter of all white migrants to Philadelphia were born in North America; the remainder were European. But the fastest growing group in Philadelphia were African Americans, their numbers expanded by migrants to the city from the countryside, the Upper South, and the Caribbean. Philadelphia was dirty and disease-ridden, but thousands of people sought refuge and economic opportunity there—an indication that as bad as conditions were in the city, they were sometimes worse elsewhere.[12]

If immigration brought infected mosquitoes from the Caribbean, and nonimmune immigrants from Europe, it also stimulated the city's phenomenal population growth during the 1790s. New arrivals contributed

10. Because Episcopalians were comparatively wealthy and financially more able to flee the city during the epidemic, their deaths from yellow fever undoubtedly were not as high as other Philadelphians. Contemporary calculations of Philadelphia's life expectancy are from Barton, "Duration of Human Life," 56.

11. Ibid., 26.

12. The statistics for Gloria Dei are based on my analysis of the Burial Records, 1786–1828, Gloria Dei (Old Swedes' Church), Pennsylvania Genealogical Society, Philadelphia. On the growth of the African American population, see Nash, *Forging Freedom*.

to Philadelphia's economic development. Using Paul Uselding's figures, the monetary contribution of the migrants can be estimated: the social savings (the amount that immigration saved the city in the cost of rearing, educating, and training 21,405 productive members of society) totaled about $7.6 million, and the gross human capital generated by these people (their contributions to the productivity of the city) equaled approximately $31.2 million. As a point of comparison, Pennsylvania's bank capital amounted to less than $13 million in the early nineteenth century.[13]

The large number of migrant laborers affected the course of Philadelphia's industrialization. Local dependence on skilled workers, on labor-intensive work processes, and a slow adaptation of mechanization characterized many of the city's highly specialized industries throughout the nineteenth century. Low capitalization requirements allowed skilled workers to become employers; others fared moderately well in monetary terms but lost their status as independent artisans. Those with few skills faced low wages and increasing competition for work. Immigration provided an abundance of skilled and unskilled labor, and the dominant nineteenth-century pattern of Philadelphia's economy had its roots in the events of the 1790s.[14]

13. The growth of Philadelphia's population during the 1790s was exceeded only in the second decade of the eighteenth century, at the beginning of heavy German immigration, and during the 1840s, when famine stimulated massive migration from Ireland. On the calculation of the monetary value of migration, see Paul Uselding, *Studies in the Technological Development of the American Economy During the First Half of the Nineteenth Century* (New York: Arno Press, 1975), chap. 3. Uselding estimates that 39,300 people (net immigration) arrived in the United States during the 1790s. If, as is estimated above, three-quarters of the white migrants to Philadelphia came from Europe, then roughly one-third of all European immigrants settled in Philadelphia. Uselding uses traditional immigration figures, but another estimate gives 131,800 as the net number of immigrants during the decade. Henry A. Gemery, "European Emigration to North America, 1700–1820: Numbers and Quasi-Numbers" *Perspectives in American History*, n.s., 1 (1984): 304. Even at this higher figure, 10 percent of all migrants must have settled in Philadelphia, which according to the census of 1790 contained just 1 percent of the nation's population. Hans-Jurgen Grabbe, "European Immigration to the United States in the Early National Period, 1783–1820," in Klepp, ed., *Demographic History*, 82, finds 40,810 immigrants to the Delaware Valley in the 1790s. Pennsylvania's bank capital is from Samuel Blodget, *Economica: A Statistical Manual for the United States of America* (1806; reprint, New York: A. M. Kelley, 1964), 159.

14. Many historians have documented the cost of industrialization to individual workers. See Cynthia Shelton, "The Role of Labor in Early Industrialization: Philadelphia, 1787–1837," *Journal of the Early Republic* 4 (1984): 365–94; Bruce Laurie and Mark Schmitz, "Manufacture and Productivity: The Making of an Industrial Base, Philadelphia, 1850–1880," in *Philadelphia: Work, Space, Family, and Group Experience in the Nineteenth Century*, ed. Theodore Hershberg (New York: Oxford University Press, 1984); and Stuart

The different demographic experiences of women and men, and of African Americans and European Americans, during the final decade of the century are evident in Poulson's data. White males suffered high death rates in Philadelphia. European males formed the bulk of the migrants to the city, and because yellow fever was virtually unknown in Europe, none of these men had any resistance to the disease. But lack of immunity was not the only reason for higher death rates among males. Infant boys are more vulnerable to disease than girls, while male laborers experienced job-related hazards, which contributed to their higher mortality levels.[15]

White women generally enjoyed lower death rates than white men. The greater restrictions on women's mobility helped preserve their lives, since they were less likely to be exposed to new disease environments. A greater proportion of women were native to Philadelphia and had contracted the common diseases of the area as children. Females gained protection as well from their greater biological resistance to infection; from the fact that their work, although often debilitating, was not usually as dangerous as men's; and from the custom among the affluent of sending women and children into the country during epidemics. Only in their childbearing years did women face higher probabilities of death than men. But the risk of childbirth began to decline as Philadelphia women increasingly reduced their fertility during the 1790s. Crude birth rates of 50 or more per 1,000 had been the norm in Philadelphia during much of the eighteenth century. The decline in the birth rate to 30 per 1,000 by 1801 signaled the start of a long decline in fertility.[16]

Because the federal censuses of 1790 and 1800 do not distinguish the age or sex of African Americans, the accuracy of estimates of their crude birth and death rates by sex is open to question. But Poulson's data do indicate that African Americans generally had higher crude

---

Blumin, "Mobility and Change in Ante-Bellum Philadelphia," in *Nineteenth-Century American Cities: Essays in the New Urban History*, ed. Stephen Thernstrom and Richard Sennet (New Haven: Yale University Press, 1969), 165–208.

15. Smith, *The "Lower Sort,"* 53–56.

16. For example, women accounted for one-third of the 3,168 recorded arrivals at the port during the 1790s. These figures are calculated from data in Ralph B. Strassburger and William John Hinke, *Pennsylvania German Pioneers: A Publication of the Original Lists of Arrivals in the Port of Philadelphia from 1727 to 1808*, 3 vols. (1934; reprint, Baltimore: Genealogical Publishing Company, 1966), 1:11. For discussions of fertility and mortality, see Klepp, *Philadelphia in Transition*, chaps. 3 and 4.

birth rates and ratios of births to deaths than whites did, a reflection of
the younger age structure of the former group. In nonepidemic years,
blacks suffered higher death rates as well. In part, this resulted from
infant mortality, since a higher birth rate will necessarily produce a
larger proportion of vulnerable individuals. But higher death rates
among African Americans also stemmed from poverty and the resulting malnutrition and lack of affordable medical care. During outbreaks
of yellow fever, blacks sometimes enjoyed lower mortality rates than
whites, because many blacks had previously acquired immunity to the
disease.[17]

This introduction to Poulson's remarkable collection of Bills of Mortality has outlined a few basic points on the demographic conditions of
Philadelphia. More analysis can be done. The different experiences of
the various churches in Philadelphia can be examined in more detail by
looking at births and deaths for evidence of growth or stagnation. The
major yellow fever epidemics had different effects on different par-
ishes. The church's nearness to the waterfront, the relative wealth of
the different congregations, and the number and origins of immigrants
in the churches would all affect the mortality rates. The experiences of
black and white church members, who tended to be wealthier and
better established, can be compared with the experiences of the poorer
and more transient Strangers, both black and white. The impact of the
major epidemics on the birth rate can be examined. Tax records, lists of
immigrants, naturalization papers, court records, medical records and
more could be used in conjunction with these demographic records to
illuminate the experiences of late eighteenth-century urban dwellers.
The rich literature on contraception and falling fertility rates in the
United States can be consulted in light of the information in these
tables. The debates about life expectancy—the impact of new standards
of cleanliness, public sanitation, and nutrition, and of medical advances,

---

17. The 1790 census records 2,150 African Americans in the city, but using the birth
and death records to estimate the population yields a figure of 2,998 (assuming that the
"missing" blacks ended up in the total for whites) or 3,146 (assuming that the missing
blacks were not counted). There would be no major discrepancies with the 1800 census
total using this method of estimation. Data from the first two federal censuses are recorded
in the U.S. Bureau of the Census, *Heads of Families of the First Census;* and the U.S. Census
Office, *Return of the Whole Number of Persons Within the Several Districts of the United States:
Second Census* (Washington, D.C.: Government Printing Office, 1800). Sex ratios among
blacks and whites appear to have been similar. Both groups had a ratio of 118 male deaths
to every 100 female deaths between 1787 and 1801.

changing living standards, and developing immune responses—can be weighed in light of Philadelphia's experience. A series of tables tabulating the statistics published by Poulson, as well as a summary of data on the city's population growth at the end of a crucial decade in the city's history, follows.[18]

18. Poulson's data did not cover the standard calendar year. Instead, figures for the years between 1787 and 1790 include the period between September 1 of one year and September 1 of the next. Statistics for the years between 1790 and 1798 and for 1801 include the period from August 1 of one year to August 1 of the next; figures for 1798–1800 include the period between May 1 of one year and May 1 of the next. Baptisms and burials in St. Peter's Episcopal Church were included in the totals for Christ Church for all but four years in the tables. Poulson offered no information about births and burials among "Negro Strangers" in 1801. The burial data for that year are derived from the Christ Church Bills of Mortality for 1801, while the number of births in that year is an estimate. The total births and deaths in the city in 1801 have been adjusted accordingly. I have corrected the total baptisms and burials in the city in 1799 and 1800, respectively, both of which Poulson had printed incorrectly.

Table 4. Total Baptisms in Philadelphia, 1788–1801

Institution/Group	1788	1789	1790	1791	1792	1793	1794	1795	1796	1797	1798	1799	1800	1801
Christ Church	156	170	165	161	182	175	155	193	177	91	110	207	89	100
St. Peter's	0	0	0	0	0	0	0	0	0	100	117	—*	111	60
St. Paul's	87	68	66	80	101	123	135	73	80	67	41	39	27	55
St. Mary's	268	234	249	254	361	353	240	262	383	417	488	496	320	406
Holy Trinity	0	0	0	50	47	51	68	86	120	72	51	74	93	92
Swedish Lutheran	7	13	15	17	47	49	31	38	45	52	48	25	30	31
German Lutheran	429	413	415	432	436	479	506	437	359	298	292	302	332	308
German Reformed	181	125	158	139	203	218	153	232	198	238	230	127	171	170
Presbyterian														
First	94	50	58	101	37	56	52	43	52	62	55	27	48	47
Second	45	55	67	76	73	69	58	65	96	71	52	53	62	69
Third	121	132	126	134	147	159	161	77	124	121	123	140	136	84
Scotch	28	14	31	26	25	17	21	19	39	17	21	12	9	14
Associate	0	0	0	0	9	7	6	7	7	11	9	9	14	6
Baptist	30	29	30	33	32	33	36	42	52	58	59	41	40	42
Moravian	7	4	7	7	5	6	8	7	9	12	10	9	7	14
Methodist	0	45	40	20	40	39	52	39	32	48	57	14	12	82
Universalist	0	3	4	5	7	9	7	8	4	4	1	0	4	2
Jewish	5	2	3	2	4	3	3	3	3	3	6	4	6	2
Friends	342	308	313	334	340	347	350	363	319	311	308	343	340	163
Free Quakers	28	24	21	11	13	11	17	13	17	18	24	19	17	26
Strangers (white)	218	187	179	178	165	167	181	182	399	402	403	445	524	150
African Episcopal	0	0	0	0	0	0	0	0	15	35	53	61	62	55
African Methodist	0	0	0	0	0	0	0	0	0	47	23	28	49	80
Strangers (Negro)	146	143	146	138	133	140	139	135	317	139	174	173	154	131
Total	2,192	2,019	2,094	2,256	2,407	2,511	2,379	2,324	2,847	2,694	2,755	2,648	2,657	2,189

Source: Poulson's *Town and Country Almanac*, 1789–1802.

*Number not recorded.

Table 5. Baptisms of Males in Philadelphia, 1788–1801

Institution/Group	1788	1789	1790	1791	1792	1793	1794	1795	1796	1797	1798	1799	1800	1801
Christ Church	66	81	79	80	97	90	78	100	91	42	51	107	43	52
St. Peter's	0	0	0	0	0	0	0	0	0	45	45	—*	58	27
St. Paul's	47	31	30	39	48	67	59	41	38	36	21	20	9	28
St. Mary's	145	114	127	125	159	182	100	131	195	195	246	220	166	197
Holy Trinity	0	0	0	26	25	27	33	40	59	38	28	40	48	47
Swedish Lutheran	4	7	7	8	26	23	12	13	26	25	26	14	16	13
German Lutheran	229	216	219	219	221	244	255	227	178	154	151	153	170	156
German Reformed	91	64	85	106	95	123	70	108	100	108	114	66	83	80
Presbyterian														
First	56	23	27	48	15	30	27	17	27	29	28	14	24	26
Second	23	29	29	42	37	34	29	37	51	37	28	26	29	37
Third	67	57	59	61	76	77	82	40	61	59	66	73	69	43
Scotch	17	6	18	12	15	12	11	9	22	11	10	7	1	9
Associate	0	0	0	3	5	4	3	3	3	7	4	5	8	4
Baptist	17	15	14	16	17	15	17	19	25	27	31	22	19	19
Moravian	5	3	3	4	1	5	3	4	3	8	4	3	1	10
Methodist	0	23	19	9	19	21	25	18	15	22	30	6	5	38
Universalist	0	1	2	2	3	4	3	4	1	2	0	0	2	2
Jewish	3	1	1	1	3	2	3	2	2	2	2	2	2	1
Friends	178	151	153	161	164	169	171	176	152	152	160	169	163	77
Free Quakers	16	11	9	5	6	5	8	6	9	8	11	10	8	16
Strangers (white)	125	91	94	87	84	81	92	94	209	197	207	231	291	86
African Episcopal	0	0	0	0	0	0	0	0	7	18	24	26	28	29
African Methodist	0	0	0	0	0	0	0	0	0	26	10	13	20	44
Strangers (Negro)	76	69	67	65	64	69	67	65	157	71	85	90	83	—*
Total	1,165	993	1,042	1,119	1,180	1,284	1,148	1,154	1,430	1,319	1,382	1,317	1,346	1,041

SOURCE: Poulson's *Town and Country Almanac*, 1789–1802.

*Number not recorded.

Table 6. Baptisms of Females in Philadelphia, 1788–1801

Institution/Group	1788	1789	1790	1791	1792	1793	1794	1795	1796	1797	1798	1799	1800	1801
Christ Church	90	89	87	81	85	85	77	93	86	49	59	100	46	48
St. Peter's	0	0	0	0	0	0	0	0	0	55	72	—*	53	33
St. Paul's	40	37	36	41	53	56	76	32	42	31	20	19	18	27
St. Mary's	123	120	122	129	202	171	140	131	188	222	242	276	154	209
Holy Trinity	0	0	0	24	22	24	35	46	61	34	23	34	45	45
Swedish Lutheran	3	6	8	9	21	26	19	25	19	27	22	11	14	18
German Lutheran	200	197	196	213	215	235	251	210	181	144	141	149	162	152
German Reformed	90	61	73	83	108	95	83	124	98	130	116	61	88	90
Presbyterian														
First	38	27	31	53	22	26	25	26	25	33	27	13	24	21
Second	22	25	38	34	36	35	29	28	45	34	24	27	33	32
Third	54	75	67	73	71	82	79	37	63	62	57	67	67	41
Scotch	11	8	13	14	10	5	10	10	17	6	11	5	8	5
Associate	0	0	0	5	4	3	3	4	4	4	5	4	6	2
Baptist	13	14	16	17	15	18	19	23	27	31	28	19	21	23
Moravian	2	1	4	3	4	1	5	3	6	4	6	6	6	4
Methodist	0	22	21	11	21	18	27	21	17	26	27	8	7	44
Universalist	0	2	2	3	4	5	4	4	3	2	1	0	2	0
Jewish	2	1	2	1	1	1	0	1	2	1	4	2	4	1
Friends	164	157	160	173	176	178	179	187	167	159	148	174	177	86
Free Quakers	12	13	12	6	7	6	9	7	8	10	13	9	9	10
Strangers (white)	93	96	85	91	81	86	39	88	190	205	196	214	233	64
African Episcopal	0	0	0	0	0	0	0	0	8	17	29	35	34	26
African Methodist	0	0	0	0	0	0	0	0	0	21	13	15	29	36
Strangers (Negro)	70	74	79	73	69	71	72	70	160	68	89	83	71	—*
Total	1,027	1,026	1,052	1,137	1,227	1,227	1,231	1,170	1,417	1,375	1,373	1,331	1,311	1,017

Source: Poulson's *Town and Country Almanac*, 1789–1802.

*Number not recorded.

Table 7. Total Burials in Philadelphia, 1788–1801

Burial Grounds	1788	1789	1790	1791	1792	1793	1794	1795	1796	1797	1798	1799	1800	1801
Christ Church	131	154	136	171	131	168	400	232	218	82	96	212	78	76
St. Peter's	0	0	0	0	0	0	0	0	0	84	98	—*	74	49
St. Paul's	22	38	36	39	38	44	86	38	46	42	27	58	20	27
St. Mary's	90	65	67	73	130	176	365	189	217	194	226	335	158	170
Holy Trinity	0	0	0	24	13	29	66	56	62	19	16	80	76	39
Swedish Lutheran	15	9	9	11	20	26	96	57	79	97	63	104	78	74
German Lutheran	176	159	203	285	217	253	782	292	295	220	217	512	259	173
German Reformed	79	30	69	128	74	96	309	145	155	123	125	255	100	103
Presbyterian														
First	40	35	35	40	32	41	99	47	50	51	50	69	48	23
Second	34	47	47	57	51	49	157	62	78	59	76	103	52	41
Third	28	47	25	39	24	80	144	92	134	69	111	89	56	45
Scotch	15	13	5	9	11	8	41	21	25	8	14	15	7	9
Associate	0	0	0	4	5	4	15	8	6	8	9	25	15	7
Baptist	12	13	14	17	20	19	67	40	47	40	52	62	32	26
Moravian	4	7	1	2	4	5	17	8	9	9	10	19	8	4
Methodist	0	20	19	13	17	19	60	21	23	21	36	63	18	63
Universalist	0	1	1	2	1	3	3	3	4	5	6	10	2	4
Jewish	2	0	3	1	2	3	3	0	3	2	3	3	2	1
Friends	141	141	154	171	140	146	474	195	210	155	138	214	157	145
Free Quakers	12	11	7	24	15	18	51	19	31	26	30	34	23	18
Strangers (white)	124	142	136	130	184	194	1,598	128	365	187	768	1,878	388	254
African Episcopal	0	0	0	0	0	0	0	0	0	69	33	42	23	19
African Methodist	0	0	0	0	0	0	0	0	0	7	13	13	23	20
Strangers (Negro)	73	64	68	69	116	116	159	106	226	89	139	268	65	343
Total	998	996	1,035	1,309	1,245	1,497	4,992	1,759	2,283	1,666	2,356	4,463	1,762	1,733

SOURCE: Poulson's *Town and Country Almanac*, 1789–1802.

*Number not recorded.

Table 8. Burials of Males in Philadelphia, 1788–1801

Burial Grounds	1788	1789	1790	1791	1792	1793	1794	1795	1796	1797	1798	1799	1800	1801
Christ Church	71	75	67	91	69	92	221	118	115	40	52	103	40	33
St. Peter's	0	0	0	0	0	0	0	0	0	42	47	—*	43	24
St. Paul's	12	14	16	17	18	18	40	17	26	19	14	28	8	15
St. Mary's	51	37	29	38	62	90	198	101	120	104	128	211	98	83
Holy Trinity	0	0	0	11	8	14	41	34	35	9	6	33	43	20
Swedish Lutheran	8	5	6	5	8	12	46	26	40	55	39	53	38	34
German Lutheran	99	32	107	141	112	125	403	156	149	105	108	285	131	96
German Reformed	37	16	48	50	34	45	179	64	71	66	61	138	47	59
Presbyterian														
First	25	15	16	17	15	17	69	21	26	29	27	40	25	12
Second	16	23	26	30	24	23	89	30	41	26	42	56	25	22
Third	17	29	12	16	10	43	87	43	73	41	59	51	32	22
Scotch	9	8	3	5	6	5	23	11	14	5	8	8	3	7
Associate	0	0	0	2	2	2	7	4	3	5	4	13	9	4
Baptist	6	6	6	9	9	10	35	18	21	17	23	29	14	12
Moravian	3	3	0	0	2	4	12	4	1	3	4	10	6	1
Methodist	0	3	10	7	9	9	34	11	12	10	19	37	10	36
Universalist	0	1	0	1	1	1	2	1	1	4	3	7	1	3
Jewish	1	0	2	1	2	2	2	0	2	1	2	2	0	0
Friends	67	58	75	80	62	66	236	88	98	75	65	110	74	72
Free Quakers	7	6	4	11	5	11	34	12	20	12	17	19	13	8
Strangers (white)	85	89	87	79	120	124	1084	77	200	101	419	1,113	240	147
African Episcopal	0	0	0	0	0	0	0	0	0	36	16	23	12	8
African Methodist	0	0	0	0	0	0	0	0	0	4	6	5	8	9
Strangers (Negro)	46	38	35	34	67	65	91	61	120	48	76	141	36	—*
Total	560	514	549	645	644	778	2,933	897	1,188	857	1,245	2,515	956	727

SOURCE: Poulson's *Town and Country Almanac*, 1789–1802.

*Number not recorded.

Table 9. Burials of Females in Philadelphia, 1788–1801

Burial Grounds	1788	1789	1790	1791	1792	1793	1794	1795	1796	1797	1798	1799	1800	1801
Christ Church	60	79	69	80	62	76	179	114	103	42	44	109	38	43
St. Peter's	0	0	0	0	0	0	0	0	0	42	51	—*	31	25
St. Paul's	10	24	20	22	20	26	46	21	20	23	13	30	12	12
St. Mary's	39	28	38	35	68	86	167	88	97	90	98	124	60	87
Holy Trinity	0	0	0	13	5	15	25	22	27	10	10	47	33	19
Swedish Lutheran	7	4	3	6	12	14	50	31	39	42	24	51	40	40
German Lutheran	77	77	96	144	105	128	379	136	146	115	109	227	128	77
German Reformed	42	14	21	78	40	51	130	81	84	57	64	117	53	44
Presbyterian														
First	15	20	19	23	17	24	30	26	24	22	23	29	23	11
Second	18	24	21	27	27	26	68	32	37	33	34	47	27	19
Third	11	18	13	23	14	37	57	49	61	28	52	38	24	23
Scotch	6	5	2	4	5	3	18	10	11	3	6	7	4	2
Associate	0	0	0	2	3	2	8	4	3	3	5	12	6	3
Baptist	6	7	8	8	11	9	32	22	26	23	29	33	18	14
Moravian	1	4	1	2	2	1	5	4	8	6	6	9	2	3
Methodist	0	11	9	6	8	10	26	10	11	11	17	26	8	27
Universalist	0	0	1	1	0	2	1	2	3	1	3	3	1	1
Jewish	1	0	1	0	1	1	1	0	1	1	1	1	2	1
Friends	74	83	79	91	78	80	238	107	112	80	73	104	83	73
Free Quakers	5	5	3	13	10	7	17	7	11	14	13	15	10	10
Strangers (white)	39	53	49	51	64	70	514	51	165	86	349	765	148	107
African Episcopal	0	0	0	0	0	0	0	0	0	33	17	19	11	11
African Methodist	0	0	0	0	0	0	0	0	0	3	7	8	12	11
Strangers (Negro)	27	26	33	35	49	51	68	45	106	41	63	127	29	—*
Total	438	482	486	664	601	719	2,059	862	1,095	809	1,111	1,948	803	663

SOURCE: Poulson's *Town and Country Almanac*, 1789–1802.

*Number not recorded.

Table 10.   Deaths by Age, Philadelphia, 1801

Burial Grounds	Under Age 11	Age 11–25	Age 25–50	Over Age 50	Total Deaths
Christ Church	22	24	15	15	76
St. Peter's	24	7	10	8	49
St. Paul's	17	3	2	5	27
St. Mary's	100	20	35	15	170
Holy Trinity	28	4	5	2	39
Swedish Lutheran	57	3	6	8	74
German Lutheran	87	11	39	36	173
German Reformed	63	—*	40	—*	103
Presbyterian					
First	12	7	2	2	23
Second	14	11	12	4	41
Third	25	9	8	3	45
Scotch	6	2	1	0	9
Associate	3	2	2	0	7
Baptist	9	7	4	6	26
Moravian	3	0	0	1	4
Methodist	20	21	14	8	63
Universalist	1	2	1	0	4
Jewish	1	0	0	0	1
Friends	66	11	24	44	145
Free Quakers	7	6	2	3	18
Strangers (white)	45	86	106	17	254
African Episcopal	7	6	3	3	19
African Methodist	14	2	3	1	20
Strangers (Negro)	—*	—*	—*	—*	—*
Total	631	244	334	181	1,390

SOURCE: Poulson's *Town and Country Almanac,* 1802.

*Number not recorded.

Table 11. Baptisms and Burials in Philadelphia, 1788–1801

Institution	Baptisms					Burials					Baptisms per 100 Burials
	No. Males	No. Females	Total No.	Males per 100 Females	%	No. Males	No. Females	Total No.	Males per 100 Females	%	
Christ Church	1,232	1,288	2,250	96	7.4	1,343	1,247	2,590	108	9.3	97
St. Peter's	0	0	0	0	0	0	0	0	0	0	0
St. Paul's	514	528	1,042	97	3.1	262	299	561	88	2.0	186
St. Mary's	2,302	2,429	4,731	95	14.0	1,350	1,105	2,455	122	8.8	193
Holy Trinity	411	393	804	104	2.4	254	226	480	112	1.7	168
Swedish Lutheran	220	228	448	96	1.3	375	363	738	103	2.6	61
German Lutheran	2,792	2,646	5,438	106	16.1	2,099	1,944	4,043	108	14.7	134
German Reformed	1,293	1,300	2,593	99	7.7	915	876	1,791	104	6.4	145
Presbyterian											
First	391	391	782	100	2.3	354	306	660	116	2.4	118
Second	468	443	911	106	2.7	473	440	913	108	3.3	100
Third	890	895	1,785	99	5.3	535	448	983	119	3.5	182
Scotch	160	133	293	120	.9	115	86	201	134	.7	146
Associate	49	44	93	111	.3	55	51	106	108	.4	88
Baptist	273	284	557	96	1.6	215	246	461	87	1.7	121
Moravian	57	55	112	104	.3	53	54	107	98	.4	105
Methodist	250	270	520	92	1.5	213	180	393	118	1.4	132
Universalist	26	32	58	81	.2	26	19	45	137	.2	129
Jewish	26	23	49	113	.1	16	12	28	133	.1	175
Friends	2,196	2,285	4,481	96	13.2	1,226	1,355	2,581	90	9.3	173
Free Quakers	128	131	259	98	.8	179	140	319	128	1.1	81
Strangers (white)	1,969	1,811	3,780	109	11.2	3,965	2,511	6,476	158	23.4	58
African Episcopal	132	149	281	88	.8	95	91	186	104	.7	151
African Methodist	113	114	227	99	.7	32	41	73	78	.3	311
Strangers (Negro)	1,028	1,049	2,077	98	6.1	858	700	1,558	122	5.6	133
Total	16,920	16,921	33,841	100	100.0	15,008	12,740	27,748	118	100.0	122

SOURCE: Poulson's *Town and Country Almanac*, 1789–1802.

Table 12. Population Change, Philadelphia, 1790–1800

Group	Population in 1790	Population in 1800	Percent Increase	No. Births	No. Deaths	Percent Natural Increase	Net Migration	Percent Migration
Total	44,096	67,811	+ 54	24,915	22,605	+ 5	21,405	+ 48
Whites	41,946	61,728	+ 47	23,019	21,072	+ 5	17,835	+ 42
Blacks	2,150	6,083	+183	1,896	1,533	+17	3,570	+166
					(1,692)	(+ 9)	(3,729)	(+173)
White males	20,374	30,674	+ 50	11,451	11,423	0	10,272	+ 50
White females	21,572	31,054	+ 44	11,568	9,649	+ 9	7,563	+ 35
Black males[a]	1,045	3,023	+189	924	828	+ 9	1,882	+180
					(919)	(0)	(1,973)	(+189)
Black females[a]	1,105	3,060	+177	972	705	+24	1,688	+152
					(773)	(+18)	(1,756)	(+159)

SOURCE: The number of births and deaths is from Poulson's *Town and Country Almanac*, 1791–1801. The population in 1790 is from the U.S. Bureau of the Census, *Heads of Families of the First Census of the United States taken in the Year 1790: Pennsylvania* (Washington, D.C.: Government Printing Office, 1908); and the population in 1800 is from the U.S. Census Office, *Return of the Whole Number of Persons Within the Several Districts of the United States: Second Census* (Washington, D.C.: Government Printing Office, 1800).

NOTE: Figures in parentheses are estimates based on the assumption of a higher mortality among blacks in 1793.

[a]Figures for these black groups are based on the assumption that their sex ratio was identical to that of whites.

Table 13. Crude Birth and Death Rates, 1788–1801

Year	Total	White	Black	White Males	Black[a] Males	White Females	Black[a] Females
				Crude Birth Rates			
1788	56	54	74	—	—	—	—
1789	48	47	69	—	—	—	—
1790	48	46	68	48	64	45	71
1791	49	48	54	49	52	47	56
1792	49	50	45	50	44	49	46
1793	49	50	42	52	42	47	42
1794	44	45	37	44	36	46	38
1795	42	42	33	43	32	42	34
1796	19	47	74	48	73	46	74
1797	44	44	45	44	47	45	43
1798	44	43	47	44	45	42	49
1799	40	40	46	40	46	40	46
1800	39	39	44	40	43	38	44
1801	31	30	(41)	30	—	30	—
				Crude Death Rates			
1788	25	24	37	—	—	—	—
1789	24	23	31	—	—	—	—
1790	24	23	32	25	33	21	30
1791	28	28	27	28	27	28	27
1792	26	25	40	26	46	24	33
1793	29	29	35	30	40	27	30
1794	93	97	(85)	116	(100)	78	(72)
1795	31	32	26	33	29	31	22
1796	39	38	50	40	54	36	46
1797	27	27	34	28	36	26	31
1798	37	38	35	40	37	35	32
1799	68	69	57	78	60	60	54
1800	26	27	18	29	18	24	17
1801	25	22	(53)	24	—	20	—

SOURCE: Poulson's *Town and Country Almanac,* 1789–1802.

NOTE: Figures in parentheses are estimates based on the assumption of a higher mortality among blacks in 1793.

[a]Figures for these black groups are based on the assumption that their sex ratio was identical to that of whites.

PART FIVE

Politics and Ideology

CHAPTER 9

Equality and Justice

Philadelphia's Popular Revolution
1775–1780

STEVE ROSSWURM

Acquiescence and resignation, not revolt and insurrection, mark world history. The great majority of humanity, no matter how awful their living conditions, no matter how tyrannical and arbitrary the behavior of those in authority, accept things as they are. Assuming or learning that the central circumstances of their lives cannot be changed, most people try to make the best of it. The readily available examples of others who are worse off, whose lives are filled with even greater misery, provide a balm for many people who do question the injustices of their lives.

A revolution changes all this, but citizens participate in such an event only after rejecting the belief that their lives are beyond their control.

For individuals to reach this conclusion, two developments are required. First, the commitment to the existing political and social system, both as an idea and as it is controlled by the wealthy and the powerful, must weaken and ultimately disappear. Second, there must be evidence, either ideological or practical, that ways exist to improve people's lives.

Applying this framework to the American Revolution is complicated, because the colonists lived under two different, if related, systems of rule. As subjects of the British Empire, they belonged to an imperial network directed by authorities in London primarily for the benefit of British interests. But Americans also resided in particular colonies, each of which had its own government, similar in form to the British state, but not identical to it.

During the American Revolution, most colonists rebelled against the imperial domination of London and the perceived threat to their liberties from the King and Parliament rather than against their local systems of government. For this reason, historians sometimes refer to the "American Revolution" as the "American War for Independence." That this event was primarily a struggle for "home rule," however, should not disguise its radical aspects, nor should it obfuscate the reactionary consequences of a Revolution that both sealed the tragic fate of many Native Americans and solidified the institution of slavery in the South.[1]

In Pennsylvania the dual struggles for independence from imperial domination and for the shape of the new domestic government became inextricably intertwined. Historians generally have concluded that the American Revolution assumed its most radical form in Pennsylvania and that the conflict among the classes was as extensive in Philadelphia as in any other area in the nation. A brief examination of Philadelphia's "dramatic dialectical dance of revolution" will demonstrate why.[2]

1. Carl Becker, *The History of Political Parties in the Province of New York, 1760–1776* (Madison: University of Wisconsin Press, 1909), 22. Two of the best discussions of these issues are Pauline Maier, *From Resistance to Revolution: Colonial Radicals and the Development of American Opposition to Britain, 1765–1776* (New York: Knopf, 1972); and Edward Countryman, *The American Revolution* (New York: Hill & Wang, 1985).

2. Quotation from E. J. Hobsbawm, *The Age of Revolution, 1789–1848* (New York: New American Library, 1962), 84. The most important studies of the Revolution in Pennsylvania include Charles H. Lincoln, *The Revolutionary Movement in Pennsylvania, 1760–1776* (Philadelphia: University of Pennsylvania Press, 1901); J. Paul Selsam, *The Pennsylvania Constitution of 1776: A Study in Revolutionary Democracy* (1936; reprint, New York: Octagon, 1971); David Hawke, *In the Midst of a Revolution* (Philadelphia: University of Pennsylvania

The struggle among the urban classes was crucially important to defining the nature of Pennsylvania's revolutionary actions. Affluent merchants and professionals and wealthy artisans—the "better sort," as they were called by contemporaries—originally led Philadelphia's early militant movement against British tyranny between 1765 and 1769. But the events of those years mobilized and politicized the "middling sort," consisting primarily of master craftsmen and shopkeepers of moderate means, and sharpened their self-awareness as a distinct economic and social group. When the colony's leaders demonstrated either that they were incapable of effectively directing the resistance movement or that they actually preferred British rule to the danger of political change orchestrated by poorer citizens, the middling sort broke with the better sort in 1769 and 1770. After the Tea Act of 1773, people of modest means assumed leadership in the resistance movement themselves (see Chapter 10). Nor did the challenge stop there. The radicals among them went on to question the tradition that "gentlemen of property and understanding" should control the political power of the state.[3]

At this point the "lower sort," primarily poor artisans and wage-earners, walked onto history's stage. Mainly politically inert and outwardly deferential before 1775, but nurturing within themselves and their communities a sense of self-worth and egalitarianism, Philadelphia's laboring poor became actors in the political drama when war broke out at Lexington and Concord. Led by their popularly elected representatives in the Committee of Privates, the lower sort became politicized as the conflict neared, especially during the debate about

---

Press, 1961); Charles S. Olton, *Artisans for Independence: Philadelphia Mechanics and the American Revolution* (Syracuse, N.Y.: Syracuse University Press, 1975); Eric Foner, *Tom Paine and Revolutionary America* (New York: Oxford University Press, 1976); Richard Alan Ryerson, *The Revolution Is Now Begun: The Radical Committees of Philadelphia, 1765–1776* (Philadelphia: University of Pennsylvania Press, 1978); Nash, *Urban Crucible;* Alexander, *Render Them Submissive;* Richard Alan Ryerson, "Republican Theory and Partisan Reality in Revolutionary Pennsylvania: Toward a New View of the Constitutional Party," in *Sovereign States in an Age of Uncertainty,* ed. Ronald Hoffman and Peter J. Albert (Charlottesville: University Press of Virginia, 1981), 95–133; and Rosswurm, *Arms, Country, and Class.*

3. On the role of the city's "middling sort" and the "better sort," see especially Olton, *Artisans for Independence;* Ryerson, *The Revolution Is Now Begun;* Nash, *Urban Crucible;* and Richard Bauman, *For the Reputation of Truth: Politics, Religion, and Conflict Among the Pennsylvania Quakers, 1750–1800* (Baltimore: Johns Hopkins University Press, 1971).

which rules should govern the newly organized militia. Many of the city's poorer inhabitants felt passionately about two issues in particular. First, a just and equitable militia policy, which would provide adequate pay for poor soldiers and ensure that everyone (including the wealthy) fulfilled their military responsibilities, could be achieved only by overthrowing the existing government structure. Second, a successful struggle to determine the shape of the new government was essential for a victorious battle for independence from Great Britain.[4]

An alliance of the radical middling sort, the lower sort, a handful of moderates, and their allies in the Continental Congress fashioned the "genuine revolution" needed to "sweep aside Quaker rule," which had long dominated Pennsylvania politics.[5] This coalition not only overthrew the proprietary government but also brought the colony solidly into the pro-Independence camp and established Pennsylvania's Constitution of 1776. Under this new form of government, probably the most democratic of any other American state, the urban lower sort were able to exercise political power during the war years in ways not possible in any other area. The relatively equitable militia system that also resulted meant that the militia remained the embodiment of the political power of poor artisans and wage-earners well into the early 1780s.

Despite internal strains, the popular movement that emerged from this coalition supported a four-point program: (1) a staunch anti-Tory policy, which would include harsh penalties for those who supported the British or who remained neutral during the war; (2) a "just price" for specific items of food, clothing, and fuel, which would keep the necessities of life within the economic reach of laboring people and would prevent wealthy merchants from taking advantage of wartime scarcity to augment their own fortune; (3) an equitable militia law that would ensure that every man fulfilled his military obligation; and (4) a strong defense of Pennsylvania's democratic Constitution.[6]

4. The political activities of Philadelphia's "lower sort" are discussed in Rosswurm, *Arms, Country, and Class*; Nash, *Urban Crucible*; and Foner, *Tom Paine*. Studies of the lower sort before and after the Revolution include Salinger, *"To Serve Well and Faithfully"*; Smith, *The "Lower Sort"*; Smith and Wojtowicz, eds., *Blacks Who Stole Themselves*.

5. John M. Murrin, "Political Development," in *Colonial British America: Essays in the New History of the Early Modern Era*, ed. Jack P. Greene and J. R. Pole (Baltimore: Johns Hopkins University Press, 1984), 440.

6. For lengthier discussions of these issues, see Steven Rosswurm, " 'As a Lyen Out of His Den': Philadelphia's Popular Movement, 1776–1780," in *The Origins of Anglo-American Radicalism*, ed. Margaret Jacob and James Jacob (London: Allen & Unwin, 1984), 300–323; Steven Rosswurm, "The Philadelphia Militia, 1775–1783: Active Duty and Active Radical-

Out of this popular movement came the documents reproduced below. The writers of these texts discuss such practical issues as the type of militia uniform to be required, enforcement of militia legislation, and the rising price of goods during the war, and they express their antipathy toward rich men who avoided their military duty or who made money while their fellow Revolutionaries fought the enemy. These documents, moreover, tell us a great deal about the concerns of Philadelphia's common folk and their radical notions about "justice" and "equality," ideals that did not hold the same meaning for all classes of people who participated in the Revolution. And the authors of these texts did not shy away from political struggle, as they demanded that the state authorities, the militia, and the popular movement implement their ideals. Four of these documents (I, II, III, and VI) emanated from people or authorities close to the lower sort and express their demand for equality. The other three (IV, V, and VII) appear to have been written by the laboring poor and share many of the characteristics of the "anonymous threatening letter" of eighteenth-century England.[7]

These documents are transcribed literally, except for a few dashes that have been changed to proper punctuation. I resisted the temptation to alter other spelling and punctuation to make them easier to read, because that would lessen the distance between a modern reader and the eighteenth-century text. In our own age, which too often views the world as a never-changing present, we need to understand the separateness, the "pastness of the past." A brief introduction establishes the context for each of the documents.[8]

---

ism," in Ronald Hoffman and Peter J. Albert, eds., *Arms and Independence: The Military Character of the American Revolution* (Charlottesville: University Press of Virginia, 1984), 75–119; and Rosswurm, *Arms, Country, and Class.*

7. According to E. P. Thompson, the "anonymous threatening letter is a characteristic form of social protest in any society which has crossed a certain threshold of literacy, in which individuals who can be identified as the organizers of protest are liable to immediate victimization." For a superb discussion of these letters and their social context, see Thompson, "The Crime of Anonymity," in Douglas Hay et al., *Albion's Fatal Tree: Crime and Society in Eighteenth-Century England* (New York: Pantheon Books, 1975), 255–344; and Peter Linebaugh and Marcus Rediker, "The Many Headed Hydra: Sailors, Slaves, and the Atlantic Working Class in the Eighteenth Century," *Journal of Historical Sociology* 3 (1990): 225–52.

8. I thank the Library Company of Philadelphia (LCP); the Pennsylvania Historical and Museum Commission, Harrisburg, Pennsylvania (PHMC); the American Philosophical Society (APS); the Historical Society of Pennsylvania, Philadelphia (HSP); and the *Pennsylvania Magazine of History and Biography* for permission to print these materials.

Documents from Philadelphia's Popular Revolution

I

[Pennsylvania had no established militia system in the eighteenth century, but it rapidly created one after the Revolution began. The following broadside (the term for a short notice widely distributed by hand and often posted in public places) appeared just a few weeks after the first organizing meeting for "the Association," as the militia was called until the spring of 1777. The militia apparently lost this battle for a uniform that would "level all distinctions."[9]]

To The ASSOCIATORS Of The CITY of PHILADELPHIA[10]
[Handwritten notation: May 18, 1775]
A Considerable number of the Associators of this city, on considering the plan of an uniform recommended by a Committee of the Officers, at a late meeting, are of opinion that it will be found too expensive for the generality, as well as inconvenient to them; that the aforesaid Officers could not, with propriety, take upon them to adopt of themselves an uniform for the whole city, without the approbation of the people, who are entitled to an equal consultation. That by adopting the cheapest uniform, such as that of a HUNTING SHIRT, as it will level all distinctions, answers the end of coat and jacket, and is within the compass of almost *every* person's ability, not costing at the utmost above ten shillings. The officers say that they did not mean to impose any particular uniform upon the people, but then they should have given the privates an opportunity of making known *their* sentiments. An uniform

9. Silas Deane to Elizabeth Deane, Philadelphia, June 3, 1775, in *Letters of Delegates to Congress, 1774–1789*, ed. Paul H. Smith et al., 14 vols. (Washington, D.C.: Library of Congress, 1976–), 1:437.
10. 962.F.114, LCP.

is granted by *all* to be absolutely necessary, but let it be something cheap, which the generality can afford. A very material advantage which the HUNTING SHIRTS have above the present uniform recommended, is that they will answer all seasons of the year, as a person may wear neither coat nor jacket in warm weather, and in winter he may cloath under them as warm as he pleases. Had the hunting shirts been recommended by the Officers, it would have met the approbation of ninety-nine out of an hundred. It is very far from being the intention of the author of this, to make any dissention among the people; and he is sorry to be under the necessity of proposing any alteration in what is seemingly fixed upon. A meeting of the Associators ought to be called immediately, that each man may have a voice in what so nearly concerns himself. The author is informed that some of the Captains of the different companies have proposed, that any of the men, who think they are not able to buy uniforms, may be supplied by *them*; now there are *hundreds* who could not afford it, yet would never submit to *ask any* man for a coat, neither would they appear in the ranks to be pointed at by those who *had* uniforms. The author begs leave to assure his fellow citizens that no interested motives are the occasion of these strictures, actuated only by a wish for the general welfare, the economy of the uniform, and its being peculiarly adapted to the climate, he hopes will induce those gentlemen, who have partly fixed upon an expensive uniform, to concur in sentiment with him.

II

[The Philadelphia militia went to war in New Jersey in July and August 1776. On November 25, 1776, the Continental Congress, after hearing a report of the meeting between its committee and General Thomas Mifflin, recommended to the Pennsylvania Council of Safety that it again call out the Philadelphia associators.[11] In the following document, the Council of Safety informed the Pennsylvania Assembly of the morale, condition, and political sentiments of the militia.]

11. *The Journals of the Continental Congress, 1774–1789*, ed. W. C. Ford, 9 vols. (Washington, D.C.: Government Printing Office, 1904–37), 6:979.

To The General Assembly of the State of Pennsy[lvania][12]
[November 26, 1776]
The Council of Safety beg leave with the utmost respect,

To lay before this House their proceedings in consequence of divers resolutions laid before them by a Committee of Congress, and of several Resolutions since passed by that Hon[ora]ble House.

In addition to these proceedings contained in the papers now before you, the Council beg leave to say that they have called together such of the Field officers of the several Battalions, in and near this City[,] as cou'd be Convened on a Short notice[,] to consult their opinion on the best mode of calling forth the Militia of the City and the four Counties mentioned in the Resolve of Congress. they have expressed the utmost readiness to do their duty[,] but they with us lament the present Situation of our Militia as a public Calamity. it is unsupported by Law.[13] the people are disgusted at the Inconveniences, hardships and Losses which they Suffered in their late Service,[14] while Non Associators were permitted to remain at home in the peaceable Enjoyment of their posessions, and many of them increasing their Wealth by grasping the Trade of the absent Associators, whose patriotic Exertions have been Sneered at, and their hardships & fatigues, [and] the distresses of their families, insultingly made jest of. and above all their just & reasonable expectations of seeing the Nonassociators obliged to [p]ay something for the indulgences which had been granted them, wholly disappointed.[15] It has been [pr]oposed to call out the Battalions of the City and [Li]berties[16] tomorrow morning, but under circumstances, with the hardships of a Winter Campaign [an]d the dread of their leaving their Families to perish from the want of the necessaries of Life. what can we Expect from the Class of Men who live from day to day on the produce of their Industry[,] Mechanicks, Tenants & Laborers, of which to the Scandal of Men in more

12. Reel 11, frame 275, Series: Executive Correspondence File, Record Group 27, Records of Pennsylvania's Revolutionary Governments, 1775–90, Division of Archives and Manuscripts, PHMC. All RG 27 items cited hereafter are from this file.

13. The Assembly had passed a militia law in April 1776, but it was not in effect after the overthrow of proprietary government. The first Revolutionary Assembly began work on a militia bill on November 29, 1776, but did not finally pass legislation until April 1777.

14. "[L]ate Service" refers to the Philadelphia militia's duty in New Jersey in July and August 1776.

15. Although the Constitutional Convention passed a law establishing heavy fines for nonassociation ("An Ordinance to render the Burthen nearly Equal as may be," September 14, 1776, Ab 1776–44, HSP), there is no evidence that authorities collected them.

16. The Northern Liberties, Philadelphia's northern suburb.

easy circumstances the Associators of this State are chiefly composed?
Can it be expected, under these discouragements and Insults, that they
will Consent to bear the whole Burthen and face alone the dangers of
defending the State? What shall we say to them when they are called
together? shall we depress the[ir] Spirits by describing the vast number
of our Enemi[es] and assuring them of the certainty of their intenti[ons]
of invading [their] [illegible]. Shall we trace out to them the footsteps of
desolation, marked by [illegible] [illegible] insulting conquerors? shall we
point to them Cities in Flames, with their wretched inhabitan[ts] flying
naked before their Enemies? Shall we Remind them of the heartrending
Cries of abused Infants, and the Shrieks of Violated Virgins, their Sisters, their daughters, when no relief can be give[n] them? Shall we describe the Chains w[hic]h will be heaped upon us, if we are conquered, by
men who have lost every Character, but the form of human nature? Such
things may Chill their Blood with horror or produce a rage of momen-
ta[ry] Madness, but will it induce men to leave their tender Connexions
unprovided for, or to forget the unequal Burthens which have been laid
on them? NO. They will demand Justice and we are Convinced that,
unless this is granted them, it i[s] in vain that we call on them in this hour
of danger.

The Council, therefore are constrain'd, to address this Honorable
House, while we may yet do it as [illegible] and to Conjure you by all the
sacred ties which Unite to us, and to our Bleeding Country, to Postpone
all other Business and every other Consideration, however necessary,
proper & important. in any other Situation of our Affairs it might be and
[illegible] at the Single Object of saving your Country from that destruction which will inevitably be the Consequence of the least delay. And they
beg leave to intimate that it would be attended with many Salutary Effects if a fine of [blank] Pounds were ordered to be Levied immediately
on every Able Bodied Man from the age of 16 to 50 years, who [s]hall
refuse or Neglect to go into Service when called upon to do. and that a
reasonable assessment be [m]ade on the Estates of those above that age.
proper Persons may be appointed in each Ward of the City and in each
Township in the respective (four) Counties to Enrol the Men and to
Collect the Fines of Delinquents, with power to levy the same on their
goods and Chattells and to make Sale thereof, returning the Surplusage
if any, after paying the Charges &c.[17] the Money so raised to be divided

17. On November 30 the Assembly resolved that half the associators should immediately take the field and remain in service for four weeks, but it took no further action until

among those who shall be in actual Service as Militia[,] or some other Effectual Plan, adapted to the present Emergency, for making the Burthen of those who stay at home in some degree equal to that of those, who go into [the] Field to meet the Enemy. But it is to the Wisdom of their Representatives that the People look [illegible] for a Remedy of the Evils of which they Complain and from the Vigour of their Counsels, expect to derive that Confidence which is necessary to Enable them to Exert themselves in the Common Cause.

As to this Council it shall be their Glory to exerci[se] [w]ith persevering firmness every power they are or shall be intrusted with to rouse and animate the People to distinguish themselves and do honour to their Country, by seizing with a manly and patriotic Spirit the present glorious opportunity of signalizing their Courage in the defense of Liberty. And they have no doubt but that this Hon[ora]ble House will on the present occasion, prove to the World, that dangers do not intimidate [themselves?][,] but on the Contrary will urge them to do all that is possible for Men who ask the Blessing of God on their Endeavours, and leave Events to him who governs the Universe.

Signed By order of Council[,] D[avid] Rittenhouse V. P. copy

III

[The Philadelphia militia served effectively during its tour of duty in December 1776 and January 1777 even though many associators were angry because state authorities did not enforce the militia law impartially. Some of the reasons for their indignation are detailed in the following letter concerning the case of James Allen.]

December 12, when it offered bounties to those who turned out; *Journal of the House of Representatives of the Commonwealth of Pennsylvania: Beginning the Twenty-Eighth Day of November, 1776 and Ending the Second Day of October, 1781* (Philadelphia, 1782), 98, 101–2. The Council of Safety apparently considered levying fines but did not do so (reel 11, frames 784–85, RG 27, PHMC; *Minutes of the Provincial Council of Pennsylvania* (Colonial Records), ed. Samuel Hazard, 16 vols. [Harrisburg, Pa.: J. Severns, 1851–53], 11, December 7, 1776, 38). A group of "Real Whigs" suggested a set of fines on December 1 (see "At a Meeting of Real Whigs . . . ," Society Hall, December 1, 1776, reel 11, frame 350, RG 27, PHMC).

To the Honourable the Council of Safety.[18]
[Bristol, December 26, 1776]

Gentlemen

We the officers of the fifth Company in the Second Philadelphia Battalion of Militia for our Selfs and our Company,[19] take this Method to inform you, that it gave us General Satisfaction on hearing that James Allen Esq. was apprehended and Conducted as a Prisoner in order to be examined by your Honourable Board and to be dealt with according to his desarts[20] the behaviour of his nearest relations in flying from their fellow Citisenes and Seeking refuge amongst our Comon onprovoked Cruel Enemys,[21] we thought was Sufficient cause for the Securing Such a Person as the afore mentioned James Allen Esq. but to our great astonishment we [are] informed that he is Set at Liberty. now Gentlemen if eve[r] there was no foundation for Confining him as a dangerous person to the Comon State, you Cannot be ignorant that he is an associator belonging to our Company, and Sorry we are to Say it, a Man that has been the Cause of more Confusion than half of the Company Could have made had they had ever So great a mind to it. For to be particulare in regard to him you must be informed that he was waited upon by Mr. Adam Foulk & Henry Kammerer[22] to get him

18. Reel 11, frame 609, RG 27, PHMC.

19. There were sixty-six men in Alexander Boyd's company, according to "A Muster Roll of Captain Alexr Boyd's Company," n.d., Cadwalader Collection, General John Cadwalader, Box 15, folder returns and muster rolls, 1776, HSP. I found the 1775 taxable wealth for twenty of these men: the mean was £8.35 and the median was £3.0. The mean taxable wealth for all Philadelphia taxpayers was £20 and the median £3.5. The occupations recorded for eighteen of the men indicate that the company was comprised predominantly of the laboring classes: 4 laborers, 2 shopkeepers, 2 bakers, 2 shoemakers, and a schoolmaster, a fanmaker, a butcher, a tobacconist, a barber, a stonecutter, a cooper, and a skinner. The tax and wealth information is from the Provincial County Tax Duplicate, 1775, Philadelphia City Archives (PCA). At some point during the campaign, someone made the following notation about the company on the muster: "many of them gone & some not dependable."

20. State authorities seized Allen on December 19. After he pledged not to harm the Revolutionary cause, both sides parted "amicably & as we began, with great politeness." Allen returned home on December 28 ("Diary of James Allen," Pennsylvania Magazine of History and Biography 9 [1885]: 193–95).

21. Andrew, John, and William Allen, brothers of James Allen, fled to the British army earlier in December.

22. Foulk does not appear on the Provincial County Tax Duplicate, 1775 (PCA), but he was actively involved in the Revolution. He served on the city's radical price-fixing committee in August 1779 ("The Independent & Constitutional Ticket for a General Committee," August 2, 1779, 962.F.147, LCP), and in 1780 he was a militia captain (Bradford Manu-

to Sign the association in order to induce the poorer kind of the Company to doo the Same.[23] he refused by & blank to do it and declared in presence of them both he never would Sign them. Some time after that the Late Assemble passed a Resolve that the Several Back Counties Should have a porportionable & Honable Number of Members, James Allen put him Self up for a Member for Northampton County,[24] making them believe he was a propper associator in one of the Companies in the City of Philadelphia, which was a positive falshood, and by that means was Elected a Member for Said County. on the hearing of the deceived good people of Said County that Mr. Allen was no regulare associator and had never Signed the association it occassioned a General dissatisfaction. Mr. Allen finding his being a Member of the House in that Situation So disagreeable, goes on his own accord to Mr. Phile,[25] Late Captain of this Company and Signs the association, and evidently it appears [S]ince not to Serve his bleeding Country but to betray it with the assistance of his Brother Andrew & the rest of their party. now Gentlemen as much as the hearing of Mr. Allen being Apprehended by order of your Honourable House gave satisfaction to us our Company and all well wishers to their Country, So much and more it moritified them on hearing that he was acquitted. now let us be free to tell you Gentlemen that if there was no Sufficient Cause for keeping him Confined as a dangerous person to the Safety of the different States at Large, it was your duty to keep him Safe as an associator propperly belonging to our Company, and have Send him under a propper Guard to the Camp for a Satisfaction of the different poor people belonging to our and the Several Companies in the Batallion. for let us be free with you, that if you only mean to force the poorer kind in to the field and Suffer the rich & the Great to remain at home who ought to Sett an

---

scripts, British Army Prisoners, Volume 3, 137, HSP). Foulk probably was a member of the Democratic Society of Pennsylvania as well. Kammerer, a shopkeeper assessed for £4 of taxable wealth in 1775, was the co-publisher of the *Philadelphische Correspondenz*, the newspaper that first published the address of the German Republican Society in 1793. He served as the Society's president.

23. In January 1776 the Committee of Privates urged Philadelphians to sign the articles of association despite its flaws ("Gentlemen and Fellow-Soldiers," 962.F.95, LCP). By mid-February the signing of the articles had become "very general" (*Pennsylvania Gazette* [Philadelphia], February 14, 1776).

24. This occurred in the May 1776 by-election.

25. The two "Philes" on the city's 1775 tax list were both named Frederick; one was a doctor, the other was a chandler.

example to the rest, you may rest assured that at a future Calling out of
the Malitia you woud have Two Hundred Men from the Whole City
that will obey. their is a General disatisfaction amongst our people on
account of the Several Gentlemen who formerly Paraded in our Company and now in time of the greatest danger have turn'd their backs,
and indeed a good many out of other Companies make onquirenies
after them, So that their going at first Serv'd to incourage the poorer
Sort[,] now Serves to discourage them. and by all inqurery we Can
make we Cant learn of any Steps being taken in order to Send them to
the Camps. they are as liable to be made to go in their Company as the
meanest Man belonging their to. their being no difference between the
Rich & the poor associator[,] of the two the Rich ought to be foremost
and the poor will Certainly follow. it is realy astonishing to View the
Batallion and to find that their is heardly one Man in Ten a Man of
property. the future Steps Gentlemen will either make the Association
flourish or Twintle to nothing. these Sentiments Gentlemen we hope
will be taken in kind light as nothing but the well fair of our Cause
induced us to acquaint you there with; we remain Honourable Gentlemen your devoted Humble Servants

Alexr Boyd Capt[,] Henry Kammerer, Lieut.[,]
Adam Foulk [illegible]

IV

[Prices rose dramatically and paper money depreciated greatly during
the second half of 1778 and the spring of 1779, creating extreme hardship for poorer Philadelphians. On May 23, an observer noted that
"every article" was raised to "an immense price" and "many" chose not
"to sell at all."[26] Increasing anger about the rising food prices, a sched-
uled militia muster day on May 24, and rumors that the militia would go
about "discovering monopolizers &c" led wealthy Quaker Elizabeth
Drinker (see Chapter 5) to confide to her diary that "many" were "appre-

26. John Mitchell to Nathaniel Greene, May 23, 1779, Nathaniel Greene Correspondence, vol. 66, APS.

hensive of a mob rising."[27] On May 24, when "many families" went without bread because there was "not a bit to be bought," Philadelphians found "Come on Coolly's" broadside posted at "ye Corners."[28]]

For our Country's good![29]

[May (23 or 24), 1779]

The depreciation of our Money and the high prices which every thing is got to, is one and the same thing. We ask not who introduced the evil, how it arose, or who encouraged it. In the midst of money we are in poverty, and exposed to want in a land of plenty. You that have money, and you that have none, down with your prices, or down with yourselves. For by the living and eternal God, we will bring every article down to what it was last Christmas, or we will down with those who oppose it.[30]

We have turned out against the enemy and we will not be eaten up by monopolizers and forestallers.[31]

Come on Coolly

V

[The following broadside, which Elizabeth Drinker characterized as "mischievous and ridiculous in its kind,"[32] appeared three weeks after the price-fixing committee election of August 2, 1779. This committee,

---

27. Elizabeth Drinker Diary (typescript), May 22, 1779, HSP. Excerpts from Drinker's diary are included in Chapter 5.

28. Mrs. Bache to her father, May 25, 1779, as cited in John William Wallace, *An Old Philadelphian: Colonel William Bradford* (Philadelphia: Sherman & Company, 1884), 304–5. Drinker Diary, May 24, 1779.

29. This is clearly a nonliteral transcription included in a letter from William Blodgett to Nathaniel Greene, May 24, 1779, Greene Correspondence, vol. 64.

30. The town meeting on May 25 decided to roll back prices on a month-by-month basis (*Pennsylvania Packet* [Philadelphia], May 27, 1779).

31. "Monopolizers" and "forestallers" were two favorite targets of the wrath of laboring people. A monopolizer (usually a merchant) bought large quantities of a specific item, created an artificial scarcity by removing it from the market, then realized large profits by selling the item at a high price. A forestaller withheld goods from the marketplace to drive up the price.

32. Drinker Diary, August 30, 1779.

dominated by the radical middling sort, met with increasing opposition in its efforts to maintain price levels and to keep Philadelphia supplied with goods. The popular movement did not respond to the following call for direct action, but subsequent events indicate that many shared his anger. Note the heavy sprinkling of biblical allusions in this broadside.[33]]

GENTLEMEN AND FELLOW CITIZ[ENS][34]
[August 29, 1779]

The time is now arrived to prove whether the suffering friends of [our] country, are to be enslaved, ruined and starved, by a few over-bearing Merchants, a swarm of Monopolizers and Speculaters, an infernal gang of Tories, &c. &c.

Now is the time to prove, whether we will support our Committee or not, whether we shall tamely sit down and see the resolves of the Town-meeting and Committee,[35] violated every day before our faces, and the Delinquents suffered to go unpunished; the case is just this, your opponents are rich and powerful, and they think by their consequence, to over-awe you into slavery, and to starve you in the bargen. But I say it is a shame and disgrace to the virtuous sons of Liberty, while the AL-MIGHTY is fighting our battles without, to suffer those Devils of all colours within us, to overturn all that God and Man has done to save us. My dear [frien]ds, if our Committee is overturned, our Money is inevitably gone, the British Tyrant will then think his Golden bribe has not been misapplied. But I call upon you all, in name of our Bleeding Country, to rouse up as a Lyon out of his den, and make those Beasts of Pray, to humble, and prove by this days conduct, than any person whatever, though puffed like a Toad, with a sense of his own consequence, shall dare to violate the least Resolve of our Committee, it were better for him, that a Mill-stone was fastened to his neck, and he cast into the depth of the Sea, or that he had never been born, *Rouse! Rouse! Rouse!* and

COME on WARMLY

33. On this point, see Thompson, "The Crime of Anonymity," 300–303; and Peter Linebaugh, "Jubilating; or, How the Atlantic Working Class Used the Biblical Jubilee Against Capitalism, with Some Success," *Radical History Review* 50 (1991): 143–80.

34. Ab 1774-46, HSP. Elizabeth Drinker provides the correct date, August 30, 1779, in her diary entry for that day.

35. The references are to the town meetings of May 25 and July 26–27, 1779, and to the price-fixing committee elected on August 2, 1779.

VI

[On October 4, 1779, radical militia men battled state authorities, the City Light Horse, and Continental troops in Philadelphia in a bloody fight that has come to be known as "Fort Wilson."[36] In the following petition, militia officers offered their analysis of the causes of the battle, reiterating long-standing militia grievances and explaining why they failed to support their men.]

To his Excellency the President Vice President and the Honorable the Executive Council of the Common Wealth of Pennsylvania[37]

The Memorial and Representation of a Deputation from the Several Battalions of Militia of the City and Liberties of Philadelphia Respectfully Sheweth

That your Memorialists in behalf of themselves and their respective Battalions being deeply affected by the Melancholy Events which happened on the 4th Instant beg to lay before you, what we believe after the most Minute enquiry and deliberation to be the principal causes thereof, humbly requesting this Honorable Board to take such Measures thereon as in your Wisdom shall seem necessary for preventing the like fatal consequences in future.

The exceeding lenity which has been shewn to persons notoriously disaffected to the Independence of the United States has rather tended to encourage them in their misconduct than to convert them to reason and sound Policy and although for the sake of order and good Government we cannot but disapprove every attempt to punish them otherwise then by the Laws of the State yet we humbly beg leave to represent in behalf of tho[se] of our fellow Citizens who lately assembled on the Commons for the purpose of removing such Obnoxious persons that their intended Conduct proceeded from an Attachment to the cause of

---

36. See John K. Alexander, "The Fort Wilson Incident of 1779: A Case Study of the Revolutionary Crowd," *William and Mary Quarterly*, 3rd ser., 31 (1974): 589–612; and Rosswurm, *Arms, Country, and Class*, chap. 7.

37. Stauffer, 633, HSP.

their suffering Country, from a remembrance of the hardships they have endured in defence thereof and the numerous Grievances they at present undergo.

The enormous Price of all the necessaries of Life many of which are now beyond the power of the Poor to purchase is an Evil which has long threatened this place with Confusion. We believe that great pains have been taken by several worthy Characters to appease and quiet the minds of the suffering Poor under their accumulated hardships and to represent to them the inconveniences that would arise from any forceable attempt to redress themselves,[38] but what are persuasions when compared with the iniquitous Price of Salt and every other foreign Article or how little will argument prevail upon families that are in want of Bread.

We entreat your Honorable Board to recommend to the Importers and Merchants of this State to fall on some plan for appeasing the [animosities] which their own Conduct has in a great measure been the cause of, and in this place we cannot help taking notice that although these Gentlemen argue in a memorial to your Excellency to sell [these] [goods] at a Certain price[,] namely Rum for 7.10.1[,][39] Coffee £1.2.6[,] Salt at £15.0.0[.] yet they no [sooner] made the proposal but they departed from it, forfeiting thereby their reputation with the Public and embittering their minds against them.

The excessive price of House Rent and the stipulations for Ground Rents to be paid in hard Money are matters which fall exceedingly heavy on Numbers of well Affected Inhabitants of this State.

The inequality likewise of the Militia law whereby a labouring Man is subject to a fine equal to him of Affluent Fortune is a Circumstance which we humbly request may be taken into consideration.

In making the representations to this Honorable Board we beg leave to assure you that we shall to the utmost of our Power endeavour to prevent any disorders from arising and as far as the Civil duty of a Citizen can extend shall always Assist in suppressing them. And as a Necessary provision thereto we request that the Persons hitherto deemed the Light Horse of this City may be put immediately

38. The militia officers here refer to the efforts of Charles Willson Peale, James Hutchinson, and Alexander Boyd to convince the militia not to march at Fort Wilson on October 4. See "Statement of Peale" in William B. Reed, *Life and Correspondence of Joseph Reed*, 2 vols. (Philadelphia: Lindsay & Blakiston, 1847), 2:423–24.

39. Seven pounds, 10 shillings, and 1 pence.

under the Militia Law or disbanded.[40] Sign'd in behalf of the Militia of the City & Liberties of Philadelphia by this deputation Oct. 8th 1779[.]

John [Mc]Culoh Capt	Wm Thorne Capt Lt Art
Thos. Hale	Robt. McGee
John Byrne Capt.	Robert Smith Capt
John Reynolds	Cadr. Dickinson
Paul Cox Lt. Coll.	Derick Peterson Capt
John Snowden	William Peltz
[J.] Pickering Capt	Alex Quarries
Leeson Simmons	George Nelson
Alexr Boyd Major	Charles Willson Peale
Thomas Francis	Charles Stulty
Richard Saltar Capt	Absalom [illegible]
John Kling	Alexander [Miller]
John Jones	Richd Dennis
James Rowan	Warwick Coates Jr Capt

VII

[The laboring poor suffered grievously through the winter of 1779–1780. Trade revived after price-fixing ended, but prices rose to extraordinary heights, and paper money depreciated even more rapidly. The extremely cold winter weather also took its toll, and the poor-relief system proved inadequate to the increased demands placed on it. On March 29, 1780, the Pennsylvania Assembly passed the state's second militia law. Although it continued many of the democratic features of previous legislation, the brunt of militia duty continued to fall on the laboring poor, as it had since 1776. The militia law and its requirement for new elections of officers provided the occasion for the broadside by "Slow and Sure."]

40. This private troop of horsemen played a prominent role in the suppression of the militia at Fort Wilson.

To the Inhabitants of Philadelphia & its respective districts, who
compose the militia Artillery & Musketry. Gentlemen[41]

Philadelphia, April 14, 1780

You are earnestly requested to attend (without Arms) a meeting to be
held on monday next the 17th Inst. at nine O'Clock in the forenoon on
the Commons near Byrnes's tavern in order to consider on matters of
great importance respecting our present circumstances in regard to the
necessaries of life, as well as the present militia Act & its consequential
bad effects on the laboring poor, as all the fines & forfeitures together
with their own tour of duty will center on themselves, also the partiality
exhibited in the said act—those least entitled to it.

Slow and Sure

N.B.[42] Perhaps a certain great personage & his B[aylor's] Guards[43] will
favor us with their Company, but we are determined to be free. . . .

the poor are humbly requested . . . to obey Cerberus's Sumons in respect to the Election of their different Officers. . . .[44]

41. This is a nonliteral transcription from Anna Wharton, Morris, ed., "Journal of
Samuel Rowland Fisher, 1779–1781," *Pennsylvania Magazine of History and Biography* 41
(1917): 283.

42. The abbreviation for the Latin *nota bene*, meaning to mark well and pay particular
attention to that which follows.

43. This refers to Joseph Reed, president of the Supreme Executive Council, who had
strenuously opposed the militia at Fort Wilson. B[aylor's] Guards, Continental Dragoons,
again refers to the defeat of the militia at "Fort Wilson."

44. I have not found the broadside signed "Cerberus" (the three-headed dog in Greek
mythology who guarded the gate of Hades).

CHAPTER **10**

Small-Producer Thought

The Argument About Capitalism

RONALD SCHULTZ

The American Revolution, like the other Atlantic revolutions of the seventeenth and eighteenth centuries, witnessed a dramatic outpouring of popular thought. In the course of the Revolutionary upheaval, ordinary Americans, whose ideas were normally confined to the oral culture of the home, farm, and workshop, joined in public debate with America's leading merchants, planters, and lawyers about the new direction of the postwar society and economy. Nowhere was this dispute sharper than in Philadelphia.[1]

1. Popular thought in the Atlantic revolutions is the subject of a large historical literature. On the English Revolution of 1640–60, see Christopher Hill, *The World Turned Upside Down: Radical Ideas During the English Revolution* (New York: Viking Press, 1972); and Brian Manning, *The English People and the English Revolution, 1640–1649* (London: Heinemann,

Philadelphia's Revolutionary era artisans—skilled craftspeople who fashioned products by hand—were heirs, with working people in general, to a tradition of popular thought and political opposition that predated the Revolution by at least half a century. Vocal opponents of the city's self-serving elite since the founding of Pennsylvania in 1681, working people played a pivotal role in 1769 and 1770 in the nonimportation movement that banned the purchase of British goods and forced recalcitrant merchants to sacrifice a measure of their own wealth for the good of the community as a whole.[2] In 1776, when they were frustrated by the Provincial Assembly's refusal to take a pro-Independence stance, working people again formed the backbone of the popular Revolutionary movement that drove Pennsylvania's Quaker and Anglican oligarchy from power and pulled Pennsylvania into the Revolutionary camp.[3]

Despite their sacrifice and contribution to the Revolutionary cause, however, most Philadelphia artisans suffered during the war. Currency devaluation, the burdens of militia service that fell disproportionately on their shoulders (see Chapter 9), and the general scarcity of food and essential goods made their everyday lives more difficult than at any time in the past. These causes of discontent came to a head in the summer of 1779 when the popularly elected Committee of Trade called on the city's merchants to reduce their inflated prices to prewar levels. Hoping to sell flour and other foodstuffs to the French and Continental armies at much higher prices than could be found in Philadelphia markets, some Quaker City merchants had begun to hoard these items early in the summer. As a result, the cost of food and necessities skyrocketed.[4]

Against this backdrop, one of the most remarkable debates of the Revolutionary era took place. At the immediate level, the discussion between

1976). On the French Revolution, see Albert Soboul, *The Sans-Culottes: The Popular Movement and Revolutionary Government, 1793–1794* (Princeton: Princeton University Press, 1980); and George Rudé, *Ideology and Popular Protest* (New York: Pantheon Books, 1980). On the American Revolution, see Nash, *Urban Crucible;* Foner, *Tom Paine and Revolutionary America;* Edward Countryman, *A People in Revolution: The American Revolution and Political Society in New York, 1760–1790* (Baltimore: Johns Hopkins University Press, 1981); and Schultz, *Republic of Labor.*

2. The story of laboring-class opposition in early Pennsylvania is told in Gary B. Nash, *Quakers and Politics: Pennsylvania, 1681–1726* (Princeton: Princeton University Press, 1968).

3. The conflicts between Philadelphia artisans and the city's merchant oligarchy are detailed in Nash, *Urban Crucible;* Rosswurm, *Arms, Country, and Class;* Ryerson, *The Revolution Is Now Begun;* Olton, *Artisans for Independence;* and Schultz, *Republic of Labor.*

4. The 1779 price control movement is discussed in Foner, *Tom Paine,* chap. 5; Rosswurm, *Arms, Country, and Class,* chaps. 7–8; and Schultz, *Republic of Labor,* chap. 2.

Philadelphia merchants and the popularly based Committee of Thirteen concerned the propriety and feasibility of price controls. But at a more fundamental level, the argument pitted two opposing conceptions of community and individual property rights against each other. The merchants' delegation claimed that an unfettered marketplace was the most salutary device for meeting the needs of the community. A free market, they declared, harnessed individual greed for the well-being of all citizens, and any intervention in the marketplace disrupted the "natural" forces of supply and demand to the detriment of everyone involved.[5]

The Committee of Thirteen, whose chairman, Blair McClenachan, was one of the political leaders of the city's craftsmen, thought differently. From the perspective of the ordinary artisan and working person, mercantile greed had driven up the prices of life's necessities and devalued the paper money, on which laboring people depended for payment of services, wages, and the purchase of raw materials, food, and rent. To many laboring-class Philadelphians, an unrestrained market meant the continued polarization of their community into a small class of the truly wealthy and a larger class of impoverished, or nearly impoverished, working people. After all, both poverty and economic inequality had intensified markedly in the city during the decade preceding the Revolution.[6]

By making a distinction between ownership and service, the Committee of Thirteen drew on the moral force of a small-producer ethic that had long informed the thoughts of the city's artisans and less-skilled working people. This ethic, rooted in the culture of the medieval guilds, the popular assertiveness of the English Reformation, and the upheavals of the seventeenth-century English civil war, viewed labor as the cornerstone of social existence and placed the producing artisan and ordinary laborer at the center of community life. This popular version of the "labor theory of value" had wide currency among the working people of early America and is here expressed as the notion of service: the idea that by investing their labor in building, outfitting, and provisioning ships for Philadelphia's merchants, workers established a claim on the use to which these ships were put. Only the collective toil of ship carpen-

5. This point of view, which predated Adam Smith by more than a century, is discussed in Albert O. Hirshman, *The Passions and the Interests: Political Arguments for Capitalism Before Its Triumph* (Princeton: Princeton University Press, 1977); and Joyce Oldham Appelby, *Economic Thought and Ideology in Seventeenth-Century England* (Princeton: Princeton University Press, 1978), esp. chap. 7.

6. McClenachan's role as a popular leader is treated in Schultz, *Republic of Labor*, chap. 3. For the plight of Philadelphia's working people and the growth of poverty and inequality during this period, see Rosswurm, *Arms, Country, and Class*; and Smith, *The "Lower Sort."*

ters, caulkers, riggers, and many other laboring people, the artisan-based committee argued, enabled Philadelphia merchants to practice their profession. In return, city workers expected an equal exercise of community responsibility on the part of merchants. By hoarding flour and shipping it to more lucrative markets at a time when many of the city's poorer residents could not even obtain bread, merchants blatantly violated the small-producer ethic of Philadelphia workers.

In the event, the price control movement failed, hobbled by the unwillingness of Committee of Trade leaders to use force to reduce prices. But the artisans' small-producer ethic continued to form the basis of artisan and laboring-class thought in the post-Revolutionary world. By the turn of the nineteenth century, Philadelphia journeymen would again seek to create a republic of labor by joining their small-producer traditions to the emerging Democratic-Republican party of Thomas Jefferson.[7]

The price control movement of 1779 thus provided the setting for one of the most important moral confrontations of the Revolution. By pitting the merchants' laissez-faire philosophy against the artisans' small-producer ethic, the struggle of 1779 asked Philadelphians to decide the future shape of American society, including its social structure, the power relationship between capitalists and workers, and the nature of the marketplace itself. Even though capitalism has triumphed throughout much of the modern world, these issues continue to be hotly debated today.[8]

The document below is the Committee of Thirteen's rationale for price control as it originally appeared in one of the city's newspapers, the *Pennsylvania Packet*, on September 10, 1779.

The Committee of Thirteen Reply

. . . Considering ourselves either as members of the general committee elected for the purpose of executing the resolves of the town-meeting, or as members of the sub-committee appointed by the general committee

7. The city's artisans were aided in this project by William Duane, publisher of the Philadelphia newspaper *Aurora* and one of the intellectual leaders of the city's early working-class movement. On Duane's role, see Schultz, *Republic of Labor*, chaps. 5–7.

8. The small-producer ethic is analyzed in Ronald Schultz, "The Small-Producer Tradition and the Moral Origins of Artisan Radicalism in Philadelphia, 1720–1810," *Past and Present*, no. 127 (1990): 84–116.

for receiving information or making enquiries, . . . we beg leave to offer
a few remarks on such parts [of the merchants' memorial] as appear
most to deserve or require it.

The [merchants'] memorial opens with a declaration on the part of the
memorialists that from the earliest time of the stamp-act they took a
decided part in favour of the liberties of America, and have invariably
continued the same unto the present day. Against this we can have nothing to object, more than that, from the want of years several of them
were not then sufficiently interested in the concerns of life to subscribe
collectively under the same character, and therefore the declaration,
however well intended, seems to convey an idea of durable importance
which is not altogether the case.[9]

Page the 1st, the [merchant] memorialists say that "the limitation of
prices is in the principle unjust," and the reasons they assign for this
declaration are, "because," say they, "it invades the laws of property, by
compelling a person to accept of less in exchange for his goods than he
could otherwise obtain."

To this we reply, that the claiming a right to an unlimited extortion,
such as prevailed before the [price] limitation took place, and to be able
to enforce that claim because that the foreign necessaries of life are in
the hands of a few, and the use of them wanted by many who cannot
otherwise procure them, nor conveniently subsist without them, *is a
principle far more unjust.* And therefore admitting their position to be true
(which we do not) and determining between two evils by a comparison of
causes and consequences, we are led to prefer the least as the wisest
choice.

We likewise think it a far greater invasion of property that any one
man or set of men should, at their own unlimited discretion, distress
others to give as much again for a thing as it is worth, because such
persons cannot do without . . . it, than it can be in the 1st mentioned
persons to limit such articles to a just and reasonable profit.

Neither can we subscribe to the doctrine that "*the limitation of prices is in
the principle unjust.*" We observe that the limiting of prices, where extortion
might otherwise be easily practiced, has been the custom, not only of our
own but of other countries in particular times and cases. The limiting the
interest of money by law, to prevent extortionous usury, is on the same
principle. The limiting tavern expenses, porters and carriers charges,

---

9. This refers to the 1765 Stamp Act crisis, when many merchants joined with laboring
Philadelphians to oppose the stamp tax imposed by the British Parliament.

ferriages, and numerous other matters, by the former laws of this state, are founded on the probability, that if no such restraints were laid on, that the persons practicing those employments would take an unjust advantage of the immediate necessity of others, and compel them to pay just what they pleased. Yet we never remember the merchants exclaiming that the principle, thus applied to their advantage, was unjust.

The state of foreign trade is now in the same predicament with the matters already mentioned. It is in the hands of a few. These few have it in their power to exact what they please, and to assume a discretionary command over the purses of their fellow citizens. And we are sorry to have occasion to say that both in their dealings and in their memorial they have discovered too much of that principle which requires restraint. . . .

We further hold that the social compact or state of civil society, by which men are united and incorporated, requires that every right or power claimed or exercised by any man or set of men should be in subordination to the common good, and that whatever is incompatible therewith must, by some rule or regulation, be brought in subjection thereto.

The [merchant] memorialists claim an unlimited right of setting what price they please on their commodities, and from the present situation of trade they have it in their power to enforce those prices. The right without the power would produce no ill effect, as is evidently seen in times when trade is free, open and plentiful; but the present situation of trade has introduced a union of the right with the power, and therefore it becomes dangerous, and requires that kind of restraint which shall make it otherwise.

To illustrate this we shall instance the case of a single person, for if the right and power which the [merchant] memorialists contend for is well founded, it will be as true in one person as in a body of men making it a common cause between them. Suppose that every article of foreign produce or manufacture in this state was in the hands of a single merchant, has he or has he not a right to exact what prices he pleases, however extortionous, or to shut up his warehouses and refuse selling them till the accumulated wants of the community shall distress them to compliance?

We are free to declare he has not such a right; and that not only on account of the fatal or dangerous consequences attending it, but on the ground he stands with regard to the supplies themselves, for as he could not possess himself of those articles without first deriving assistance from the collected efforts of the community, it follows as an act of duty, that having first received advantage from their service he owes them his in return, at a price proportioned to what he gave; and, therefore, whenever the avarice of individuals occasions them to transgress this line, the principles of public justice and common good require it to be limited. In short, we wish the [merchant] memorialists to see that it is the extortion which has been so extensively practiced that we wish to restrain and prevent; and there is no way to reach or check it than by a limitation of prices, therefore those limitations, operating as a boundary to the extortion, become at once both necessary and just.

[The Committee of Trade had presented a proposed Articles of Association to the city's merchants in the summer of 1779. In an effort to ensure that enough European manufactured goods were available in Philadelphia, the Association would have committed merchants not to import and sell European products directly to other American ports where they might earn a greater profit.]

As this matter naturally connected with an article in the proposed association against which the [merchant] memorialists likewise object, we shall . . . reply to the [merchants'] objections . . . against the aforesaid article, which article is in the following words:

"And we do further engage and promise that we will not order any of our ships or vessels loaded or to be loaded with foreign produce or manufactures . . . into any port out of this state, there to unload, or permit any commander or master in our employ so to do . . . and that we will to the utmost of our power use our best endeavours to keep the state supplied with such produce and manufactures, whether foreign or domestic, as we in our several dealings and occupations are or shall be concerned in, and having done so, will likewise endeavour to supply the wants of any of the United States."

To this, [the merchant] memorialists object and say, —"That the American merchants" (*meaning themselves*) "would pursue a different line of conduct" (*that is, send their vessels to other places*) was easily foreseen, and "therefore," say they, "an association is proposed, by which we are to covenant that we will order our vessels to this port and conform to your regulations. We cannot," say they, "but observe that the proposal of such an association clearly demonstrates the impropriety of any limitations, because it shows a conviction that we should have pursued a different line of conduct, and that these evils have taken place which are before hinted at. But the association would be more unjust and impolitic than the limitation itself. For first, as it is confessedly the *only* measure which can support the other, it is chargeable with the like injustice. Secondly, it would direct our enemies where to cruise, in order to intercept supplies; and thirdly, it would oblige us to continue a trade which we can demonstrate to be ruinous."

To this we reply, first, in general terms, that we can see no injustice in requiring from them a service which it would be their duty to perform if no such assurance was required; and that for the following reasons:

On our return to this city after it was evacuated by the enemy, there was not a vessel, scarcely a boat, to be seen in the river.[10] It was therefore impossible that those who then professed themselves merchants, or have since denominated themselves by that character, could exercise their professions without the accumulated assistance of the several trades and manufacturers concerned in the art of building and fitting out vessels for sea. Ship carpenters, joiners, blacksmiths, gunsmiths, rope makers, block makers, tanners, curriers, painters and laborers of numerous kinds, contributed their several portions of service to this purpose. When the vessel was on float and capable of sailing, another set of men were employed to victual her, and a third to man her; and without the previous assistance of all these, the merchant would have been only an unserviceable name applied to an occupation extinct and useless.

We conceive that those men and all others concerned had something more in view than their mere wages when employed in the constructing and fitting out vessels for mercantile purposes, and that they naturally considered themselves as furnishing such vessels, not so much for the particular emoluments of the merchant who employed them as for the more beneficial purposes of supplying themselves and fellow citizens with foreign necessaries; and there-fore we hold, that though by the acceptance of wages they have not, and cannot have any claim in the *property* of the vessel, after she is built and paid for, we nevertheless hold, that they and the state in general have a right in the *service* of the vessel, because it constitutes a considerable part of the advantage they hoped to derive from their labors.

That the *property* of the vessel is the immediate right of the owner, and the *service* of it the right of the community collectively with the owner, is so naturally deduced from the purposes for which all mercantile vessels are built, that we undertake to declare as our opinion, that the proposed article in the association, whereby the service of such vessels is so claimed

10. During the military occupation of Philadelphia in the winter of 1777–78, the British destroyed most of the city's maritime fleet as well as many buildings and homes.

and stipulated for, is founded on a matter of right in the community, and therefore is not and cannot be unjust.

To illustrate this point by a farther argument, and to shew that an exclusive right to the service of vessels is not vested in the owner, we will suppose a case that will clearly prove them to be distinct and separate, which is,

That if the owner has a right to employ his vessels without any regard to the interest or convenience of the community he resides among, he has a right *not* to employ them for any purpose whatever, or to burn or otherwise destroy them, and consequently the merchants claim a collective right of suspending the commerce of a country whenever they please, which never can be admitted, because, in this case, the claim of a few individuals is opposed to the good of the community; to which . . . separate claims must be subordinate. Thus much for the general principles on which the aforesaid article in this proposed association is founded. We now proceed to take notice of the particular objections stated against it in the memorial:

The [merchant] memorialists say, that as the aforementioned article in the association is "confessedly the *only* measure that can support the limitation of prices, it is chargeable with the like injustice."

In replying to this position we would first observe that the reasoning in it is defective, because the supposed injustice in the article is placed on its being the "*only*" measure that can support the limitations, which mode of reasoning appears to us to be neither truth nor argument because it will from thence follow, that *any* measure which can be applied or thought of for that purpose must of course be chargeable with injustice; an assertion we likewise deny, unless it can [be] proved that the banishment of extortion is an act of criminality.

We would further observe that the [merchant] memorialists, by allowing the aforesaid article in the association to be the "*only*" measure that can support the regulations, confess thereby that the regulations are supportable, and that the committee have luckily or wisely hit on the very thing which will give it that support; which confession we cannot but consider as a very powerful reason why the service of the vessels here constructed or fitted out should be applied to the purpose expressed in the association. And we have yet further to observe, that they have likewise furnished us with additional reasons for requiring from them this part of a citizen's duty, because they have in several parts of their memorial thrown out hints that the hope of a little more gain in any other place will induce the importers to desert the convenience of the community they reside among by carrying their vessels and cargoes elsewhere.

In reply to their second objection, we do not conceive that the directing their vessels to this port will be any further inducement to the enemy than the directing them to other ports; because the time of their return being always uncertain the enemy can have no more hope in one place than another, and their coming in will in any case be safer than their going out. Beside which, the present condition of the enemy at sea and the superiority of the combined fleets of France, Spain and America, will render it impossible for the enemy to keep stationary vessels in the manner they formerly did, and as most of our armed vessels are superior to the little half manned privateers of New-York, we do not look on this objection as having sufficient weight, and the less so, as the aforesaid article in the association admits their putting into other ports under circumstances or distress or danger.[11]

To their third objection, namely, that "it is obliging them to continue a commerce which they can demonstrate to be ruinous," we have only reply, that whenever they please to quit it by disposing of their vessels they will find persons enough to succeed them who will not start the same objections, and as we have yet heard of no importer becoming a bankrupt, we think the fact somewhat contradicts the assertion.

As an appendage to their objections against the aforesaid article in the association, the [merchant] memorialists . . . say "that the measure of preventing exports from this state to the neighboring states will be found pernicious to her in the same manner that all selfish plans of policy have ever been." To this we answer that we know of no article in the proposed association that admits of such an explanation or justifies such an assertion. We only enjoin that persons resident in this state and fitting out vessels from hence, shall import their returns into it, and we recommend the same measure to every state in the union while the war lasts; because we are of opinion that it is not only just in itself but will likewise abolish the custom of hawking cargoes from state to state, by which means the prices are unnecessarily kept up, and also prevent those artificial scarcities being produced by withholding the supplies, and thereby enforcing exorbitant prices on the stock in hand. But it is, and ever has been, and ever will be, our wish and endeavour to supply the rest of the states, especially such as do not or cannot import, and in order to do this, it is in

11. Before France formally allied with the United States in 1778 and supplied naval protection, the British maintained an effective maritime blockade of American ports.

the first instance necessary that the imports should be confined to the supply of that market from whence those after supplies are to proceed, and therefore it is not we, but the importers, who prevent the supplying such states, by not making a sufficiency of returns into this, or by concealing them after they are arrived. . . .

The frequent declarations and reasonings interspersed through the [merchant] memorial in favour of a *free trade* are in our opinion delusively applied to cases they have no concern with, unless it can be proved that a right to extort and a power to enforce that extortion is one of the descriptive principles of a free trade, which we deny: A *free trade* consists in the right of every one to partake of it, and to deal to the best advantage he can, on just and equitable principles subordinate to the common good; and as soon as this line is encroached on, either by the one extorting more for an article than it is worth, or the other for demanding it for less than its value, the *freedom* is equally invaded and requires to be regulated. Neither can we help observing that the freedom of trade as the freedom of extorting, and as we consider extortion to be incompatible with the right and advantages of a free trade, therefore the limitations by being levelled against the one are calculated to support the other. But if the freedom of trade is to be taken on the scale which the [merchant] memorialists have affixed to it, then must all and every species of forestalling, monopolizing and engrossing[12] be sanctioned thereby, because their idea of a free trade is for every man to do what he pleases; a right, which if claimed and exercised by individuals in that line, may for the same reason be claimed and exercised by individuals in matters of government, and therefore the practice is inadmissable, because it is repugnant to the very principles on which society and civil governments are founded. We likewise think it needless in the [merchant] memorialists to advance any thing on this head to us, who are ourselves tradesmen, and several of us importers, and consequently are as much interested in supporting the fair and just freedom of trade as themselves.

That we may not be thought to have introduced the words *forestalling, monopolizing* and *engrossing* with an ill-natured design . . . we shall quote

---

12. "Forestallers," "monopolizers," and "engrossers"—all usually merchants—were favorite villains of laboring people. A monopolizer bought large quantities of an item, then created an artificial scarcity by removing it from the market, then realized large profits by selling it at a high price. A forestaller withheld goods from the marketplace to drive up their price. An engrosser was a monopolizer of vital commodities necessary for the maintenance of life.

what [merchants] themselves have advanced in . . . their memorial, and sorry we are to say that such practices should find such public advocates.

"We know," say the [merchant] memorialists, "how great is the popular odium against men of this case" (meaning the persons above-mentioned) "and we would avoid saying any thing upon the occasion, if it were not necessary to convey to you in the fullest manner the just sentiments of our hearts. It must be remembered that those men relieved the necessities of Pennsylvania when the enemy were in possession of her capital, by introducing articles of consumption from the extremes of the continent. It is true they were prompted by the love of gain, but whatever may have been the cause the effect certainly was to relieve the necessities of the people. Leaving this however out of the question, it will readily be admitted that the trade of an engrosser consists in hoarding up those articles which will probably become scarce and dear, to take advantage of that circumstance, creating thereby an artificial previous to a natural scarcity. By the high price consequent upon the artificial scarcity, the actual consumption is lessened, the natural scarcity is lessened, and an actual want prevented. Thus the interested views of these men, like the provident foresight of a Captain who puts his people on short allowance, prevents in both cases sufferings of the most alarming nature."

To this we reply that we know of no kind of vice that cannot be palliated, but we insist that none can be justified. Neither are the arguments they have advanced consistently founded under any circumstances they can suppose, because the same quantity of goods in their first distributed state will supply the same quantity of wants as they will in their collected or monopolized state, and that with greater convenience to the purchaser, and loaded with less expense; and therefore as monopolizing does not increase the quantity of goods, but only collects them, it will follow, that the same *short allowance* will take place in one case as in another; and admitting the same profits to be put on them by the first holders as are afterwards put on them by the monopolizer, yet the unnecessary expense of carriage is saved upon the goods, and the charges of travelling is lessened to the consumer. But it often happens that the most plentiful articles may be and are monopolized, and a scarcity produced from no other cause, and therefore in whatever light it may be viewed, we conceive that no vindication can be set up for a practice which in no probable case can do good, and in every known case must do hurt.

We hear much of a scarcity of several articles in the city, and we think it necessary to call on the [merchant] memorialists for the reason. The

imports, since the regulations took place, have, we believe, been more
plentiful than before, and therefore no scarcity could happen unless the
importers and wholesale dealers have either concealed their goods or
collusively disposed of them. To say they have sent them elsewhere,
because they could get a few more shillings per pound or per gallon, is to
confess the offence for which themselves must answer. And desirous as
we may be to execute the trust committed to us, it is impossible for us
without further assistance, to watch men who from inclination or avarice
may be disposed to thwart every public measure, and to justify such
conduct by the pretence of a *free trade*.

We were in hopes the [merchants'] memorial would have afforded us a
ground whereon to establish a plan of mutual confidence and dependence, between the several parts of the community; and it is matter of
surprise to us to find so considerable a number of the same names
subscribed to the memorial as were proposed in a ticket for members of a
committee at the last election, because it proves to us that the disposition
of such persons, though at that time partially concealed, was directly
contrary to the purposes for which they were proposed to be chosen; and
that the powers they so endeavoured to possess were intended to be
applied to oppose the measures they seemed to countenance.

The repeated experience of four years has convinced us of the abso-
lute necessity of limiting the prices, in order to stop the depreciation.
Every penny taken from the former will be so much, at least, added to
the value of the money, and when it is considered how great a part of the
property of America is invested in the money, it is certainly not only a
national object but an object of individual advantage to endeavour to
give to it as much permanent value as the quantity will admit of.

But this is not all. We cannot go on with the currency if the rise of the
prices is to continue. Every calculation for the maintenance of the army
and of government is unhinged thereby. Had we no army, no government expenses to support, the emissions might stop whether there was
money in the treasury or not, but this not being the case, and the daily
demands for money being increased by the advance of prices, the emissions are thereby unavoidably forced on, and as soon as they are out in
circulation are as instantly swallowed up by the new increase of prices
which succeed them.

Limit those prices so that the expenses of government will admit of
calculation, and promote, at the same time, the measures for collecting
money into the public treasury either by a subscription of taxes or by

levying them directly on such persons as shall neglect to subscribe, and the emissions may then be stopped. But we think it worthy of remark, that in our opinion, the stoppage can only take place in *consequence* of those measures and not be made the *means* for producing them, because the treasury must have an ability to go on at the very instant in which the emissions shall cease.

APPENDIX:
MONETARY VALUES

The values of monetary amounts that appear in the various documents can be evaluated by comparing them against some basic prices and wages in late eighteenth-century Philadelphia provided below. Throughout the period, 1770–1810, there were 12d. (pence) in 1s. (shilling), and 20s. in £1 (pound). During the 1790s, when the new nation was in the process of changing its currency to a dollar-based system, 7s. and 6d. equaled $1.

Monetary Values

	Average Price or Wage[a]	
Item	1772	1795
Monthly wages		
Laborer	£ 3.90	$ 22.04
Mariner	£ 3.13	$ 23.95
Ship mate	£ 4.63	$ 30.99
Ship captain	£ 6.98	$ 36.00
Washerwoman	£ 3.12	$ 11.33
Annual rent		
Laborer	£10.08	$ 41.88
Mariner	£11.85	$ 49.23
Shoemaker	£21.99	$ 91.34
Tailor	£22.81	$ 94.79
Annual minimal cost		
for family of four		
Firewood	£ 5.10	$ 29.42
Clothing	£ 7.22	$ 25.84
Food	£30.35	$169.24
Price per pound		
Meat	3.58d.	$ 0.06
Rice	2.36d.	$ 0.06
Chocolate	1.30s.	$ 0.24
Coffee	1.35s.	$ 0.21
Bohea tea	4.58s.	$ 0.46
Common flour	2.14s.	$ 0.69
Price per gallon		
Milk	0.89s.	$ 0.24
Philadelphia rum	5.00s.	$ 1.00
Molasses	1.92s.	$ 0.78

Source: Calculated from data in Billy G. Smith, *The "Lower Sort": Philadelphia's Laboring People, 1750–1800* (Ithaca: Cornell University Press, 1990), 101, 110, 114, 232–37.

[a]All amounts are in Pennsylvania currency.

GLOSSARY

augue: An acute fever marked by regularly recurring chills.

barrow: A castrated hog.

boreal: A wind from the north.

bound servant: People, usually Europeans, who sold themselves into servitude for three or four years in return for passage to America, maintenance, and perhaps freedom dues at the conclusion of their term. A few Americans also indentured themselves as bound servants for several years.

castor hat: A hat originally either made of beaver's fur or intended to imitate such. By the late eighteenth century it was often made of rabbit's fur.

chain: The horizontal threads crossing the warp in a woven fabric.

chattels: Movable personal property.

coarse tow: Coarse broken flax or hemp fiber prepared for spinning.

consumption: A progressive wasting away of the body, particularly by tuberculosis.

country born: Born in America.

disorderly house: A brothel or an illegal tavern.

dropsy: An abnormal accumulation of serous fluid in connective tissue causing puffy swelling.

engrosser: A person who purchased large quantities of a vital commodity (such as flour) necessary for the maintenance of life, then withheld it from the market in order to drive up its price and to make a large profit.

filling: An inferior cloth used primarily to occupy space in a garment.

flux: Diarrhea.

forestaller: A person who withheld goods from the marketplace to drive up the price.

freedom dues: The clothing, cash, and other items that indentured servants sometimes received from their masters at the completion of their years of service.

friend: A Quaker.

fustian: A type of cloth originally manufactured at Fusht on the Nile; it contained a warp of linen thread and a woof of thick cotton.

gaol: Jail.

gathering: A festering abscess.

Germantown: A small town several miles north of Philadelphia.

grazer: A person who fattened cattle for the market by allowing them to graze.

hank: 560 yards of yarn.

hat fiddles: Ornaments on hats.

Hispaniola: An island in the West Indies.

hives: A corruption of the word "heaves." It signified a childhood disease characterized by extremely difficult breathing and a hoarse, rasping cough.

hostler: A person who takes care of horses, generally at an inn or stable.

instant: Of or occurring in the immediate month.

lax: Diarrhea.

leading strings: Two cords attached to the shoulders of the dresses worn by toddlers, used by parents to steady a child's movements.

linsey: Coarse woolen stuff first made at Linsey in Suffolk, England, and very popular in early America.

lousy: Infected with lice.

magnum bonum (*Magnumbonums*): A large yellow plum.

monopolizer: A person, usually a merchant, who bought large quantities of a specific item, created an artificial scarcity by removing it from the market, then gained large profits by selling the item at a high price.

muslin: Generally a delicately woven cotton fabric.

N.B.: The abbreviation for the Latin *nota bene*, meaning to mark well and pay particular attention to that which follows.

nankeen: An imported yellow cotton cloth manufactured in Nanjing, China.

neat's leather: Made from the hide of a bovine animal.

necessary: A toilet.

Northern Liberties: Philadelphia's northern suburb.

palsied: Paralyzed in some part of the body.

patrol: The city's night watchmen.

phthisick: Any type of debilitating affliction.

pinchbeck watches: A toy watch, or one made of cheap alloy resembling gold.

relict: A widow.

roram hat: A hat made of a woolen cloth with a fur face.

schooner: A vessel with two or more masts.

shaloon: A woolen fabric made in Chalons, France.

shirting: A kind of stout cotton cloth used to make shirts.

shoat: A young hog.

sloop: A small, single-mast vessel.

snow: A small ship.

Society of Friends: The Quakers.

Southwark: Philadelphia's southern suburb.

St. Kitts: A British colony in the West Indies.

stranguary: A slow, painful discharge of urine produced by spasmodic muscular contractions of the urethra and bladder.

surtout coat: A man's large overcoat.

swanskin: A fleecy cloth like Canton flannel used especially for linings.

ticking: A case or covering containing feathers, flocks, or the like to form a mattress or pillow, or the strong, hard linen or cotton material used for making such cases.

ticklenburg: A kind of coarse linen cloth.

toilinet: A kind of fine woolen cloth.

ultimo: Of or occurring in the month preceding the present.

velveret: A variety of fustian with a velvet surface.

waitingman: A personal servant.

westcoats: An underjacket or a vest.

worsted: A woolen fabric or stuff made from well-twisted yarn spun of long-staple wool combed to lay the fibers parallel. First made at Worstead in England.

SELECTED BIBLIOGRAPHY
AND FURTHER READING

Alexander, John K. "Deference in Colonial Pennsylvania and That Man from New Jersey." *Pennsylvania Magazine of History and Biography* 102 (1978): 422–36.

———. "The Fort Wilson Incident of 1779: A Case Study of the Revolutionary Crowd." *William and Mary Quarterly*, 3rd ser., 31 (1974): 589–612.

———. "Institutional Imperialism and the Sick Poor in Late Eighteenth-Century Philadelphia: The House of Employment vs. The Pennsylvania Hospital." *Pennsylvania History* 51 (1984): 101–17.

———. "The Philadelphia Numbers Game: An Analysis of Philadelphia's Eighteenth-Century Population." *Pennsylvania Magazine of History and Biography* 98 (1974): 314–24.

———. *Render Them Submissive: Responses to Poverty in Philadelphia, 1760–1800.* Amherst: University of Massachusetts Press, 1980.

Aries, Philippe. *Centuries of Childhood: A Social History of Family Life.* New York: Vintage, 1962.

Armes, Ethel, ed. *Nancy Shippen: Her Journal Book.* Philadelphia: J. B. Lippincott, 1935.

Baron, Ava, and Susan E. Klepp. " 'If I Didn't Have My Sewing Machine . . .': Women and Sewing Machine Technology." In *A Needle, a Bobbin, a Strike: Women Needleworkers in America,* edited by Joan M. Jensen and Sue Davidson, 20–59. Philadelphia: Temple University Press, 1984.

Bauman, Richard. *For the Reputation of Truth: Politics, Religion, and Conflict Among the Pennsylvania Quakers, 1750–1800.* Baltimore: Johns Hopkins University Press, 1971.

Becker, Carl. *The History of Political Parties in the Province of New York, 1760–1776.* Madison: University of Wisconsin Press, 1909.

Biddle, Henry D., ed. *Extracts from the Journal of Elizabeth Drinker.* Philadelphia: J. B. Lippincott Company, 1889.

Boydston, Jeanne. *Home and Work: Housework, Wages, and the Ideology of Labor in the Early Republic.* New York: Oxford University Press, 1990.

Carson, Ann. *The History of the Celebrated Mrs. Ann Carson, Widow of the Late Unfortunate Lieutenant Richard Smith. . . .* Philadelphia, 1822.

Clement, Priscilla F. *Welfare and the Poor in the Nineteenth-Century City: Philadelphia, 1800–1854.* Rutherford, N.J.: Fairleigh Dickinson University Press, 1985.

Cooke, Jacob Ernest, et al., eds. *Encyclopedia of the North American Colonies.* 3 vols. New York: Charles Scribner's Sons, 1993.

Countryman, Edward. *The American Revolution.* New York: Hill & Wang, 1985.

———. *A People in Revolution: The American Revolution and Political Society in New York, 1760–1790.* Baltimore: Johns Hopkins University Press, 1981.

Crane, Elaine F. "The World of Elizabeth Drinker." *Pennsylvania Magazine of History and Biography* 107 (1983): 3–28.

Crane, Elizabeth Forman. *The Diary of Elizabeth Drinker.* 3 vols. Boston: Northeastern University Press, 1991.

Cray, Robert E., Jr. *Paupers and Poor Relief in New York City and Its Rural Environs, 1700–1830.* Philadelphia: Temple University Press, 1988.

Davidson, Cathy N. *Revolution and the Word: The Rise of the Novel in America.* New York: Oxford University Press, 1986.

Doerflinger, Thomas M. *A Vigorous Spirit of Enterprise: Merchants and Economic Development in Revolutionary Philadelphia.* Chapel Hill: University of North Carolina Press, 1986.

Duffy, John. *Epidemics in Colonial America.* Baton Rouge: Louisiana State University Press, 1953.

Fitzroy, Herbert W. K. "The Punishment of Crime in Provincial Pennsylvania." *Pennsylvania Magazine of History and Biography* 60 (1936): 242–69.

Foner, Eric. *Tom Paine and Revolutionary America.* New York: Oxford University Press, 1976.

Goldin, Claudia. "The Economic Status of Women in the Early Republic: Quantitative Evidence." *Journal of Interdisciplinary History* 16 (1986): 375–404.

Gough, Robert. "Towards a Theory of Class and Social Conflict: A Social History of Wealthy Philadelphians, 1775 and 1800." Ph.D. diss., University of Pennsylvania, 1977.

Greene, Jack P., and J. R. Pole, eds. *Colonial British America: Essays in the New History of the Early Modern Era.* Baltimore: Johns Hopkins University Press, 1984.

Hawke, David. *In the Midst of a Revolution.* Philadelphia: University of Pennsylvania Press, 1961.

Hirshman, Albert O. *The Passions and the Interests: Political Arguments for Capitalism Before Its Triumph.* Princeton: Princeton University Press, 1977.

Hoerder, Dirk. *Crowd Action in Revolutionary Massachusetts, 1765–1780.* New York: Academic Press, 1977.

Hoffer, Peter Charles. "Crime and Law Enforcement: The British Colonies." In *Encyclopedia of the North American Colonies,* 3 vols., edited by Jacob Ernest Cooke et al., 1:391–402. New York: Charles Scribner's Sons, 1993.

Hoffman, Ronald, and Peter J. Albert, eds. *Arms and Independence: The Military Character of the American Revolution.* Charlottesville: University Press of Virginia, 1984.

———. *Sovereign States in an Age of Uncertainty.* Charlottesville: University Press of Virginia, 1981.

Jensen, Joan M. "Needlework as Art, Craft, and Livelihood Before 1900." In *A Needle, a Bobbin, a Strike: Women Needleworkers in America,* edited by Joan M. Jensen and Sue Davidson, 1–19. Philadelphia: Temple University Press, 1984.

Jensen, Joan M., and Sue Davidson, eds. *A Needle, a Bobbin, a Strike: Women Needleworkers in America.* Philadelphia: Temple University Press, 1984.

Johnson, Amandus. *The Journal and Biography of Nicholas Collin.* Philadelphia: New Jersey Society of Pennsylvania, 1936.

Jones, Douglas Lamar. "The Strolling Poor: Transiency in Eighteenth-Century Massachusetts." *Journal of Social History* 8 (1975): 28–54.

Katz, Michael B. *In the Shadow of the Poorhouse: A Social History of Welfare in America.* New York: Basic Books, 1986.

Kerber, Linda K. *Women of the Republic: Intellect and Ideology in Revolutionary America.* Chapel Hill: University of North Carolina Press, 1980.

Klepp, Susan E. "Demography in Early Philadelphia, 1690–1860." *Proceedings of the American Philosophical Society* 133 (1989): 85–111.

———. *Philadelphia in Transition: A Demographic History of the City and Its Occupational Groups, 1720–1830.* New York: Garland, 1989.

Klepp, Susan E., ed. *The Demographic History of the Philadelphia Region, 1600–1860.* Philadelphia: American Philosophical Society, 1989.

———. *"The Swift Progress of Population": A Documentary and Bibliographic Study of Philadelphia's Growth, 1642–1859.* Philadelphia: American Philosophical Society, 1991.

Lemisch, Jesse, ed. *Benjamin Franklin: The Autobiography and Other Writings.* New York: New American Library, 1961.

Lermack, Paul. "Peace Bonds and Criminal Justice in Colonial Philadelphia." *Pennsylvania Magazine of History and Biography* 100 (1976): 173–90.

Lincoln, Charles H. *The Revolutionary Movement in Pennsylvania, 1760–1776.* Philadelphia: University of Pennsylvania Press, 1901.

Linebaugh, Peter. "Jubilating; or, How the Atlantic Working Class Used the Biblical Jubilee Against Capitalism, with Some Success." *Radical History Review* 50 (1991): 143–80.

Linebaugh, Peter, and Marcus Rediker. "The Many Headed Hydra: Sailors, Slaves, and the Atlantic Working Class in the Eighteenth Century." *Journal of Historical Sociology* 3 (1990): 225–52.

McColley, Robert. "Slavery: The British Colonies." In *Encyclopedia of the North American Colonies,* 3 vols., edited by Jacob Ernest Cooke et al., 2:67–86. New York: Charles Scribner's Sons, 1993.

McManus, Edgar J. *Black Bondage in the North.* Syracuse, N.Y.: Syracuse University Press, 1973.

Maier, Pauline. *From Resistance to Revolution: Colonial Radicals and the Development of American Opposition to Britain, 1765–1776.* New York: Knopf, 1972.

Miller, Richard G. *Philadelphia—The Federalist City: A Study of Urban Politics, 1789–1801.* Port Washington, N.Y.: Kennikat Press, 1976.

Mitchell, James T., and Henry Flanders, comps. *The Statutes at Large of Pennsylvania from 1682 to 1801.* 18 vols. Harrisburg, 1896–1911.

Mohl, Raymond A. *Poverty in New York, 1783–1825.* New York: Oxford University Press, 1971.

Morgan, Philip D. "Bound Labor: The British and Dutch Colonies." In *Encyclopedia of the North American Colonies,* 3 vols., edited by Jacob Ernest Cooke et al., 2:17–31. New York: Charles Scribner's Sons, 1993.

Nash, Gary B. *Forging Freedom: The Formation of Philadelphia's Black Community, 1720–1840.* Cambridge: Harvard University Press, 1988.

————. "Poverty and Poor Relief in Pre-Revolutionary Philadelphia." *William and Mary Quarterly,* 3rd ser., 23 (1976): 3–30.

————. *The Urban Crucible: Social Change, Political Consciousness, and the Origins of the American Revolution.* Cambridge: Harvard University Press, 1979.

————. "Urban Wealth and Poverty in Pre-Revolutionary America." *Journal of Interdisciplinary History* 6 (1976): 545–84.

Nash, Gary B., and Jean R. Soderlund. *Freedom by Degrees: Emancipation in Eighteenth-Century Pennsylvania.* New York: Oxford University Press, 1991.

Norton, Mary Beth. *Liberty's Daughters: The Revolutionary Experience of American Women, 1750–1800.* Boston: Little, Brown, 1980.

Olton, Charles S. *Artisans for Independence: Philadelphia Mechanics and the American Revolution.* Syracuse, N.Y.: Syracuse University Press, 1975.

Patrick-Stamp, Leslie. "The Prison Sentence Dockets for 1795." *Pennsylvania History* 60 (1993): 353–82.

Powell, J. H. *Bring Out Your Dead: The Great Plague of Yellow Fever in Philadelphia in 1793.* 1949. Reprint, Philadelphia: University of Pennsylvania Press, 1993.

Rorabaugh, W. J. *The Craft Apprentice from Franklin to the Machine Age in America.* New York: Oxford University Press, 1986.

Rosswurm, Steven. *Arms, Country, and Class: The Philadelphia Militia and the American Revolution.* New Brunswick, N.J.: Rutgers University Press, 1987.

————. " 'As a Lyen Out of His Den': Philadelphia's Popular Movement, 1776–1780." In *The Origins of Anglo-American Radicalism,* edited by Margaret Jacob and James Jacob, 300–323. London: Allen & Unwin, 1984.

————. "The Philadelphia Militia, 1775–1783: Active Duty and Active Radicalism." In *Arms and Independence: The Military Character of the American Revolution,* edited by Ronald Hoffman and Peter J. Albert, 75–119. Charlottesville: University Press of Virginia, 1984.

Rowe, G. S. "*Femes Covert* and Criminal Prosecution in Eighteenth-Century Pennsylvania." *American Journal of Legal History* 32 (1988): 138–56.

————. "Women's Crime and Criminal Administration in Pennsylvania, 1763–1790." *Pennsylvania Magazine of History and Biography* 109 (1985): 335–68.

Ryerson, Richard Alan. "Republican Theory and Partisan Reality in Revolutionary Pennsylvania: Toward a New View of the Constitutional Party." In *Sovereign States in an Age of Uncertainty,* edited by Ronald Hoffman and Peter J. Albert, 95–133. Charlottesville: University Press of Virginia, 1981.

————. *The Revolution Is Now Begun: The Radical Committees of Philadelphia, 1765–1776.* Philadelphia: University of Pennsylvania Press, 1978.

Salinger, Sharon V. "Colonial Labor in Transition: The Decline of Indentured Servitude in Late Eighteenth-Century Philadelphia." *Labor History* 22 (1981): 165–91.

————. *"To Serve Well and Faithfully": Labor and Indentured Servants in Pennsylvania, 1682–1800.* New York: Cambridge University Press, 1987.

Salmon, Marylynn. "The Court Records of Philadelphia, Bucks, and Berks Counties in the Seventeenth and Eighteenth Century." *Pennsylvania Magazine of History and Biography* 107 (1983): 249–62.

Scharf, J. Thomas, and Thompson Westcott. *History of Philadelphia, 1609–1884*. 3 vols. Philadelphia: L. H. Everts & Company, 1884.

Schultz, Ronald. *The Republic of Labor: Philadelphia Artisans and the Politics of Class, 1720–1830*. New York: Oxford University Press, 1993.

———. "The Small-Producer Tradition and the Moral Origins of Artisan Radicalism in Philadelphia, 1720–1810." *Past and Present* 127 (1990): 84–116.

Selsam, J. Paul. *The Pennsylvania Constitution of 1776: A Study in Revolutionary Democracy*. 1936. Reprint, New York: Octagon, 1971.

Shelton, Cynthia. "The Role of Labor in Early Industrialization: Philadelphia, 1787–1837." *Journal of the Early Republic* 4 (1984): 365–94.

Shryock, Richard Harrison. *Medicine and Society in America, 1660–1860*. New York: New York University Press, 1960.

Smith, Abbot Emerson. *Colonists in Bondage: White Servitude and Convict Labor in America, 1607–1776*. New York: Norton, 1947.

Smith, Billy G. "Death and Life in a Colonial Immigrant City: A Demographic Analysis of Philadelphia." *Journal of Economic History* 37 (1977): 863–89.

———. *The "Lower Sort": Philadelphia's Laboring People, 1750–1800*. Ithaca, N.Y.: Cornell University Press, 1990.

———, "Poverty and Economic Marginality in Eighteenth-Century America." *Proceedings of the American Philosophical Society* 132 (1988): 85–118

———. "Poverty in Early America." In *Encyclopedia of the North American Colonies*, 3 vols., edited by Jacob Ernest Cooke et al., 1:483–94. New York: Charles Scribner's Sons, 1993.

Smith, Billy G., and Richard Wojtowicz, "The Precarious Freedom of Blacks: Excerpts from the *Pennsylvania Gazette*, 1728–1776." *Pennsylvania Magazine of History and Biography* 113 (1989): 237–64.

———, eds., *Blacks Who Stole Themselves: Advertisements for Runaways in the Pennsylvania Gazette, 1728–1790*. Philadelphia: University of Pennsylvania Press, 1989.

Smith, Tom W. "The Dawn of the Urban-Industrial Age: The Social Structure of Philadelphia, 1790–1830." Ph.D. diss., University of Chicago, 1980.

Soderlund, Jean R. "Women in Eighteenth-Century Pennsylvania: Toward a Model of Diversity." *Pennsylvania Magazine of History and Biography* 115 (1991): 163–84.

Stansell, Christine. *City of Women: Sex and Class in New York, 1789–1860*. Chicago: University of Illinois Press, 1987.

Thompson, E. P. "The Crime of Anonymity." In *Albion's Fatal Tree: Crime and Society in Eighteenth-Century England*, edited by Douglas Hay et al., 255–344. New York: Pantheon Books, 1975.

Trattner, Walter I. *From Poor Law to Welfare State: A History of Social Welfare in America*. New York: The Free Press, 1989.

Turner, Edward Raymond. *The Negro in Pennsylvania: Slavery—Servitude—Freedom, 1639–1861*. Washington, D.C.: American Historical Association, 1911.

Ulrich, Laurel Thatcher. *A Midwife's Tale: The Life of Martha Ballard, Based on Her Diary, 1785–1812*. New York: Knopf, 1990.

U.S. Bureau of the Census. *Heads of Families of the First Census of the United States taken in the Year 1790: Pennsylvania.* Washington, D.C.: Government Printing Office, 1908.

U.S. Census Office. *Return of the Whole Number of Persons Within the Several Districts of the United States: Second Census.* Washington, D.C.: Government Printing Office, 1800.

Warner, Sam Bass, Jr. *The Private City: Philadelphia in Three Periods of Its Growth.* Second edition. Philadelphia: University of Pennsylvania Press, 1987.

Weigley, Russell F., ed. *Philadelphia: A 300-Year History.* New York: Norton, 1982.

Williams, William H. *America's First Hospital: The Pennsylvania Hospital, 1751– 1841.* Wayne, Pa.: Haverford House, 1976.

Wolf, Stephanie Grauman. *Urban Village: Population, Community, and Family Structure in Germantown, Pennsylvania, 1683–1800.* Princeton: Princeton University Press, 1976.

CONTRIBUTORS

SUSAN BRANSON is assistant professor of history at Southwest Texas State University. Her research interests include social history of the Early National Era and American women's history. Her most recent article is "The Invisible Woman: The Family Economy in the Early Republic—The Case of Elizabeth Meredith" (forthcoming). In addition to writing a book with Susan E. Klepp on Ann Baker Carson, she is currently finishing a book about Philadelphia women and the shaping of popular political culture in the 1790s.

CATHERINE GOETZ has taught courses in the departments of history, English, and architecture at Montana State University and has served as historic preservation officer for Bozeman, Montana. Her research and writing interests range widely, from women's history to African American novelists to daily life in Butte, Montana. She presently is working on various projects as a public historian.

SUSAN E. KLEPP is professor of history at Rider University. She has written and edited several books on the demography of eighteenth-century Philadelphia, as well as articles on race and health and on abortive and contraceptive technology in the early mid-Atlantic region. Her most recent book, co-edited with Billy G. Smith, is *The Infortunate: The Voyage and Adventures of William Moraley, an Indentured Servant* (Penn State Press, 1992). She is currently working with Susan Branson on the life and time of Ann Baker Carson (1785–1824) and with Karin Wulf on the diary of Hannah Callender Sansom (1737–1801).

STEVE ROSSWURM teaches history at Lake Forest College. He is the author of *Arms, Country, and Class: The Philadelphia Militia and the American Revolution* (1987). He is the editor of *The CIO's Left-Led Unions* (1992) and of *J. Edgar Hoover Reader: Communism, Masculinity, and Crime* (forthcoming). He is also working on a book on the relationship between the Federal Bureau of Investigation and the Catholic Church from 1935 to 1960.

G. S. ROWE, professor of history at the University of Northern Colorado, is the author of *Thomas McKean: The Shaping of an American Republicanism* (1978) and *Embattled Bench: The Pennsylvania Supreme Court and the Forging of a Democratic Society, 1684–1809* (1994), as well as numerous articles on early Pennsylvania and Delaware history. He is working on a study of crime and criminal administration in pre-nineteenth-century Pennsylvania.

RONALD SCHULTZ teaches early American history at the University of Wyoming. He is the author of *The Republic of Labor: Philadelphia Artisans and the Politics of Class, 1720–1830* (1993) and "Alternative Communities: American Artisans and the Evangelical Appeal, 1790–1830" (1995). He is working on two books: *Between Revolutions: American Society, 1790–1830*, and *God and Workingmen: Popular Religion and the Creation of the American Working Class, 1730–1830*.

BILLY G. SMITH is professor of history at Montana State University. He is concerned about issues of class, race, and resistance in early America. He is the author of *The "Lower Sort": Philadelphia's Laboring People, 1750–1800* (1990), "Poverty in Early America" (1993), and "Runaway Slaves in the Mid-Atlantic Region During the Revolutionary Era" (forthcoming). He is currently engaged in studying blacks who fled slavery in eighteenth-century America.

RICHARD WOJTOWICZ is an independent scholar and co-editor of *Blacks Who Stole Themselves: Advertisements for Runaways in the Pennsylvania Gazette, 1728–1790* (1989), "The Precarious Freedom of Blacks: Excerpts from the *Pennsylvania Gazette* 1728–1776" (1989), and "Advertisements in the *Pennsylvania Gazette* for Runaway Slaves, Servants, and Apprentices, 1795–1796" (1987). He is working on several local histories of Montana.

NAME INDEX

SUBJECT INDEX